First World War
and Army of Occupation
War Diary
France, Belgium and Germany

14 DIVISION
42 Infantry Brigade
King's (Shropshire Light Infantry)
5th Battalion
9 May 1915 - 7 February 1918

WO95/1902/1

The Naval & Military Press Ltd
www.nmarchive.com
Published in association with The National Archives

Published by

The Naval & Military Press Ltd

Unit 10 Ridgewood Industrial Park,

Uckfield, East Sussex,

TN22 5QE England

Tel: +44 (0) 1825 749494

www.naval-military-press.com

www.nmarchive.com

This diary has been reprinted in facsimile from the original. Any imperfections are inevitably reproduced and the quality may fall short of modern type and cartographic standards.

© Crown Copyright
Images reproduced by permission of The National Archives, London, England, 2015.

Contents

Document type	Place/Title	Date From	Date To
Heading	14th Division 42nd Infy Bde 5th Bn Shropshire L.I. May 1915-Feb 1918		
Heading	14th Division 5th Shropshire L.I. Vol I May To Oct 22		
War Diary	Aldershot	09/05/1915	20/05/1915
War Diary	Ostrohove Rest Camp Boulogne	21/05/1915	21/05/1915
War Diary	Erkelsbrugge	22/05/1915	27/05/1915
War Diary	Eecke	28/05/1915	30/05/1915
War Diary	Dug-Outs 2 Miles S W of Ypres	31/05/1915	31/05/1915
War Diary	Dug-Outs S.W. of Ypres	01/06/1915	01/06/1915
War Diary	Dug-Outs 2 Miles S.W. of Ypres	02/06/1915	02/06/1915
War Diary	Canada Huts	03/06/1915	05/06/1915
War Diary	Locre	06/06/1915	12/06/1915
War Diary	Canada Huts	13/06/1915	14/06/1915
War Diary	Vlamertinghe	15/06/1915	15/06/1915
War Diary	Trenches E. Of Ypres.	16/06/1915	16/06/1915
War Diary	Vlamertinghe	17/06/1915	18/06/1915
War Diary	Trenches E Of Ypres	19/06/1915	24/06/1915
War Diary	Zwynland	25/06/1915	07/08/1915
War Diary	Ypres Ramparts	08/07/1915	19/07/1915
War Diary	Busseboom	20/07/1915	26/07/1915
War Diary	Ypres	27/07/1915	10/08/1915
War Diary	Vlamertinghe	11/08/1915	23/08/1915
War Diary	Ypres	24/08/1915	29/08/1915
War Diary	Vlamertinghe	30/08/1915	06/09/1915
War Diary	Ypres	07/09/1915	14/09/1915
War Diary	Near Poperinghe	15/09/1915	23/09/1915
War Diary	Ypres	24/09/1915	25/09/1915
War Diary	Near Poperinghe	26/09/1915	27/09/1915
War Diary	Ypres	13/10/1915	22/10/1915
Miscellaneous	5th Division G. 411	31/05/1915	31/05/1915
Heading	5th K.S.L.I Vol 2 Oct 21st-Dec 31st 1915		
Miscellaneous	5th, Bn, King's Shropshire Light Infantry		
Miscellaneous	A Company		
Miscellaneous	B Company		
Miscellaneous	5th Batt. King's Shropshire Light Infantry		
Miscellaneous	D Company		
Heading	War Diary Of 5th King's Shropshire L.I. from 21.10.15 to 31.12.15. (Volume 2)		
War Diary	Ypres	21/10/1915	21/10/1915
War Diary	Houtkerque	22/10/1915	08/11/1915
War Diary	Ypres	18/11/1915	21/11/1915
War Diary	Brandhoek	22/11/1915	23/11/1915
War Diary	Ypres	24/11/1915	26/11/1915
War Diary	Brandhoek	27/11/1915	29/11/1915
War Diary	Ypres	30/11/1915	10/12/1915
War Diary	St. Jan Ter. Biezen	11/12/1915	11/12/1915
War Diary	Ypres	12/12/1915	15/12/1915
War Diary	A Huts	16/12/1915	16/12/1915
War Diary	Houtkerque	17/12/1915	29/12/1915
War Diary	Brandhoek	30/12/1915	31/12/1915

Heading	5th K.S.L.I Vol 3 42 Bde		
Heading	War Diary Of 5th King's Shropshire L.I. from January 1st to 31st 1916 (Volume 3)		
War Diary	Brandhoek	01/01/1916	07/01/1916
War Diary	Elverdinghe	08/01/1916	23/01/1916
War Diary	Bradhoek	24/01/1916	26/01/1916
War Diary	Elverdinghe	27/01/1916	31/01/1916
Heading	War Diary Of 5th King's Shropshire L.I from February 1st to 29th 1916 (Volume 3)		
War Diary	Elverdinghe Sheet 28 Belgium	01/02/1916	05/02/1916
War Diary	Brandhoek	06/02/1916	08/02/1916
War Diary	Elverdinghe	09/02/1916	09/02/1916
War Diary	Elverdinghe Sheet 28 Belgium	10/02/1916	11/02/1916
War Diary	Poperinghe a.1.D.8.5 Sheet 28 Belgium & France	12/02/1916	12/02/1916
War Diary	Houtkerque E. 14. D Sheet 27	13/02/1916	13/02/1916
War Diary	Wormhoudt C. 10.d.9.5 Sheet 27	14/02/1916	21/02/1916
War Diary	Berteaucourt Les-Dames	22/02/1916	25/02/1916
War Diary	Hem	26/02/1916	26/02/1916
War Diary	Grand Rullecourt	27/02/1916	29/02/1916
Miscellaneous	Report On Relief On Night Of 11th-12th February Of 31 & 32		
Heading	War Diary Of 5th King's Shropshire L.I from March 1st to 31st 1916 (Volume 4)		
War Diary	Sombrin (O.23. Sheet 51c) France	01/03/1916	01/03/1916
War Diary	Berneville (R.I.C. 51c Sheet) France	02/03/1916	05/03/1916
War Diary	Arras (G.28.a. Sheet 57B) France	06/03/1916	13/03/1916
War Diary	Ronville G.28.C (Sheet 51B France)	14/03/1916	21/03/1916
War Diary	Simencourt Q.10.d-Q.11.C. Sheet 51C France	22/03/1916	29/03/1916
War Diary	Simencourt Q 10 d. Q 11 c Sheet 51.C France Ronville G.28.C Sheet 51C. France	29/03/1916	31/03/1916
Heading	War Diary Of 5th King's Shropshire L.I. from April 1st to 30th 1916 (Volume 5.)		
War Diary	Ronville G.28.C. Sheet 51B France	01/04/1916	04/04/1916
War Diary	Arras G 28.a Sheet 51 B	05/04/1916	13/04/1916
War Diary	Ronville G. 28. C. Sheet 51B France	13/04/1916	21/04/1916
War Diary	Simencourt Q.10.d and Q.11.C. Sheet 51C France	22/04/1916	29/04/1916
War Diary	Ronville	30/04/1916	30/04/1916
Heading	War Diary Of 5th King's Shropshire L.I. from May 1st to 31st 1916. (Volume 6.)		
War Diary	Ronville G.28.C 51 B France	17/05/1916	22/05/1916
War Diary	Berneville Q.6.d. Sheet 51. C. France	23/05/1916	31/05/1916
War Diary	Arras	31/05/1916	31/05/1916
War Diary	Ronville G 28 C Sheet 51 B France	01/05/1916	06/05/1916
War Diary	Arras G. 28.a Sheet 51. B France	07/05/1916	14/05/1916
War Diary	Ronville G 28. C 51 B. France	15/05/1916	16/05/1916
Heading	War Diary Of 5th King's Shropshire L.I From June 1st To 30th 1916 (Volume 7)		
War Diary	Ronville G. 28. C 51 B France	01/06/1916	08/06/1916
War Diary	Arras Sheet 51 B.	09/06/1916	18/06/1916
War Diary	Arras Sheet 51B France	19/06/1916	19/06/1916
War Diary	St. Sauveur Sheet 51B France	20/06/1916	30/06/1916
Heading	War Diary Of 5th King's Shropshire L.I. from July 1st to 31st 1916 (Volume 8)		
War Diary	St. Sauveur Sheet 51B France	01/07/1916	09/07/1916
War Diary	Arras (G 28.a.51B)	10/07/1916	11/07/1916
War Diary	Arras (G. 28.a. 51b) France	12/07/1916	12/07/1916

War Diary	Achicourt (H. Right. Sector) (Sheet. 51B France)	13/07/1916	18/07/1916
War Diary	Arras (Sheet 51B) France	19/07/1916	21/07/1916
War Diary	Blangy (G. 23. Sheet) 51B France	22/07/1916	25/07/1916
War Diary	Blangy (G. 28 Sheet 51B) France	26/07/1916	27/07/1916
War Diary	Agnez-Les. Duisans (K.12 Sheet 51c) France	27/07/1916	27/07/1916
War Diary	Agnez-Les-Duisans & Grand Roullecourt (0.9 Sheet. 51c France)	28/07/1916	28/07/1916
War Diary	Grand Roullecourt. (0.9. Sheet) 51.C 1 France	29/07/1916	29/07/1916
War Diary	Barly (Lens II) 1/100,000	30/07/1916	30/07/1916
War Diary	Barly & Candas (Lens. II) 1/100,000)	31/07/1916	31/07/1916
Heading	42nd Brigade. 14th Division. 1/5th Battalion King's Shropshire Light Infantry August 1916		
Heading	War Diary Of 5th King's Shropshire L.I. from August 1st to 31st 1916 (Volume 9)		
War Diary	Candas. (Lens II)	01/08/1916	06/08/1916
War Diary	Candas (Sheet 62 D) France	07/08/1916	07/08/1916
War Diary	Buire-Sur-L'ancre. (Sheet 62D) France	08/08/1916	12/08/1916
War Diary	F 14.a (Sheet 62 D)	13/08/1916	18/08/1916
War Diary	Ref. Albert. (Combined Sheet)	19/08/1916	19/08/1916
War Diary	Albert France (Combined Sheet)	20/08/1916	21/08/1916
War Diary	Delville Wood (S.12 c & d) Albert (Combined Sheet)	22/08/1916	24/08/1916
War Diary	Delville Wood (S.12 c & d) Albert (Combined Sheet) & F.14.a.	25/08/1916	25/08/1916
War Diary	(Sheet 62 D) France	26/08/1916	26/08/1916
War Diary	F.14.a (Sheet 62 D) France	27/08/1916	28/08/1916
War Diary	(Albert) Combined Sheet	29/08/1916	30/08/1916
War Diary	(Albert) Combined Sheet Airaines & Vergies (Map. Dieppe 16)	31/08/1916	31/08/1916
Miscellaneous	5th Shrops L.I.	27/08/1916	27/08/1916
Heading	War Diary Of 5th King's Shropshire L.I. from September 1st to 30th 1916 Volume 10		
War Diary	Vergies. (Map. Dieppe 16)	01/09/1916	11/09/1916
War Diary	F. 13. C. South (62 D. France)	12/09/1916	14/09/1916
War Diary	Sheet France 57 C S W	15/09/1916	15/09/1916
War Diary	Sheet 57 C S W	16/09/1916	16/09/1916
War Diary	Sheet 57 C.S.W & 62. D. France	17/09/1916	17/09/1916
War Diary	62. D. France	18/09/1916	20/09/1916
War Diary	Sheet 62 D France	21/09/1916	21/09/1916
War Diary	Sheet 62 D France & Grand Roullecourt (0.9 b 51c) France	22/09/1916	22/09/1916
War Diary	Grand Roullecourt. (0.9.b) Sheet 51. C France	23/09/1916	24/09/1916
War Diary	Grand Roullecourt. (0.9.b) Sheet 51. C France & K. 28.d 51c K 36 D	25/09/1916	25/09/1916
War Diary	Warlus (K 36 D) 51. C France	26/09/1916	26/09/1916
War Diary	Agny M 8d (Sheet 51 B S W)	27/09/1916	30/09/1916
Miscellaneous	14th Division.	06/09/1916	06/09/1916
Miscellaneous	2/Lieut J.C. Jinks		
Heading	War Diary Of 5th King's Shropshire L.I. from October 1st to 31st 1916 (Volume II)		
War Diary	Agny (M.8.D) Sheet (51B S.W) France	01/10/1916	04/10/1916
War Diary	Agny (Sheet 51B) France	05/10/1916	06/10/1916
War Diary	Agny (Sheet 51B) France & Dainville (L. 29 C Sheet 51c) France	07/10/1916	07/10/1916
War Diary	Dainville (L. 29 C) Sheet 51C France	08/10/1916	12/10/1916
War Diary	Dainville (L.29.C) Sheet 51 C (France) & G. Left Sector	13/10/1916	13/10/1916

War Diary	Agny (M.8.d) Sheet (51B S.W)	14/10/1916	19/10/1916
War Diary	Agny. M.8.D. (Sheet 51B S.W) France	20/10/1916	25/10/1916
War Diary	Agny (51B S W) & Wanquetin (51 C France)	26/10/1916	26/10/1916
War Diary	Wanquetin (51 C France) Blavincourt & Ligneruil (51 C France)	27/10/1916	27/10/1916
War Diary	Lignereuil & Blavincourt (51 C France)	28/10/1916	31/10/1916
Heading	War Diary Of 5th King's Shropshire L.I. from November 1st to 30th 1916 (Volume 12)		
War Diary	Blavincourt (1. 27.d.) Lignereuil 1.71.b (51 C France)	01/11/1916	06/11/1916
War Diary	Blavincourt (1.27.d.) Lignereuil 1.21.b. (51 C France) & Ivergny (N 71) 51c France	07/11/1916	09/11/1916
War Diary	Ivergny (N. 21) (51c France)	10/11/1916	22/11/1916
War Diary	Ivergny (N. 21) (51 C France) & Dainville (L. 29 C) 51c. France	23/11/1916	23/11/1916
War Diary	Dainville (L.29.C.) 51 C France	24/11/1916	30/11/1916
Heading	War Diary Unit.-5th King's Shropshire L.I. from 1st December 1916 To 31st December 1916 Volume No. 13		
War Diary	Dainville (L. 29. C) 51 C France	01/12/1916	08/12/1916
War Diary	Gouy-En-Ternois (B.28.d) 51 C France	09/12/1916	09/12/1916
War Diary	Gouy-En-Ternois (B.28.d.51C)	10/12/1916	15/12/1916
War Diary	Gouves & (K 16.d) Montenescourt. (K.21.A) Agny (M.8.D) 51B S W	16/12/1916	16/12/1916
War Diary	Agny (M.8.D.) Sheet 51 B.S.W.	17/12/1916	22/12/1916
War Diary	G. Left Sector (M.8.d) 51 B.S.W.	23/12/1916	26/12/1916
War Diary	G. Left Sector	27/12/1916	27/12/1916
War Diary	Dainville (L. 29.C) 51C. France	28/12/1916	31/12/1916
Heading	War Diary Unit, 5th King's Shropshire Light Infantry. Period From Jan 1st 1917 To Jan 31st 1917 Volume No. 14		
War Diary	Dainville (L. 29. C) 51C. France	01/01/1917	01/01/1917
War Diary	G. Left. Sector Agny 51. B.S.W	02/01/1917	06/01/1917
War Diary	G. Left Sector Agny	07/01/1917	07/01/1917
War Diary	Agny (M.8.d) (51 B.S.W)	08/01/1917	13/01/1917
War Diary	G Left Sector Agny (51. B.S.W)	14/01/1917	17/01/1917
War Diary	G. Left Sector Agny (51. B.S.W) & Dainville (L 29 C) 51 C France	18/01/1917	18/01/1917
War Diary	Dainville L. 29 C. (51 C. France)	19/01/1917	22/01/1917
War Diary	Dainville L 29 C (51 C. France) & G Left Sector Agny	23/01/1917	23/01/1917
War Diary	Agny (G Left Sector)	24/01/1917	25/01/1917
War Diary	G Left Sector (Agny)	26/01/1917	27/01/1917
War Diary	G. Left Sector (Agny) & Agny (51 B.S.W) (M.8.d)	28/01/1917	30/01/1917
War Diary	Agny (51 B.S.W M.8.d)	31/01/1917	31/01/1917
Heading	War Diary Unit 5th Shrops L.I. Date From 1-2-17 To 28-2-17 Vol No 15		
War Diary	Agny (M.8.d) 51 B.S.W	01/02/1917	02/02/1917
War Diary	G Left (Agny) (M.8.d)	03/02/1917	03/02/1917
War Diary	G Left Agny (51 BSW)	04/02/1917	05/02/1917
War Diary	G Left Sector (51 BSW) Achicourt & Arras (51B)	06/02/1917	06/02/1917
War Diary	Arras (G 27.d.5.6) 51B	07/02/1917	13/02/1917
War Diary	Arras (G 27.d.5.6)	14/02/1917	15/02/1917
War Diary	Arras (G 27 d.5.6) & Ronville	16/02/1917	16/02/1917
War Diary	H. Left Sector. (Ronville)	17/02/1917	18/02/1917
War Diary	N. Left Sector	19/02/1917	21/02/1917
War Diary	Ronville	22/02/1917	23/02/1917
War Diary	Ronville (G.34.a) 51. B	24/02/1917	26/02/1917

War Diary	Ronville (G 34.a) 51 B & (L. 29. C) 51 C. France	27/02/1917	27/02/1917
War Diary	Ronville (G 34.a) 51 B & (L. 29. C) 51 C. France (L. 29. C.) France	28/02/1917	28/02/1917
Heading	War Diary Unit. 5th Shrops L.I. Period From 1-3-1917 To 31-3-1917 Volume No. 16		
War Diary	Dainville (L. 79.C) France 51 C	01/03/1917	10/03/1917
War Diary	Dainville (L 29 C) France 51 C & Ronville (G.34.a 51 B France)	11/03/1917	11/03/1917
War Diary	Ronville (G. 34.a.50. B France)	12/03/1917	12/03/1917
War Diary	Ronville (G. 34.a.50. B France)	13/03/1917	17/03/1917
War Diary	H. Sector (Left) Ronville (G. 35. C. 1 To (G. 35.d.8.8) Arras Trench Map	18/03/1917	18/03/1917
War Diary	H. Left Sector Ronville	19/03/1917	20/03/1917
War Diary	Ronville Sector	21/03/1917	23/03/1917
War Diary	Ronville Sector & Dainville	24/03/1917	27/03/1917
War Diary	Dainville & Fosseaux (Sheet 51C. France)	28/03/1917	28/03/1917
War Diary	Fosseaux	29/03/1917	31/03/1917
Heading	War Diary Of 5th King's Shropshire L.I. Period Apl 1st To 30th 1917 Volume No 18		
War Diary	Fosseax (P 10.d) 51c	01/04/1917	02/04/1917
War Diary	Fosseax & Simencourt (Q.10.b) Sheet 51.C. France	03/04/1917	03/04/1917
War Diary	Simencourt (51.C. France) (Q.10.b)	04/04/1917	04/04/1917
War Diary	Simencourt (51.C. France) & Dainville	05/04/1917	05/04/1917
War Diary	Dainville (L 29 C) Sheet 51. C	06/04/1917	06/04/1917
War Diary	Dainville (L 29 C) Sheet 51 C. & H. Sector Ronville (51 C Map)	07/04/1917	07/04/1917
War Diary	H. Sector Ronville (51C France) Sheet	08/04/1917	08/04/1917
War Diary	H. Sector & Sheet. 51. B.S.W (M.6.A.8) N. Of B.	09/04/1917	09/04/1917
War Diary	Ronville H Sector (N 7 b) 51 B.S.W	09/04/1917	09/04/1917
War Diary	Telegraph Hill (N. 7 b. 37 BSW)	10/04/1917	10/04/1917
War Diary	Telegraph Hill (N. 7 b) 51 BSW Map	10/04/1917	10/04/1917
War Diary	Telegraph Hill & Wanquetin (K 32 A) 51 C Map	11/04/1917	11/04/1917
War Diary	Wanquetin & Noyelette (J 18.b)	12/04/1917	12/04/1917
War Diary	Noyelette (J.18.b) 51 C France	13/04/1917	13/04/1917
War Diary	Noyellette (J.18.a) & Liencourt (132 C) 51 C Map	14/04/1917	14/04/1917
War Diary	Liencourt 1.32. C (51 C Map)	15/04/1917	16/04/1917
War Diary	Liencourt (1.32.C) 51. C France	17/04/1917	22/04/1917
War Diary	Liencourt (1.32 C) & Hauteville (J. 35. C)	23/04/1917	23/04/1917
War Diary	Hauteville (J. 35. C) 51 C Map. & Grosville (R.25.d) 51 C & The Harp (N. Of B) 51 BSW	24/04/1917	24/04/1917
War Diary	The Harp & Wancourt (N. M. C.0.5) 51 BSW Map	25/04/1917	25/04/1917
War Diary	Wancourt (N. Nt. C. 0. 5) 51 BSW Map	26/04/1917	27/04/1917
War Diary	Wancourt (N Nt C. 0.5 & N.16.C.O.5) 51 BSW	28/04/1917	28/04/1917
War Diary	Wancourt (N 16.c. 0.5) 51 BSW	29/04/1917	30/04/1917
War Diary	14th Division G.S. 2678 Appendix I	07/04/1917	07/04/1917
Miscellaneous	Complementary Order. Appendix 3	10/04/1917	10/04/1917
Miscellaneous	All Units, 14th Division. Appendix 4	14/04/1917	14/04/1917
Miscellaneous	42nd Inf Bde. B.M. 14/167. Appendix 5	16/04/1917	16/04/1917
Miscellaneous	Appendices		
Miscellaneous	A Form. Messages And Signals. Appendix 2		
Heading	War Diary 5th Shrops L.I. 1st-31st May 1917 Vol 18		
War Diary	Nr Wancourt (N. 16 C)	01/05/1917	01/05/1917
War Diary	Nr Wancourt (51 BSW)	02/05/1917	03/05/1917
War Diary	Wancourt (N Nr d 8) O.19.a (51 BSW) France	03/05/1917	03/05/1917
War Diary	Wancourt (N. Nt) 51 BSW	04/05/1917	04/05/1917
War Diary	Trenches (In N. 13.a)	05/05/1917	08/05/1917

War Diary	Trenches (In N 13 a) & N.1.a (51 BSW)	09/05/1917	09/05/1917
War Diary	N. 1.a (51 BSW)	10/05/1917	14/05/1917
War Diary	Nepal Trench (Hindenburg Line) (N.15.d.3.4)	15/05/1917	19/05/1917
War Diary	Panther & Pore Trenches N 20 B-N. 21. C-N 20.d. (51. BSW)	20/05/1917	23/05/1917
War Diary	Panther & Pore Trenches (O 26.a. & O. 25.d)	24/05/1917	25/05/1917
War Diary	Right Sector O.26.a & O 25.d (51 B S W)	25/05/1917	27/05/1917
War Diary	Right Sector O.26.a & O 25.d (51 B S W) & N. 30.b. Ac.	28/05/1917	31/05/1917
Heading	War Diary Of 5th King's Shropshire L.I. Period 1st to 30th June 1917 Volume No. 19		
War Diary	Puchevilliers (N 27.c.57)	19/06/1917	30/06/1917
War Diary	Wancourt. (Support Trenches) (N 30.b. 51 BSW)	01/06/1917	03/06/1917
War Diary	Neuville Vitasse (N. 20.a 15.50) 51 BSW	03/06/1917	03/06/1917
War Diary	Neuville Vitasse (N. 20.a 15.50) & Beurains (M.10.d)	04/06/1917	04/06/1917
War Diary	Beurains (M.10.d) (51. BSW)	05/06/1917	08/06/1917
War Diary	Beurains (M 10 d) (51. BSW) & Monchiet. (Q.71.C.9.6)	09/06/1917	09/06/1917
War Diary	Monchiet (Q 21 C 96) & Saulty Gombremetz (V.2.C)	10/06/1917	10/06/1917
War Diary	Saulty Gombremetz (V.2.C) 51 C & Puchevilliers. (N.27.b 57.D. Map)	11/06/1917	11/06/1917
War Diary	Puchevillers (N.27.C) 57 D Map	12/06/1917	18/06/1917
Miscellaneous	Programme Of Work Week ending June 16.1917		
Miscellaneous	Programme Of Work For W/E June 23rd 1917		
Miscellaneous	Programme Of Work For Week Ending June 30th		
Heading	War Diary Of 5th King's Shropshire L.I. Period 1st To 31st July 1917 Volume No. 20		
War Diary	Puchevillers. (N. 27. C) Sheet 57 C	01/07/1917	10/07/1917
War Diary	Puchevillers (N 29.d. 57 D)	11/07/1917	11/07/1917
War Diary	Puchevillers Bailleul (S.d.8.6) Sheet 28	12/07/1917	12/07/1917
War Diary	Bailleul (S. 1.d 8.6) Sheet 28	13/07/1917	15/07/1917
War Diary	Nr Bailleul (S.I.d.8.6)	16/07/1917	26/07/1917
War Diary	Nr Bailleul (S.I.d.8.6) Sheet 28	27/07/1917	31/07/1917
Miscellaneous	14th Division	08/07/1917	08/07/1917
Miscellaneous	42nd Inf. Bde. S.C. 317/6	10/07/1917	10/07/1917
Miscellaneous	Battalion Orders By Lieut-Col. H.M. Smith D.S.O. Commanding 5th King's Shropshire Light Infantry		
Miscellaneous	Operation Orders By Capt. O.S. Benbow-Rowe H.O. Commanding 5th King's Shropshire Light Infantry		
Operation(al) Order(s)	Operation Orders 2.		
Operation(al) Order(s)	Operation Orders 3.		
Miscellaneous	Operation Orders By Lieut-Col. N.M. Smith D.S.O. Commanding 5th King's Shropshire Light Infantry Appendix 5		
Heading	War Diary Unit 5th Kings Shropshire L.I. Period 1st To 31st August 1917 Volume No 21		
War Diary	Nr Bailleul 28 S 1.d.8.6	01/08/1917	05/08/1917
War Diary	Nr Bailleul & Caestre Area	06/08/1917	06/08/1917
War Diary	Caestre Area. Sheet 27 (N.5. C 51)	07/08/1917	08/08/1917
War Diary	Caestre Area. V.5.C.5.1	09/08/1917	14/08/1917
War Diary	Caestre Area N 5 C 51 & Ouderdom	15/08/1917	15/08/1917
War Diary	N Ouderdom G. 29.c	16/08/1917	16/08/1917
War Diary	Nr Ouderdom Dickebosch & Halt. Way House	17/08/1917	17/08/1917
War Diary	Halt-Way-House 1.17.C.4.8 (Zillebeke)	18/08/1917	19/08/1917
War Diary	Halt Way House & Trenches (E Of Ypres)	20/08/1917	20/08/1917
War Diary	In The Line (E Of Ypres)	21/08/1917	23/08/1917

War Diary	Halt. Way House (L.17 C 4.8) Sheet 28 N W	24/08/1917	25/08/1917
War Diary	Halt Way House & K.24.a.5.4 (Sheet 27)	26/08/1917	26/08/1917
War Diary	K 24.a. 5.4 (Sheet 27) & Q.29.d.8.3	27/08/1917	29/08/1917
War Diary	Thieushouk Area (Sheet 27) Q 29.d.8.3	29/08/1917	31/08/1917
Miscellaneous	Operation Orders by Lieut Col. H.M. Smith D.S.O. Commdg. Lobe. Appendix 1		
Operation(al) Order(s)	14th Division Order No 141 Appendix 2	31/08/1917	31/08/1917
Miscellaneous	14th Division. G.s. 177 Appendix 2	30/08/1917	30/08/1917
Heading	War Diary Unit 5th King's Shropshire L.I. Period 1st To 30th September 1917 Volume No. 22		
War Diary	Thieushoek Area (27.Q.29.d.8.3) & Neuve Eglise (28.S.12.C.8.8)	01/09/1917	01/09/1917
War Diary	Neuve Eglise 28.S.12.C.8.8 & Messines (Sheet 28 S E) & 28 SW	02/09/1917	02/09/1917
War Diary	Messines (O.32.d.b.2)	03/09/1917	06/09/1917
War Diary	Messines	07/09/1917	10/09/1917
War Diary	Neuve Eglise (28 T.15.a.0.4)	11/09/1917	13/09/1917
War Diary	Neuve Eglise	14/09/1917	14/09/1917
War Diary	Neuve Eglise & Doulieu Area L. II A.10.10 (Sheet 36A)	15/09/1917	15/09/1917
War Diary	Doulieu Area (36 A. L.II.a.10.10)	16/09/1917	17/09/1917
War Diary	Doulieu Area & Canteen Corner (28 T. 26. C.5.1)	18/04/1917	18/04/1917
War Diary	Canteen Corner	19/09/1917	21/09/1917
War Diary	Canteen Corner Camp. (28. T.26.C.5.1)	22/09/1917	24/09/1917
War Diary	Canteen Corner (28. T.26.C.5.1)	25/09/1917	30/09/1917
Heading	War Diary 5th King's (Shropshire Light Infantry) 1st To 31st October 1917 Volume No. 23		
War Diary	Messines	01/10/1917	08/10/1917
War Diary	Kortepyp (T.26.b.50.60 Ref. Sheet 27)	09/10/1917	10/10/1917
War Diary	Berthen Area Q.30.d.3.4 Ref. Sheet 27 1/40.000	11/10/1917	11/10/1917
War Diary	Ridge Wood N.5.a.8.4 Ref. Sheet 28	12/10/1917	16/10/1917
War Diary	J.14.d.90.20 Gheluvelt 28.N.E.	17/10/1917	24/10/1917
War Diary	Berthen Area X.1.b.2.2 Sheet 27	25/10/1917	30/10/1917
Heading	War Diary 5th Kings Shrops L.I. 1st To 30th November 1917 Volume No. 24		
War Diary	Berthen. Area X.I.b.2.2 Ref. Sheet. 27	01/11/1917	05/11/1917
War Diary	Berthen. Area X.I.b.2.2 Ref. Sheet. 27 And I.3.b.7.4 Ref. Sheet 28	06/11/1917	06/11/1917
War Diary	I.3.b.7.4 Ref. Sheet 28	07/11/1917	28/11/1917
War Diary	I.3.b.7.4 Ref. Sheet 28 & Q.22.d.6.2 Sheet 27	29/11/1917	29/11/1917
War Diary	Q.22.d.6.2 Ref Sheet 27	30/11/1917	30/11/1917
Heading	War Diary 5th Shrops L.I. December 1917 Volume 25		
Miscellaneous	O.C. 5th Battn. K & L.I	03/01/1918	03/01/1918
War Diary	Q.22.d.6.2 Ref. Sheet 27	01/12/1917	02/12/1917
War Diary	Q.22.d.6.2 Ref. Sheet 27 And G.6.d.4.4 Ref. Sheet 28	03/12/1917	03/12/1917
War Diary	G.6.d.4.4 Ref. Sheet 28	04/12/1917	08/12/1917
War Diary	G.6.d.4.4 & G.37.d.1.11 Ref. Sheet 28	09/12/1917	09/12/1917
War Diary	G.37.d.1.11 Ref. Sheet 28	10/12/1917	10/12/1917
War Diary	G.18.d.5.6 Sheet 28	16/12/1917	18/12/1917
War Diary	G.37.d. 1.11 Ref. Sheet 28	11/12/1917	11/12/1917
War Diary	G.37.d. 1.11 Ref. Sheet 28 & V.29.b.6.6 Ref. Sheet 27	12/12/1917	12/12/1917
War Diary	V.29.b.6.6 Ref. Sheet 27	13/12/1917	14/12/1917
War Diary	V.29.b.6.6 Ref. Sheet 27 & C.18.d.5.6 Ref. Sheet 28	15/12/1917	15/12/1917
War Diary	G. 18.d. 5.6 Ref. Sheet 28 & D.4.d.5.4 Ref. Sheet 28	19/12/1917	19/12/1917
War Diary	D.4.d.5.4 Ref. Sheet 28	20/12/1917	21/12/1917
War Diary	D.4.d.5.4 Ref. Sheet 28 & G.27.C.8.8 Ref. Sheet 28	22/12/1917	22/12/1917

War Diary	G.27.C.8.8 Ref. Sheet 28	23/12/1917	24/12/1917
War Diary	G.27.C.8.8 Ref. Sheet 28 & Hazebrouck 5A	25/12/1917	25/12/1917
War Diary	Longuenesse Nr St Omer Ref. Hazebrouck 5A	26/12/1917	31/12/1917
Heading	War Diary 5th King's Shropshire L I January 1918 Volume 26		
War Diary	Longuenesse Ref. Amiens 1/100,000. Hazebrouck 5a 12/1/100.000	01/01/1918	01/01/1918
War Diary	Suzanne	02/01/1918	22/01/1918
War Diary	Rosiere-En-Santerre Ref. France 1/100.000 Amiens	23/01/1918	23/01/1918
War Diary	Guerbigny	24/01/1918	25/01/1918
War Diary	Beine (Ref. Map. St. Quentin, 1/100.000 & 66.C.N.W.)	26/01/1918	26/01/1918
War Diary	Montescourt Ref. St. Quentin 1/100,000 & 66.C.N.W.	27/01/1918	27/01/1918
War Diary	Left Sector B.30.C.64. To I.C.a.O.O.	28/01/1918	28/01/1918
War Diary	Ref. St. Quentin 1/100,000 66.c.N.W.	29/01/1918	31/01/1918
Heading	War Diary 5th King's Shropshire L.I. February 1918 Volume 27		
War Diary	Ref St. Quentin & 66c.N.W. Left Sector From B.30.c. 64 to I.1.a.O.O. Both Inclusive.	01/02/1918	02/02/1918
War Diary	Jussy	03/02/1918	07/02/1918

14TH DIVISION
42ND INFY BDE

6TH BN SHROPSHIRE L.I.
MAY 1915 - FEB 1918

DISBANDED 2.18

Box 1902

I.S.
19 sheets.

12/
7518

427/14/Hussein

5th Shropshire L.I.
vol I
May 15 to 22 Oct 15.
Oct '15

in attack in trenches 25/9/15

Army Form C. 2118.

WAR DIARY
or
INTELLIGENCE SUMMARY.
(Erase heading not required.)

Instructions regarding War Diaries and Intelligence Summaries are contained in F. S. Regs., Part II. and the Staff Manual respectively. Title pages will be prepared in manuscript.

Place	Date	Hour	Summary of Events and Information	Remarks and references to Appendices
ALDERSHOT	9/5/15		LIEUT. P.J. BELLASIS left for duties at the Port of disembarkation.	
ALDERSHOT	11/5/15		Regiment placed on War footing, and all surplus clothing and equipment returned to Stores. CAPT. R. MEYNELL left at 6 a.m. for duties as Brigade Billeting Officer.	

Army Form C. 2118.

WAR DIARY
or
INTELLIGENCE SUMMARY
(Erase heading not required.)

Instructions regarding War Diaries and Intelligence Summaries are contained in F. S. Regs., Part II. and the Staff Manual respectively. Title pages will be prepared in manuscript.

Place	Date	Hour	Summary of Events and Information	Remarks and references to Appendices
ALDERSHOT.	19/5/15	9.55 A.M	Fine. MAJOR J.G. FORBES, LIEUT. S.G. BEAUMONT, LIEUT. J.C.B. FIRTH, 109 Rank and file, 79 Horses and Mules and the whole of the Transport left ALDERSHOT at 9.55 A.M. for SOUTHAMPTON.	
ALDERSHOT.	20/5/15	5.20 and 5.45 P.M.	Fine. 28 Officers and 797 Rank and file under LIEUT-COL. H.M.SMITH, D.S.O. Left ALDERSHOT at 5.20 and 5.45 P.M. for FOLKESTONE. Arrived at OSTROHOVE REST CAMP. BOULOGNE. at 1.30 A.M. 21st May.	
OSTROHOVE REST CAMP. BOULOGNE.	21/5/15	9.30 A.M.	Fine. Left at 9.30 a.m. Read H.M's THE KING'S Message to the Troops. Entrained at PONT-AU-BRIQUE for CASSEL. A long and tiring march from there to Billets at ERKELSBRUGGE. Picked up Transport at PONT-AU BRIQUE, and Transport and men went in one train. Strength 32 Officers including REV FATHER AMERY Brigade Chaplain, 908 Other Ranks. SGT WEIL to BASE.	
ERKELSBRUGGE	22/5/15		Fine.	
ERKELSBRUGGE	23/5/15		Fine. Holy Communion at 7 a.m. Church Parade at 9 a.m.	
ERKELSBRUGGE	24/5/15		Fine. Regiment inspected and complimented by BRIG-GENERAL STOPFORD. A route march afterwards.	
ERKELSBRUGGE	25/5/15		Fine.	
ERKELSBRUGGE	26/5/15		Fine.	
ERKELSBRUGGE	27/5/15		Fine. Paraded 3.30 a.m. and marched about 16 miles to Billets at EECKE.	

Army Form C. 2118.

WAR DIARY
or
INTELLIGENCE SUMMARY.

(Erase heading not required.)

Instructions regarding War Diaries and Intelligence Summaries are contained in F.S. Regs., Part II. and the Staff Manual respectively. Title pages will be prepared in manuscript.

Place	Date	Hour	Summary of Events and Information	Remarks and references to Appendices
EECKE.	28/5/15		Fine.	
EECKE	29/5/15		Fine.	
EECKE.	30/5/15		Fine. Parade at 3.45 a.m. A & B Coys under MAJOR FORBES, A Coy to DICKEBUSCH.	
DUG-OUTS 2 miles S.W. of YPRES	31/5/15		Fine. Attached to 5th Division. An address by SIR JAMES FURGUSON. Marched 550 to Trenches for digging at ZILLEBEKE. Remainder of Battalion under MAJOR FORBES moved into dug-outs about 2 miles S.W. of YPRES.	
DUG-OUTS S.W. of YPRES.	1/6/15		Fine. About 12.30 A.M. whilst returning from trenches, Sgt. DISS B.Coy was killed, and Pte BOWEN B.Coy, Pte ROBERTS B.Coy, and L/Cpl McAULEY L.Coy wounded. Returned remainder of Battalion at 4 a.m. Marched out for trench digging at ZILLEBEKE at 8.15 p.m.	
DUG-OUTS 2 miles S.W. of YPRES	2/6/15		Fine. Pte Griffiths C Coy killed. Pte Smith L.Coy, Pte Long L Coy, Pte Tarbit B.Coy wounded. Returned from trench digging at 3.30 A.M. Heavily shelled all round camp, all the afternoon, but none actually dropped in camp. Paraded at 8.15 p.m. 550 men for working party at ZILLEBEKE. Regiment under MAJOR FORBES shifted back to Huts and Bivouacs at CANADA at 8.30 p.m. Killed L/Cpl Edwards A. Coy. Wounded. Ptes Hyatt, Fowler, Evans, L/Cpl Strawbridge, Pte Dodd L.Coy.	
CANADA HUTS.	3/6/15		Fine. Paraded at 7.30 p.m. for trench digging at ZILLEBEKE	
CANADA HUTS	4/6/15		Fine. Returned from trenches at 3. A.M. Pte Roberts L.Coy wounded. 300 men under MAJOR FORBES JORDAN paraded for digging.	
CANADA HUTS.	5/6/15		Fine. Returned from trenches at 3. A.M. Maxim Gun detachment under LIEUT. BEAUMONT and 2nd LIEUT. HUNT at 2 p.m. marched to LOCRE.	

Army Form C. 2118.

WAR DIARY
or
INTELLIGENCE SUMMARY.
(Erase heading not required.)

Instructions regarding War Diaries and Intelligence Summaries are contained in F.S. Regs., Part II. and the Staff Manual respectively. Title pages will be prepared in manuscript.

Place	Date	Hour	Summary of Events and Information	Remarks and references to Appendices
LOCRE.	6/6/15.		Fine. Marched at 7 a.m. to LOCRE and bivouaced in a field. C and D Coys. under MAJOR FORBES went up to the Trenches at 8.15 p.m. for instruction. Each Coy being attached respectively to 6th and 8th SHERWOOD FORESTERS. Pte Smith D. Coy Killed. Wounds left leg.	
LOCRE	7/6/15		Fine. Weather hot. C + D Coys still in the Trenches. Pte Hallett D Coy killed by Rifle grenade and buried at 9.30 p.m. in KEMMEL Chateau Cmetery. Cpl Dunn C Coy killed. Ptes Lewis and Evans C Coy wounded.	
LOCRE.	8/6/15		Fine. C and D Coys relieved by A and B Coys. Pte Hacking D Coy Killed. Pte Briggs D Coy wounded.	
LOCRE.	9/6/15		Fine. No Casualties. Visited B Coys Trenches in the afternoon. Pte Hacking buried at 9.30 p.m. in KEMMEL Chateau Cemetery.	
LOCRE	10/6/15.		Wet. A post occupied by B Coy was attacked by Bomb throwers, but enemy were driven off by rifle fire. C + D Coys relieved A and B in the Trenches. No Casualties.	
LOCRE.	11/6/15		Fine. C and D Coys returned to camp about 12 midnight. Pte Lewis C Coy wounded by rifle grenade.	
LOCRE.	12/6/15.		Fine. Marched at 7 A.M. to CANADA HUTS.	
CANADA HUTS	13/6/15.		Parade service and Holy Communion. Fine.	
CANADA HUTS.	14/6/15		Fine. Marched at 8.55 a.m. to Huts at WLAMERTINGHE. Took out a working party of 200 under MAJOR MURRAY. to dig "dug-outs" E of YPRES for occupation tomorrow. A draft of 99 men arrived from Pembroke Dock	

Army Form C. 2118.

WAR DIARY
INTELLIGENCE SUMMARY.
(Erase heading not required.)

Instructions regarding War Diaries and Intelligence Summaries are contained in F.S. Regs., Part II. and the Staff Manual respectively. Title pages will be prepared in manuscript.

Place	Date	Hour	Summary of Events and Information	Remarks and references to Appendices
VLAMERTINGHE	15/6/15		Fine. Marched at 8 P.M. to Dugouts. E. of YPRES. and Ourselves in all night.	
TRENCHES. E. OF YPRES.	16/6/15		Fine. Marched at about 10 A.M to support BRITISH attack E. of YPRES which our guns had prepared by a two hours bombardment. The Regiment came under a very heavy shell fire, high explosives etc. CAPT. AVERY and 2.LIEUT. ELLIS killed. 2.LIEUT. STARK and 2.LIEUT. V.D. FRENCH wounded. 11 Other ranks killed. 57 Other Ranks wounded. 10 O.R. Missing.	
VLAMERTINGHE	17/6/15		Fine. The Regiment withdrawn at 3 A.M. to VLAMERTINGHE. 2nd LIEUT. FRENCH died of wounds.	
VLAMERTINGHE	18/6/15		Fine.	
TRENCHES. E. OF YPRES.	19/6/15		Fine. A Draft of 82 men arrived at VLAMERTINGHE from ENGLAND in the morning. Marched at 7.55 P.M. to take over the SUFFOLKS TRENCHES Arrived at SUFFOLK H.Q at 10 P.M. Completed taking over at 12.25 A.M. C & D Coys in front trenches A & B in support.	
TRENCHES. E. OF YPRES.	20/6/15		Fine. Heavy Shelling at times. Stood to arms all night thinking we were going to attack. LIEUT. H.G BOOKER wounded. Pte. Douglas "D" Coy killed & buried at H.Q. 4 Other Ranks wounded.	
TRENCHES. E. OF YPRES.	21/6/15		Fine. Heavy Shelling at times. 6 Other ranks wounded.	
TRENCHES. E. OF YPRES	22/6/15		Fine. Oxfords made an attack at 8 P.M. on GERMAN trenches, but could not get in. The Artillery bombardment had not been very well ranged. LIEUT. LLOYD Led our Bombers in the assault. One was killed (Pte Wood) Pte Germann bombarded. our Trenches heavily when our bombardment ceased. 26 Other ranks wounded.	
TRENCHES E. OF YPRES.	23/6/15		Some rain. 3 Other ranks wounded.	

Army Form C. 2118.

WAR DIARY
or
INTELLIGENCE SUMMARY.
(Erase heading not required.)

Instructions regarding War Diaries and Intelligence Summaries are contained in F. S. Regs., Part II. and the Staff Manual respectively. Title pages will be prepared in manuscript.

Place	Date	Hour	Summary of Events and Information	Remarks and references to Appendices
TRENCHES E. of YPRES	24/6/15		Fine. Heavy Shelling on No. 15 Trench which was wrecked and one man, Pte ROBINSON O Coy, killed. 10th DURHAMS arrived in relief at 10.5 p.m. Relief complete at 1.15 A.M. 25/6/15. No Casualties to us during relief and very little firing.	
ZWYNLAND	25/6/15		Left BRIGADE H.Q. E. of YPRES with D Coy the other 3 Coys having gone on. Not meal W. of YPRES. Moved into Bivouac about 2½ miles S.W. of POPERINGHE at ZWYNLAND arrived about 6 a.m. All ranks very tired. Heavy Showers after arrival.	
ZWYNLAND	26/6/15		Fine. One Shower. Resting in Bivouac.	
ZWYNLAND	27/6/15		Fine. One Shower. Church Service 10 a.m. All men hot Baths at Brewery.	
ZWYNLAND	28/6/15		Fine. Resting.	
ZWYNLAND	29/6/15		Fine with Showers. Resting.	
ZWYNLAND	30/6/15		Fine. Resting.	
ZWYNLAND	1/7/15		Fine. Resting. A digging party of 400 men under MAJOR FORBES (100 from each Coy) paraded at 6.15 p.m. and went in Motor Buses to KRISTADT and thence to the YPRES Salient to digging. 2 Other ranks wounded.	
ZWYNLAND	2/7/15		Fine. Digging party returned 4.30 a.m. Staff of 50 men arrived this evening at 7 p.m. CAPT. SUMNER brought them but returned to the BASE on 3rd.	
ZWYNLAND	3/7/15		Fine and hot. Resting.	
ZWYNLAND	4/7/15		Church service at 11.30 a.m. and found digging party of 300 men under MAJOR JORDAN digging communication trenches. No casualties.	

Army Form C. 2118.

WAR DIARY
of
INTELLIGENCE SUMMARY.
(Erase heading not required.)

Instructions regarding War Diaries and Intelligence
Summaries are contained in F. S. Regs., Part II.
and the Staff Manual respectively. Title pages
will be prepared in manuscript.

Place	Date	Hour	Summary of Events and Information	Remarks and references to Appendices
ZWYNLAND	5/7/15		Fine. 1st Batt.n came for a Route March through our Camp, and halted there for an hour to allow the men to see one another.	
ZWYNLAND	6/7/15		Fine. 200 men under MAJOR DELMÉ MURRAY went out all night digging Communication trenches. No casualties.	
ZWYNLAND	7/8/15		Windy and Showery.	
YPRES RAMPARTS	8/8/15		Fine. Battalion marched at 4 p.m. to the RAMPARTS as reserve to the Brigade. The 5th Ox and BUCKS and 9th RIFLE BRIGADE. 9 K.R.R. also in Reserve. One man wounded. Machine Gun detachment which were attached to the 5th Ox & Bucks. A Carrying Party of 610 men for rations and engineering material went up to the Ox & Bucks trenches.	
YPRES RAMPARTS	9/7/15		Fine. Heavy German shelling in the afternoon by stink shells. 2Lieut HOLT hit by portion of shell in his dug-out also two men. Clearing Streets and Ramparts by day and carrying at night.	
YPRES RAMPARTS	10/9/15		R. Harford M.G. Section killed this morning by a German shell. He was buried by the Oxfords in RAILWAY WOOD. Clearing Streets and Ramparts by day and carrying to Trenches at night. Carrying party of 600 men rations engineering material for OXFORDS 12 men wounded.	
YPRES RAMPARTS	11/7/15		Clearing and Salving Stores by day and carrying at night. 600 men carrying. No Casualties.	
YPRES RAMPARTS	12/7/15		2 Other ranks wounded.	
"	13/7/15		4 other ranks wounded.	
"	14/7/15		7 other ranks wounded. 2 Died of wounds.	

Army Form C. 2118.

WAR DIARY
—of—
INTELLIGENCE SUMMARY.
(Erase heading not required.)

Instructions regarding War Diaries and Intelligence
Summaries are contained in F. S. Regs., Part II.
and the Staff Manual respectively. Title pages
will be prepared in manuscript.

Place	Date	Hour	Summary of Events and Information	Remarks and references to Appendices
	15/7/15		1 Other rank killed. 10 wounded.	
	16/7/15		1 " " killed 6 wounded.	
	17/7/15		4 " " wounded.	
	18/7/15		Relieved by Somersets and D.C.L.I. Machine Gunners Signallers and Bombers in the afternoon. Somersets did not arrive till 11 p.m. and the	
	19/7/15		D.C.L.I. till one a.m. The relief was not complete till 2.45 a.m. and we did not get into Camp till 5.30 a.m. 1 Other rank killed, one accidentally killed. 6 wounded.	
BUSSEBOOM	20/7/15		2 Working parties of 100 men at H.10.d.6.3 in morning and } Rfl.Brig. Belgium, France 2 " " 100 " " " " in afternoon } Wood Sheet 28.	
BUSSEBOOM	21/7/15		Men had Baths. 2 Working parties 100 men each by night to WHITE CHATEAU.	
BUSSEBOOM	22/7/15		LIEUT. COL. SMITH admitted to Hospital suffering from wounds received 16th inst in trenches. MAJOR FORBES took over Command. 2 Working parties 100 men by day H.10.D.6.3	
BUSSEBOOM	23/7/15		2 Working parties 100 each H.10.D.6.3 by day Rfl.Brig. Belgium & France Wood Sheet 28. 2 " " 50 " for 14th Signal Coy by night 2 LIEUT. OWEN went on course of M.G. with H. Motor M.G. Batt. Reinforcement of 140 O.R. arrived.	
BUSSEBOOM	24/7/15		2 Working parties 50 each by night at I.9.d.4.5. Rfl.Brig. Belgium, scale Wood Sheet 28. 2 " " 100 " day " H.10.d.6.3 " " 1 O.R. wounded.	
BUSSEBOOM	25/7/15		2 Working parties 100 each by day at H.10.d.6.3 " " Thunderstorm.	
BUSSEBOOM	26/7/15		Took over YPRES Ramparts from Somerset L.I. Relief complete 10.50 p.m.	

WAR DIARY
or
INTELLIGENCE SUMMARY.
(Erase heading not required.)

Army Form C. 2118.

Place	Date	Hour	Summary of Events and Information	Remarks and references to Appendices
YPRES.	27/7/15		Repairing Dug-outs. Cleaning up in day. Sanitary party under LIEUT WARD and 12 men. 3 N.C.O's on Carrying and working parties at night. 1 N.C.O. killed (Q.M.S. Turner) 2 Mules killed. 2 Limbered wagons damaged by shell fire in YPRES.	
YPRES.	28/7/15.		Repairing Dug-outs etc. F.G.C.M. on Pte Langford promulgated. By night 150 On working parties in H. Sector (1 wounded) " " 276 " Carrying " " " Capt C.J. FRENCH 2 R. Rif and 13 men to Course of Instruction with 177th Tunneling Coy.	
YPRES.	29/7/15		Repairing Dug-outs etc. By night working parties 150. By night Carrying parties 266. 1 killed. 8 wounded. Bomb throwers unstable.	
YPRES.	30/7/15		LIEUT BURROUGH arrived. Bat'n ordered to relieve Ox & BUCKS in trenches, but Order cancelled because of enemy attack on Crater. A & B Coys sent to G Sector. H.Q Lines N & S of MENIN ROAD. Half C Coy sent to take place of A Coy. advanced to front.	
YPRES.	31/7/15.		D Coy about 4 a.m. proceeded to H.Q Lines S of MENIN Road. LIEUT LLOYD and Bombers sent to reinforce 9th K.R.R. at G.10. Enemy having occupied portion of G.10. Casualties 1 killed. LIEUT LLOYD and 8 Bombers wounded. D Coy to F2. Half C Coy to G.H.Q. Lines S of MENIN Road.	
YPRES	1/8/15		H.Q & H.Q. Coy. to F2 and New Generals Dugout respectively. At this time position of Coys as follows:- A Coy. S9. B Coy G.H.Q. Lines. C Coy. S F2 & S 2. D Coy S F2 & S11. H.Q. F.2. Orders went to take over from 9th K.R.R. by daylight. C Coy to go to S.3A. C to G.10. B to S7, 9 +11. and D to G.H.Q Lines S of MENIN Road. Move by daylight impracticable. In consequence of D & B Coys being already in position. D Bournemann at S7.9.11 and B Coy at G.H.Q. Lines. Contrary to Army orders. Move complete by midnight. A C & D Coys placed under of Col. VILLIERS STEWART RIFLE BGDE. Casualties CAPT MEASON CAPT MEYNELL Wounded. Other ranks (3) killed. 2 Died of wounds. 20 Wounded.	

WAR DIARY
INTELLIGENCE SUMMARY

Army Form C. 2118.

Place	Date	Hour	Summary of Events and Information	Remarks and references to Appendices
YPRES	2/8/15		9th R.B's relieved by Col. GREEN and 8th K.R.R. and H.Q. moved to G.H.Q. Lines S. of MENIN Road. A.C. and D Coys under orders of LIEUT COL GREEN. Casualties 2 Died of Wounds.	
YPRES	3/8/15		Situation the same. - 8 Other ranks killed 11 wounded. Capt Bort arrived.	
YPRES	4/8/15		Situation the same. 2 Killed 2 wounded. Relieved by 1st Bn K.S.L.I. and 2nd K.O.Y.L.I.	
YPRES	5/8/15		Relief complete before midnight and Batt. now at YPRES. C Coy at Dug out near ECOLE. A and H.Q Coys at H/Q Lines N of MENIN Road. B. coy Reinforcements 10. OR arrived from Base.	
YPRES	6/8/15		Relieved 5th OX & BUCKS in H Sector relief complete before midnight. Bombardment 3 am. Col. COBB in Command of left sector. Casualties 3 Killed. 4 wounded.	
YPRES	7/8/15		Situation the same. Much shelling both sides. Casualties 1 Killed 6 wounded. 2 Coys K.R.R's on our right. K.R.R's much battered. 2 Coys R.B's relieved	
YPRES	8/8/15		Situation same. Much shelling Attack by 16th and 18th BRIGADES should have taken place but postponed. Casualties. 2 killed. 17. wounded.	
YPRES	9/8/15		2.45 A.M. Bombardment till 3.15 a.m. 16th and 18th Brigades attack. Batt. supported attack by rifle and M.G. fire. Casualties 2LIEUT R.F. TAYLOR killed. CAPT W.L. HERD CAPT. P.J. BEHASS/S. wounded. 2LIEUT S. MORINGTON killed. 36 wounded. CAPT STAFF F. MOORE LANE CAPT. F. LAKE wound in afternoon. 2 Coys 2nd R.B. relieving by 2 Coys 3rd Ox & BUCKS. Man 2 Coys much shattered.	
YPRES	10/8/15		Situation the same. Quiet day - no casualties. Relieved by 1 Platoon 10th D.L.I. and the 6th SOMERSET L.I on evening. Relief complete before midnight.	
VLAMERTINGHE	11/8/15		To Bivouac near Vlamertinghe H.1.b.7.2	

WAR DIARY
or
INTELLIGENCE SUMMARY.

(Erase heading not required.)

Army Form C. 2118.

Instructions regarding War Diaries and Intelligence Summaries are contained in F.S. Regs., Part II. and the Staff Manual respectively. Title pages will be prepared in manuscript.

Place	Date	Hour	Summary of Events and Information	Remarks and references to Appendices
VLAMERTINGHE	12/8/15		In Bivouac H.1.B.7.2 LIEUT W.F.W. SHIELDS and M.O. O.R. Reinforcement arrived from Base. Working party 1 Officer 50 men by Bus to YPRES under 62nd Coy R.E. No casualties.	
VLAMERTINGHE	13/8/15		In Bivouac H.1.B.9.2. Working party 1 Officer 50 men by Bus to YPRES under 62nd Field Coy R.E. No Casualties	
VLAMERTINGHE	14/8/15		6th Division claim Bivouac Ground. Moved before 10 am to new Bivouac G.5.C.7.7. Working party 1 Officer 50 men by Bus to YPRES under 62nd Field Coy R.E. " " 100 " G: 16 REDOUBT " " 30 " Railway Crossing for Road Repairing. No Casualties.	
VLAMERTINGHE	15/8/15		In Bivouac G.5.C.7.7. Working party 1 Officer 50 men by Bus to YPRES under 62nd Field Coy R.E. No Casualties.	
"	16/8/15		In Bivouac G.5.C.7.7.	
"	17/8/15		In Bivouac G.5.C.7.7. Major FORBES and Major JORDAN left for England LIEUT. COL. O.C. BORRETT D.S.O. Kings Own Regiment took over command of Regt.	
"	18/8/15		In Bivouac G.5.C.7.7. Sto Leigh (Stretcher Bearer) wounded (Rifle) whilst with working party under R.E. YPRES.	
"	19/8/15		In Bivouac G.5.C.7.7. Inspection 10 A.M. B.G.C. Inspection 5 P.M. G.O.C. 6th Corps. Address to Officers "The Regiment had always had a very fine name. He was proud to have one of its Battns under his command." 2 LIEUT. H.D.E. ELLIOTT from 9th Battn joined. Draft of 55 arrived from Base.	
VLAMERTINGHE	20/8/15		Moved at 5. P.m. to become Brigade Reserve in Billets at H.I.D.8.8.	

WAR DIARY
or
INTELLIGENCE SUMMARY.
(Erase heading not required.)

Army Form C. 2118.

Instructions regarding War Diaries and Intelligence Summaries are contained in F. S. Regs. Part II. and the Staff Manual respectively. Title pages will be prepared in manuscript.

Place	Date	Hour	Summary of Events and Information	Remarks and references to Appendices
VLAMERTINGHE	21/8/15		In Hutments (in Reserve) at H.I.D.8.8.	
VLAMERTINGHE	22/8/15		In Hutments (in Reserve) at H.I.D.8.8. LIEUTS:- BONNYMAN. T.G. & LLEWELLYN. J.H. 2ND LIEUTS FOSTER. R.S. SMITH. C.C. FAULKNER. E.C. DAVIS. W.L. joined.	
VLAMERTINGHE	23/8/15		In Hutments (in Reserve) at H.I.D.8.8. Company Officers visited Trenches, previous to taking over at night. On this visit 2 Coy Officers were wounded, i.e. LIEUT. F.T. BURROUGH. C Coy. CAPT. E.V.E. TUNNER B Coy. Battalion took over trenches from Ox & Bucks (5th) Bn 2nd & 13 Coy & French. C Coy. I.H.Q. A Coy. H.13.	
YPRES	24/8/15		LIEUT. R.G. BUGGEN. Killed. (otherwise quiet)	
YPRES	25/8/15		LIEUT. T.G. BONNYMAN. Wounded. Corporal & 4 Other to Wounded.	
"	26/8/15		2 LIEUT. E. GERTON joined. 2 O.R. Wounded.	
"	27/8/15		3 O.R. Wounded.	
"	28/8/15		7 O.R. Wounded.	
"	29/8/15		Relieved by 6th D.C.L.I. Arrived in Bivouacs at C.6.d.6.0. VLAMERTINGHE.	
VLAMERTINGHE	30/8/15		LIEUT. J.T. SNEALL M.O. joined. Rest.	
"	31/8/15		Rest.	
"	1/9/15		Rest	

Army Form C. 2118.

WAR DIARY
or
INTELLIGENCE SUMMARY.
(Erase heading not required.)

Instructions regarding War Diaries and Intelligence Summaries are contained in F.S. Regs., Part II. and the Staff Manual respectively. Title pages will be prepared in manuscript.

Place	Date	Hour	Summary of Events and Information	Remarks and references to Appendices
VLAMERTINGHE	2/9/15		Reinforcements of 40. O.R. arrived.	
Do.	3/9/15 to 6/9/15		Rest.	
YPRES	7/9/15		Battalion proceeded to Trenches. B.Coy G.H.Q. SOUTH of MENIN ROAD. C.Coy N of MENIN ROAD. A + D + Bn H.Q. Dugouts. I.15.b.9.9.	
YPRES	8th & 9th		Quiet.	
"	10/9/15		4. O.R. wounded	
"	11/9/15		Left Dugouts. I.15.b.9.9. to relieve 5th OX + BUCKS L.I. Bn. H.Q. + A.Coy. F.2. H.13. H.19.	
"	12th 13th 14th		Quiet.	
NEAR POPERINGHE	15/9/15		Relieved by YORKSHIRES. returned to Bivouacs F.27. C.5.8. All in Billets by 2. A.M. On returning to Bivouacs D.Coy were shelled and 2.O.R. were killed and 12. O.wounded.	
"	16/9/15		In Bivouac. Reinforcement of 46. O.R. arrived	
"	17/9/15		Battalion inspected by 2nd Army Commander. (GENERAL PLUMER) 5.30 pm	
"	18th to 23rd		In Bivouac.	

Army Form C. 2118.

WAR DIARY or INTELLIGENCE SUMMARY.
(Erase heading not required.)

Place	Date	Hour	Summary of Events and Information	Remarks and references to Appendices
YPRES.	24/9/15		The Battalion proceeded to the trenches in fighting order on the night 23rd/24th September. Strength 14 Officers + 60 O.R. The Battalion disposition was as follows :- A + D Coy H.13 to H.16 and supporting trenches B. Coy F.13. C. Coy Ramparts YPRES. Battalion H.Q. H.16. At 3.50 a.m. an intense Bombardment by our own Guns took place lasting till 4.20 a.m. This was immediately replied to by the Germans & Heavy Bombardment continued throughout the day. Casualties CAPT. S. G. BEAUMONT killed. 3. O.R. killed. 3. O.R. wounded. S. O.R.	
"	25/9/15		At 1. A.M. The Battalion was in position in the Trenches as follows :- A. Coy. H.13 & 14. D. Coy. H.15a. and H.16a. B. & S.15. C. Coy. Diagonal. At 3.50 a.m. intense Bombardment replied to by Germans immediately. At H. 5 a.m. Battalion in position for assault A. & D. Coy. and 2 platoons of B with 2 Machine Guns and Signallers in Coy Column in front of our own Lines. 2 Platoons of B & C Coys in support in the trenches. At 4.20 a.m. assault took place and we penetrated to Germans second line, but owing to the attack on the position on our right not getting home, and the Counter attack enveloping our left flank the position became untenable and the Battalion was forced to re-occupy our original line of trenches at about 8.15 a.m. The Germans bombarded heavily up till 1. P.M. and again from 9. P.M. till midnight. During the day the Battalion was reinforced by 2 platoons of the 16th Somerset L. I. and were relieved in the trenches at 11.30 P.M. by the 6th D.C.L.I. Casualties :- Officers 1. killed. Missing wounded + missing	

Killed: O.R. 3. 41.
Wounded: 5. 250.
Missing: 2. 100.
3.
7.

Army Form C. 2118.

WAR DIARY
or
INTELLIGENCE SUMMARY.
(Erase heading not required.)

Instructions regarding War Diaries and Intelligence Summaries are contained in F. S. Regs., Part II. and the Staff Manual respectively. Title pages will be prepared in manuscript.

Place	Date	Hour	Summary of Events and Information	Remarks and references to Appendices
NEAR POPERINGHE	26/9/15		Returned to Billets at F.27.c.5.8. The 5th Corps Commander visited the Battalion in Billets and congratulated them on their bearing on the 25th inst. and said they could rest assured that they had drawn considerable forces of the enemy towards YPRES and prevented them from reinforcing down south. They could therefore say that they had materially assisted in the victory round ARRAS.	
"	27/9/15 to 12/10/15		In Billets. F.27.c.5.8.	
YPRES.	13/10/15		Battalion proceeded to Trenches on night of 13th. Entrained at Poperinghe for YPRES at 8 p.m. During the train journey the Germans sent over several shells but most of them failed to explode. On arrival at YPRES the town was being shelled very heavily but there were no casualties. The Battalion relieved the 7th R.B.s. The disposition of Companies was as follows:- D Coy & 1 Platoon of B. F.13. C. & B Coys and Bombers X1a. A & B Coys and Battn. H.Q. Dug outs I15.B.8.9. Relief complete by 11.30 p.m.	
"	14/10/15 15/10/15		Quiet.	
"	16/10/15		At 5.20 a.m. an exceptional noise was heard and it was reported that H.20 Trench occupied by the OX & BUCKS. had been blown up. We were ordered to stand to in case the enemy made an attack. No attack was however, made by them. At 9 a.m. the OX & BUCKS. sent for our Bombers	

WAR DIARY or INTELLIGENCE SUMMARY.

Army Form C. 2118.

Place	Date	Hour	Summary of Events and Information	Remarks and references to Appendices
YPRES	17/10/15		D. Coy moved up to support Ox & BUCKS. A. Coy and Batth.H.Q. F.13.	
"	18/10/15		Battalion relieved 8th R.B.s. in A.Scots. A. Coy moved to A.3. B Coy to A.4. C. Coy to X.3. D Coy to A.5. Batth.H.Q. POTIJZE WOOD near Y.3.	
"	19/10/15		Situation quiet. Considerable Aeroplane activity.	
"	20/10/15		Rapid fire was opened on a German working party at 5 a.m. and 3 men were seen to fall.	
"	21/10/15		Little activity displayed by the Germans. Battalion relieved by 1ST/LEICESTERS	
"	22/10/15		Arrived in Billets at near HOUTKERQUE.	

5th Division.
G.411.

1. The 5th Bn. King's Shropshire L.I. will find a working party to night, with proper complement of Officers, for work on the ZILLEBEKE switch.
   The party to be organized in two detachments, one of 300 and one of 250.

2. The working party will march at 7.15 p.m. and will draw tools in the field east of 15th Inf. Bde. Headquarters I.21.a. 7/2, and then proceed to the rendezvous given in the attached work table.
   The party will march in detachments of 50 at an interval of 200 yards.

3. Four Officers will be at the rendezvous given in work table at 7.30 p.m. to meet the representatives R.E., to be pointed out the work that is to be done.

4. The remainder of the battalion will march at 7.30 p.m. via Cross Roads in H.16.d. 1/1 to the dug-outs in H.23.b., where they will be joined by the working party on completion of their task.

5. 5th Divisional Cyclist Company will detail 2 Officers and 20 men to be at disposal of O.C. 5th King's Shropshire L.I. as guides. They will be responsible for guiding the Officers proceeding in advance, and the working parties, both to the spot where the tools will be laid out and to the rendezvous given in work table.
   They will also be responsible for guiding the remainder of the battalion to the dug-outs in H.23.b.

6. 5th Divisional Cyclist Company will detail one Officer and 20 men to be at the Offices of C.R.E. in RENINGHELST at 4 p.m. where they will conduct three wagons to R.E. Park DICKEBUSCH H.28.c., draw 450 shovels and 100 picks and take them to the field east of 15th Bde. H.Q., lay them out and hand them over to working party. The wagons can be dismissed when the tools have been unloaded.

7. The working party on completion of work will store the tools in the neighbourhood of the rendezvous given in work table in readiness for to-morrow night's work.

8. Please acknowledge, by wire where possible.

5th Division,
31st May, 1915.

Lt.Colonel,
General Staff, 5th Division.

Copies to
42nd Infantry Bde.
5th Bn. Shrop. L.I.
5th Div. Cyclist Co.
C.R.E.
A.A & Q.M.G.

5th K.S.L.I. Vol: 2

79/121
9/10

Oct 21st — Dec 31st 1916

2.S.
8 sheets

5th, Bn, KING'S SHROPSHIRE LIGHT INFANTRY.

ROLL of OFFICERS.

Lt. Col. O. C. Borrett.
Major A.T.C. Rundle,
Capt. C.J. French
Capt. N.T. Porter (Sick)
Capt. J. H. Llewellyn
Capt. E. G. Cripps
Capt. H. E. Measer (Sick)
Lieut. C. Palmer.
" R. Yates Earl.

2/Lieut. C.H.B. Phipps
" S. G. Budgett
" D. Boumphrey
" D.W. Hughes
" D.E.G. Preece
" H.D.E. Elliott (Sick)
" O.S. Benbow Rowe
" R.D. Elliott
" W.J. Milton
" T.B. Jolly (leave)
" G. Turner (leave)
" A.K. Guyer
" L.A. Jones
" R.A. Butt
" C.S. Underhill
" C.C. Abraham
" A. Gittins,

Lieut. & QrMr. P. Bradshaw.
Lt. J.T. Smeall (Medical Officer)
Capt. W.M. Amery (R.C. Chaplain)

"A" Company.

Regtl.No.	RANK AND NAME.	REMARKS.
7935	C.S.M. Roberts. F.	
8623	C.Q.M.S. Newman, G.	
10941	Actg.Q.M.S. Manning, J.	
10855	Sgt. Bishop, T.R.	
10518	" Price, J.	
10547	" Howard, S.	
10522	" Williams, T.	
11089	" Morgan, GR.	
10589	" Burnham, C.	
8198	" Lloyd, B.	
10793	" Davies, J.	
10810	Cpl. Wright, S.	
10731	" Farrington, G.	
10773	" Maddox, J.	
10617	" Morris, G.	
11155	L/Sgt. Hawkins, T.W.	
11045	Cpl. Bullock, W.	
11436	" Johnson, J.H.	
16079	L/Sgt. Edwards, P.	
16777	Cpl. Wilkinson, T.	
9810	" Beech, G.	
6866	" Strong, F.	
10667	L/Cpl. Rogers, J.	
10676	" Barlow, J.	
10575	" Hatton, T.R.	
11088	" Tomkins, T.	
20155	" Johnson, W.	
20107	" Kenny, E.	
10303	" Norry.	
10685	" Ashton, T.	
10554	" Jones, T.W.	
10488	" Chittenden, C.	
11150	" Arrowsmith, W.	
5905	" Clarke, A. E.	
20133	" Brand, H.	
10674	" Briggs, J.	
9430	" Pugh, H.	
10505	" Shone, T.	
5978	" Potts, F.	
10763	" Annum, B.	
10689	" Ashbury, T.	
10856	" Ashworth, F.	
10630	" Ashworth, E.	
15068	" Adderley, H.	
17280	" Ashton, A.	
10591	" Buttery, J.	
10826	" Buckley, E.	
16037	" Ball, A.	
16258	" Broom, W.	
6681	" Binnersley, W.	
17441	" Biston, C.	
17233	" Baldwin, W.	
16746	" Bachegalup, P.	
16701	" Burton, J.	
11141	" Brown, W.	
17834	" Branson, S.	
17833	" Barker, A.	
20026	" Brightwell, J.	
20054	" Bailey, J.	
20023	" Birchall, F.	
17976	" Bamford, F.	

"A" Company (Continued)

Regtl. No.	RANK AND NAME.	REMARKS.
11237	Pte. Boston, C.	
17382	" Brewne, T.	
16121	" Boyd, T.	
17780	" Bailey, W.	
4133	" Blakely, A.	
10753	" Butler, J.	
10659	" Blower, J.	
16206	" Craddock, W.	
16044	" Crawshaw, J.	
10578	" Craghill, W.	
20008	" Cattlin, A.W.	
10762	" Clare, G.H.	
17853	" Coxhall, W.	
5511	" Childs, G.A.	
10606	" Deane, J.	
16745	" Davies, T.	
17027	" Davies, A.	
18166	" Davies, R.	
20072	" Davies, E.	
6617	" Davies, T.	
20109	" Denman, J.	
20122	" DeValder, A.	
17331	" Deem, C.D.	
10583	" Evans, J.E.	
10851	" Evans, A.	
10617	" Evans, C.	
16453	" Evans, F.	
10914	" Evans, T.	
17023	" Evans, W.C.	
18064	" Evans, S.	
16081	" Evans, J.T.	
17570	" Ewell, E.	
18205	" Elsby, S.	
17892	" Eccles, G.	
11842	" Edmondson, T.	
6945	" Edwards, W.	
10815	" Foster, W.	
10627	" Fearnall, B.	
16179	" Foster, T.	
8097	" Floyd, H.	
10687	" Goodwin, T.	
11574	" Goodwin, W.	
18120	" Griffiths, W.J.	
11174	" Griffiths, J.F.	
16682	" Giles, G.	
20038	" Graham, T.	
18162	" Grindrodd, H.	
17447	" Green, A.	
6625	" Grigg, W.	
10559	" Hodgson, L.E.	
10678	" Haines, R.	
10786	" Hamer, E.	
10798	" Herbert, W.	
10817	" Howells, J.	
17226	" Howells, T.	
16012	" Hayward, W.	
10623	" Hughes, J.H.	
10969	" Hughes, C.	
7278	" Holloway, W.	
10977	" Hill, E.	

"A" Company, (continued)

Regtl.No.	Rank and Name	Remarks
11158	Pte. Hill, R.E.	
17354	" Harp, S.	
20135	" Hopewell, W.A.	
17937	" Hanley, G.	
18136	" Hicks, J.	
15907	" Howlett, W.	
16048	" Heaton, H.	
16408	" Hart, F.	
18068	" Hollingshead, H.	
17632	" James, D.	
11087	" James, A.	
10664	" Johnson, G.A.	
11722	" Jones, L.H.	
16111	" Jones, J.W.	
11746	" Jones, W.	
~~15038~~	"	
17633	" Jones, R.H.	
18141	" Jones, G.R.	
18230	" Jones, B.	
6538	" Jones, T.	
17061	" Judge, C.	
18197	" Jaundrill, J.	
10748	" Kirby, H.	
18202	" Kenny, J.	
10514	" Lowe, M.W.	
10634	" Lloyd, A.	
10640	" Lloyd, F.	
6446	" Lloyd, R.	
10610	" Lewis, T.	
7996	" Lewis, E.	
16154	" Lovatt, J.	
17355	" Lynch, T.	
16093	" Lightfoot, W.	
17707	" Longworth, W.	
10671	" Lloyd, S.	Attached.
8871	" Loxham, H.	
10590	" Marsland, C.	
~~10854~~	" ~~Martin, J.~~	
~~14961~~	"	
~~00010~~	"	
11151	" Mann, J.	
10882	" Matthews, J.P.	
15043	" Morton, J.	
10203	" Maharry, R.	
16216	" Mackinson, F.	
10509	" Millineaux, J.	
18146	" Minckley, A.	
18147	" Mitchell, J.T.	
18344	" Mills, J.H.	
17649	" Merry, V.	
10811	" Neat, J.	
15035	" Norman, G.	
18179	" Newton, J.	
11738	" Nash, G.	
10694	" Newbrook, F.	
10619	" Oakley, A.	
10719	" Orwell, W.	
16169	" Orwell, J.	
17271	" Oliver, ~~S.~~	
10682	" Palin, G.	
11743	" Phillipa, R.	
11724	" Phillips, E.	
16996	" Pugh, E.	
11192	" Poston, C.	
18234	" Perry, J.	
14961	" Martin a.	

"A" Company (Continued)

Regtl.NO.	RANK AND NAME.	REMARKS.
17329	Pte, Purcell, G.A.	
11204	" Probert, W.	
~~13112~~	" ~~Prosser, T.H.~~	
18046	" Parry, E.	
11350	" Preece, J.	
10506	" Pymm, C.	
~~10558~~	"	
10558	" Rich, D.S.	
10847	" Riley, C.	
6483	" Ryan, C.	
16701	" Robb, L.	
18039	" Rowlands, J.	
8783	" Russell, H.	
10787	" Richards, J.	
11696	" Smith, W.	
11059	" Smith, H.G.	
17546	" Smith, R.M.	
16202	" Sims, A.	
17018	" Simmons, W.	
~~18031~~	"	
18183	" Stephenson, F.	
16028	" Sumner, D.	
17866	" Spragg, L.	
17275	" Smith, J.	
20183	" Searle, F.	
6480	" Stewart, E.	
11638	" Taylor, G.H.	
11156	" Taylor, H.	
10672	" Taylor, T.A.	
16699	" Thorley, W.	
18351	" Thomas, T.	
7434	" Thomas, D.H.	
10504	" Talbot, G.	
9262	" Thorne, W.	
10511	" Vaughan, T.	Hospital
10576	" Wakefield, W.	
16076	" Wilkinson, J.	
10625	" Williams, W.T.	
18174	" Williams, L.	
6581	" Williams, C.	Hospital
16132	" Workman, T.	
17727	" Waterton, C.	
18119	" Wharton, J.	
18004	" Windle, E.	
17789	" Wainwright, A.	
10436	" Webster, D.	
6566	" Ward, H.	
15010	" Warrender, H.	
18724	" Wood, H.	Hospital
16495	" Ward, J.	
17995	" Wright, E.	
11639	" Williams, H.	
8009	" Whitehead, G.B.	
8682	" Watson, B.	
16215	" Yates, J.	Hospital
18031	" Symonds D.	
17786	" Yates G.	

"B" Company-

Regtl. No.	RANK AND NAME.	REMARKS.
10802	Sgt. Tallboys, H.	
9026	" Johnson, J.	
8881	" Ferrington, J.	
16817	Cpl. House, W.	
5500	" Prue, W.	
15090	L/Cpl. Stephens, H.	
10745	" Taylor, T.	
10732	" Williams, T.	
14863	" Parsons, G.	
6353	" McGeorge, R.	
20065	" Allsopp, E.	
8489	C.S.M. Mound, S.	
0524	C.Q.M.S. Gimes, J.	
16024	Sergt. Bullock, W.	
6762	" Collins, C.	
10772	" Hailey, E.	
8635	" Jones, W.	
8358	" Lang, J.	
9636	" Martin, R.	
8597	" Purcell, H.	
10983	Cpl. Bromley, J.	
9521	" Cook.	
11513	" Cowlett, A.	
9866	" Price, W.	
6247	" Macdonald, L.	
11648	" Malt, W.	
7784	" Reed, B.	
11529	" Thomas, W.	
9616	" Williams, H.	
9881	" Williams, B.	
6498	" Allen, B.	
10975	L/Cpl. Bailey, W.	
~~20065~~		
8101	" Dodson, G.	
10967	" Griffiths, W.	
10916	" Hulbert, J.	
10963	" Lewis, W.	
~~10698~~	" ~~Ogleby, R.~~	
11687	" White, F.	
11534	" Stone, A.	
9578	" Buckley, A.	
11537	" Horner, F.	
20033	" Allsebrook, G.	
15926	" Armstrong, G.	
8030	" Astley, T.	Hospital
20066	" Allsopp, P.	
10788	" Barrett, H.	
16072	" Bywater, G.	
10865	" Blackford, G.	
17326	" Beddall, R.	
17968	" Bailey, E.	
8159	" Baugh, G.	Hospt
20007	" Beck, G.	
11043	" Brazill, J.	
17857	" Barnes, J.	
17858	" Brindle, P.	
7460	" Brewer, W.	
11558	" Breedon, H.	
17029	" Bertwhistle, R.	
6871	" Boulter, H.	
6803	" Bissell, W.	
17352	" Booth, E.	

"B" Company (Continued)

Regtl. NO.	RANK AND NAME.	REMARKS.
20061	Pte. Blackburn, C.	
20112	" Crossley, A.	
16091	" Collier, A.	
16024	" Charles, T.	
10820	" Clawley, W.	
20118	" Cambridge, G.	
18297	" Cowgill, C.	
17221	" Coyle, J.	
6523	" Cadman, R.	
16714	" Casey, J.	
16717	" Crompton, E.	
10858	" Curley, T.	
11462	" Challoner, T.	
11484	" Challoner, J.	
11652	" Chester, G.	
5223	" Cluett, A.	
20027	" Crookes, J.	
6531	" Cullen, P.	
6087	" Crompton, M.	
17785	" Davies, J.	
10912	" Davies, J.	
17666	" Downes, R.	
11880	" Davies, W.	
11587	" Durnall, G.H.	
18296	" Dudley, J.	
15833	" Dunn, G.	
10929	" Elton, H.	
17384	" Evans, E.	
17978	" Eggleston, R.	
16167	" Evans, G.J.	
10932	" Evans, W.	
6898	" Eaton, J.	
17577	" Edgar, J.T.	
17987	" Edwards, P.	
16753	" Edwards, G.	
10873	" Forrester, W.	
11536	" Forrester, W.	
11916	" Fidler, A.	
7041	" France, H.	
6686	" Faulkner, J.	
18853	" Griffiths, H.	
11015	" Gegg, F.G.	
12983	" Guntripp, F.	
~~10580~~	~~" Gavin, P.~~	
11274	" Gigg, B.	
17701	" Gogerty, H.	
10686	" Gwilliam, B.	
11625	" Gethin, J.J.	
18087	" Grindley, J.	
7593	" Goodall, J.	
10721	" Gough, H.	
7910	" Hicks, W.	
10862	" Hanley, H.	
9448	" Holland, P.	
10665	" Hanlon, G.	
7612	" Hickman, G.	
17613	" Harris, G.	
10930	" Holt, F.	
11522	" Horton, W.	
10919	" Hodges, J.	
9354	" Hill, J.	
10746	" Hill, A.	
17825	" Hodgson, J.	

"B" Company (Continued)

Regtl. No.	RANK AND NAME.	REMARKS.
17716	Pte. Horder, C.	
17488	" Hopwood, J.	
10310	" Hughes, J.	
17962	" Husband, W.	
17717	" Hill, W.G.	
17974	" Hoare, C.	
7095	" Hemmings, W.	
15157	" Harris, G.	
17879	" Hindley, J.	
17918	" Hughes, M.	
17941	" Hartshorn, J.	
17894	" Hassell, S.	
17939	" Jones, W.	
10722	" Jones, H.	
10893	" James, A.	
16101	" Johnson, F.	
17757	" Jones, J.	
~~9597~~		
6228	" Jennings, G.	
18054	" Johnson, R.	
17706	" Kinsey, W.	
6327	" Kirkham, W.	
17769	" Kemp, J.H.	
11708	" Lock, W.	
14864	" Langford, J.	
16719	" Long, H.	
16866	" Love, S.	
11624	" Lucas, H.	
17756	" Lloyd, L.	
10981	" Lloyd, J.	
17781	" Lawrence, G.	
17373	" Langford, G.	
16025	" Leach, J.	
11917	" Mabbett, A.	
~~18054~~	~~" Munday, W.~~	
10883	" Malpas, W.	
16729	" Mansell, F.	
15901	" McCarthy, P.	
17526	" Monks, R.	
18110	" Maddox, W.	
15111	" Meredith, P.	
16075	" Morris, R.	
7004	" McNeill, T.	
14962	" Manford, W.	
11009	" Meadows, G.	
16804	" Mason, W.	
15904	" Murphy, D.	
6883	" Morris, J.	
16158	" Millington, E.	
10741	" Nutt, H.	
6183	" Nicholls, C.H.	
7789	" Nicholls, A.E.	
11960	" Nash, T.	
11435	" Nickless, J.	
17963	" Neill, T.	
16443	" Nicholls, G.	
10601	" Oliver, C.	
16825	" Owens, E.	
11602	" Onions, W.	
17903	" Prior, H.	
17739	" Page, J.	
10800	" Pritchard, A.	
11365	Roberts	

"B" Company (Continued)

Regtl. No.	Rank and Name	Remarks
10587	Pte, Powell, A.	
17647	" Powell, R.	
16681	" Powell, G.	
7101	" Paterson, W.	
17243	" Parry, G.	
11433	" Pont, C.	
17917	" Perks, W.	
10062	" Phaisey, J.	
17925	" Potts, H.	
11008	" Price, A.	
8953	" Phillips, P.	
17470	" Prior, G.	
9142	" Richards, W.	
10789	" Richards, G.	
18842	" Raiswell, J.	
16183	" Russell, J.	
14904	" Richards, H.	
~~11222~~	" ~~Rees, E.~~	
17883	" Ruscoe, J.	
9401	" Rigby, J.	
11507	" Ryder, A.	
10949	" Richards, J.	
17901	" Richards, E.	Hospt
20150	" Rawlinson, W.	
9874	" Smith, A.	
17498	" Seabury, J.	
16031	" Sullivan, J.	
6960	" Slack, J.H.	
17584	" Smith, H.	
17803	" Smith, W.	
7893	" Sherbrook, W.H.	
17921	" Sylvester, G.G.	
17849	" Steventon, G.	
17651	" Southall, G.	
7549	" Scott, J.	
16034	" Smith, W.	
19878	" Turner, J.	
18782	" Taylor, J.	
11512	" Thomas, W.	
16074	" Tanner, E.	
17060	" Tringham, J.	
18092	" Treherne, G.	
5957	" Thacker, A.	
9767	" Taylor, S.	
15933	" Veevers, W.	
10894	" Vedmore, E.	
10926	" Vickery, W.	
14945	" Waterhouse, W.	
10931	" Whittle, G.	
17042	" Watkins, A.	
10861	" Wallace, T.	
11012	" Woodend, L.	
20194	" Wetherall, E.	
14497	" Wilkinson, G.	
~~11454~~	" ~~Wood, J.~~	
11525	" Wilson, G.	
17820	" Wainwright, T.	
17953	" Ward, C.	
17745	" Whalley, A.	
15106	" Wilshaw, M.	
14940	" Westwood, L.	

5th. Batt. KING'S SHROPSHIRE LIGHT INFANTRY.

NOMINAL ROLL (by Companies) of N.C.O's and MEN proceeding with the Battalion.

"C" Company.

Regtl. No.	RANK AND NAME.	REMARKS.
10843	R.Q.M.S. Grimley, F.H.	
9406	C.S.M. Furber, G.C.	
11025	C.QM.S. Morris, S.	
10986	Sgt. Hands, W.	
10985	" Powis, C.	
11076	" Oakley, J.	
8067	" Jones, B.J.	
11269	" Atkinson, C.	
11033	" Morris, F.	
9440	" Williams, S.	
7014	L/Sgt. Williams, P.	
11044	Cpl. Williams, J.	
11723	" Jarvis, W.	
11262	" Baker, W.	
7550	" Watkins, T.	
11495	" King, A.	
10327	" Carter, A.	
12327	" Wilson, A.	
8345	" Lane, D.	
9954	" Butler, F.	
11253	" Lowe, E.	
10979	" Phillips, J.	
9529	" Earl, F.	
11068	" Howells, G.	
11309	" Thomas, S.	
16903	" Sudlow, H.	
10886	L/Cpl. Narroway, R.	
16550	" Williams, L.	
11096	" Hayle, H.	
10995	" Williams, E.	
11105	" Williams, J.	
16799	" Jones, J.	
18243	" Vaughan, W.	
11103	" Llewellyn, H.	
6259	" Easther, H.	
11100	Pte. Alford, G.	
11054	" Austin, P.	
17334	" Austin, F.	
17736	" Almond, G.	
20035	" Allen, H.	
20034	" Anderson, H.	
11618	" Allen, F.	
17471	" Abraham, J.	
8849	" Anderson, W.J.	
11117	" Arrowsmigh, F.	
11066	" Baggott, C.	
11102	" Baker, F.	
11312	" Bengree, J.	
15109	" Brown, A.	
11047	" Bunn, L.	

"C" Company. (Continued)

Regtl. No.	RANK AND NAME.	REMARKS.
8326	Pte. Butter, R.	
17321	" Burton, W.	
16906	" Benbow, R.	
15891	" Butterworth, S.	
16484	" Bradley, S.	
20055	" Burrows, W.	
11118	" Bate, G.W.	
18226	" Birch, A.	
18229	" Brookes, J.	
6485	" Bullock, J.	
18206	" Broad, T.	
16288	" Beddoes, H.	
7794	" Beckworth, F.	
17877	" Blair, W.	
17874	" Butcher, E.	
17801	" Bates, T.	
20286	" Ballantyne, E.	
20051	" Braddock, W.	
14990	" Barnes, J.	
6337	" Buckley, J.	
11060	" Court, C.	
11429	" Crump, A.	
9689	" Cox, C.	
6502	" Clark, J.H.	
6623	" Craddock, G.W.	
9769	" Campbell, J.	
17993	" Cooke, H.	
10840	" Connolly, A.	
8715	" Cooke, F.	
17459	" Davies, D.	
9448	" Downes, R.	
10998	" Davies, G.	
11167	" Davies, C.	
16515	" Davies, T.	
11123	" De-Peare	
15105	" Dunn, S.	
15922	" Davies, C.	
17822	" Duffy, G.	
16100	" Davies, F.	
18268	" Davies, E.	
18053	" Downing, S.W.	
11036	" Davies, A.	
17718	" Davies, H.	
10998	" Edwards, L.	
11058	" Emmett, F.	
7137	" Evans, J.	
10121	" Evans, E.	
15084	" Edwards, T.	
6352	" Evans, W.	
17451	" Ellis, J.R.	
17021	" Edwards, W.	
6695	" Edwards, W.	
6308	" Evans, J.	
~~16940~~	" ~~Farber, W.~~	
16494	" France, W.	
10980	" Fowles, J.	
17611	" Fewtrell, W.	
17672	" Freakley, P.	
18326	" Fox, J.	
10527	" Groves, S.	
11077	" Gainham, W.	
18121	" Green, S.	

"C" Company (Continued)

Regtl.No.	RANK AND NAME.	REMARKS.
9823	Pte. Griffiths, A.	
20140	" Grey, A.	
17815	" Gosling, G.	
6622	" Greybanks, A.	
16256	" Genner, W.	
10549	" Gent, A.	
10966	" Hands, W.	
15909	" Hayden, J.	
10727	" Hicks, H.	
6089	" Hicks, T.	
11081	" Hampson, H.	
11447	" Hayward, T.	
17981	" Hayward, A.	
18192	" Hinks, W.	
6633	" Hamilton, J.	
6937	" Harris, E.	
17642	" Hotchkiss, C.	
20212	" Heaton, R.	
17751	" Harris, S.	
17863	" Heyes, W.	
10719	" Hicks, J.	
8569	L/Cpl. Ives, G.	
9020	Pte. Jordan, J.	
6392	" Jones, G.	
17797	" Jones, C.	
18200	" Jackman, H.	
10607	" Jackson, G.	
17639	" Jones, W.	
7830	" Jones, J.	
17230	" Kitson, J.	
17691	" Kelsey, W.	
17896	" Kay, W.	
11684	" Lacon, R.	
11177	" Lewis, W.	
11128	" Lloyd, R.	
6415	" Lewis, C.	
16911	" Littlehales, J.	
9595	L/Cpl. Lee, S.	
17971	Pte. Lewis, D.	
14887	" Long, D.	
20057	" Latham, W.	
10114	" Luscott, W.	
15923	" Machesney, G.	
17260	" Morris, C.	
16490	" Mason, T.	
11188	" Meakin, W.	
11255	" Morgan, A.	
11159	" Morgan, F.	
16516	" Moss, T.	
7496	" Marsland, F.	
16971	" Morgan, H.	
17553	" Millington, A.	
17293	" Martin, W.	
18099	" Millward, J.	
11220	" Macklin, F.	
17052	" Manders, H.	
6264	" Morgan, W.	
16702	" Mort, A.	
20073	" Mash, C.H.	
8782	" McAuley, W.	
17804	" Noden, W.	
10458	" Nash, F.	Hospl

"C" Company (Continued)

Regtl.No.	RANK AND NAME.	REMARKS.
18178	Pte. Needham, W.	
11021	" Oliver, E.	
11240	" Onions, H.	
16774	" Oldham, B.	
17056	" Osborne, B.	
11041	" Parsons, C.	
10725	" Pendry, G.	
11258	" Phillips, E.	
11042	" Preston, J.	
6683	" Panting, J.	
16492	" Parry, J.	
11652	" Palmer, B.	Prison,
10791	" Price, T.	
11120	" Preston, W.	
8408	" Parry, R.	
11604	" Parker, J.E.	
16929	" Pounds, C.	
11121	" Ralphs, F.	
10796	" Robinson, J.	
11178	" Rowley, T.	
11152	" Rowlands, C.	
17490	" Rogers, J.	
17872	" Rogers, J.	
16053	" Ryder, A.	
11616	" Sandells, J.	
8524	" Sullivan, J.	
17741	" Scholes, T.	
17467	" Sykes, A.	
7272	" Stacey, F.	
6525	" Shenton, E.	
17982	" Skellern, S.	
11550	" Soutar, R.	
17954	" Sxon, J.	Hospl
17762	" Sutton, G.	
15140	" Scanlon, J.	
6683	" Stones, W.	
17998	" Shotton, E.	
18010	" Skarratt, J.	
17468	" Turner, H.	
11135	" Trevor, O.	
~~18145~~	" ~~Taylor, A.E.~~	
6312	" Teague, C.	
17013	" Topps, A.	
17951	" Taylor, H.	
17922	" Thomas, M.	
6023	" Taylor, T.	
11203	" Thomas, E.J.	
16489	" Williams, H.	
16930	" Woodward, C.	
17261	" Williams, J.	
17785	" Whittingham, J.	
17950	" Wright, W.	
17814	" Wear, T.	Hospl
18022	" Williams, C.	
17250	" Williams, T.	
17380	" Williams, J.	
8977	" Wyatt, T.	
17975	" Ward, G.	
20083	" Wiltshire, R.	
14903	" White, A.	
11144	Sgt. Turner, E.	
11106	Pte. Vernalls, C.	
7195	L/Cpl. Earl.	Hospl
17956	Pte. Rowley, T.	

"D" Company.

Regtl. No.	RANK AND NAME.	REMARKS.
9135	R.S.M. Pitt, J.A.	
7805	C.S.M. Bates, G.	
8811	C.Q.M.S. Thredgold, J.	
10756	Sgt. Thomas, J.	
7133	" Langford, J.	
11292	" Addis, J.A.	
11498	" Smith, A.J.	
11693	" Urion, G.	
7275	" Bryan, J.H.	
11576	" Colley, A.	
11363	" Gilbert, A.	Hospt
13955	L/Sgt. Hughes, T.J.	
6412	" Webb, D.	
16672	Cpl. Carr, J.W.	
10291	" Clarke, W.	
20157	" Davies, E.G.	
11686	" Davies, W.E.	
11420	" Butler, J.	
11359	" Foreman, J.	
7526	" Welch, J.	
9946	L/Cpl. Boulton, J.	
6718	" Beech, W.	
17229	" Bufton, H.	
9714	" Beeston, H.	
11387	" Coppock, A.	
11599	" Watson, A.	
11539	" McAuley, J.	
10044	" Attwood, C.	
16698	" Adshead, J.	
11417	" Lloyd, R.H.	
10984	" Kynaston, A.	
11579	" Morgan, W.	
10126	" Hutchins, D.H.	
6995	" Smith, R.H.	
~~16905~~	~~" Neale, T.~~	
~~11258~~	~~" Poyner, B.~~	
11946	Pte. Allsopp, G.	
18128	" Amos, T.	
18223	" Allen, T.A.	
18227	" Amos, H.	
7828	" Adams, G.	
10537	" Attwood, A.	
11755	" Adams, J.	
16966	" Bourne, J.	
20025	" Barber, E.	
6109	" Baldwin, G.	
17209	" Breece, G.H.	
17958	" Bywater, F.	
20056	" Buckley, W.	
20018	" Blanchard, R.	
18107	" Bowen, A.	
18235	" Bickerton, W.	
18325	" Beatty, J.	
17793	" Bishop, F.	
8127	" Bailey, E.	
11504	" Beech, J.	
18170	" Bethel, J.	
18290	" Bellingham, F.	
6431	" Bubb, F.	
10498	" Ball, A.	
11236	" Bethel, R.	
6786	" Boulton, W.	
20046	" Burke, M.	

7284 Corpl Ousey.

"D" Company (Continued)

Regtl.No.	RANK AND NAME.	REMARKS.
20021	Pte. Buzzard, G.	
11764	" Briggs, J.	
11403	" Clewes, P.	
10915	" Champ, F.	
16447	" Chesters, J.	
20123	" Clarke, J.	
18228	" Chave, P.	
17837	" Coates, T.	
17829	" Campion, H.	
11344	" Corney, A.	
11712	" Cox, E.	
16350	" Challoner, P.	
11308	" Davies, R.	
~~20165~~	" ~~Davies, H.~~	
9821	" Durkin, J.	
17205	" Davies, R.J.	
18014	" Davies, J.	
17798	" Davies, J.E.	
17835	" Davies, H.	
11007	" Davies, G.	
11406	" Dodd, J.	
11297	" England, J.	
17543	" Evans, G.	
10910	" Eaves, D.	
16514	" Evans, J.	
14907	" Evans, J.	
10993	" Evans, G.	
7472	" Ecahs, H.	
7782	" Edwards, R.	
18236	" Evans, E.H.	
18033	" Evahs, J.	
6345	" Ellis, W.	
17594	" Evans, W.	
11210	" Evans, J.	
11316	" Evans, W.	
11562	" Edwards, G.	
10920	" Fleetwood, W.	
8089	" France, T.	
11767	" Furnell, W.H.	
8719	" Farr, R.	
11413	" Ferrington, T.	
8995	" Farlow, W.	
11327	" Fuller, W.	
5486	Pte. Golding, J.	
9895	" Griffiths, G.	
18301	" Griffiths	
9926	" Griffiths, T.	
14793	" Griffiths, W.	Hospl
11302	" Glassey, J.	
11382	" Griffiths, E.J.	
9586	" Gwilt, T.	
10308	" Gretton, A.	
10792	" Gambriel, E.	
8503	" Gardiner, E.	
17011	" Greaves, J.	
18418	" Hamlett, D	
10835	" Harris, E.	
9864	" Hughes, A.	
6532	" Hayes, T.	
17763	" Halliwell, A.	
17472	" Herrity, E.	
17722	" Holmes, C.	
7893	" Hallmark, H.E.	

"D" Company (Continued)

Regtl.No.	RANK AND NAME.	REMARKS.
11600	Pte, Humphries, H.	
17003	" Herring, C.	
7974	" Hodson, W.	
16879	" Hopkins, J.	
11318	" Harris, E.	
11338	" Heaford, G.	
16831	" Heycock, E.	
16117	" Harris, W.	
17342	" Harry, D.	
11413	" Highfield, T.	
17305	" Harding, W.	
17277	" Jones, G.	
10921	" Jones, A.	
18066	" Jones, W.E.	
11329	" Jones, E.	
11250	" Jones, W.W.	
11416	" Jones, A.T.	
18204	" Jones, F.	
18084	" Jones, W.O.	
11310	" Jones, E.	
11315	" Kendall, H.J.	
6723	" Kent, D.	
11508	" Laurie, J.	
17469	" Lewis, W.	
15910	" Lewis, T.	
9508	" Lloyd, G.	
18165	" Lewis, R.	
17001	" Link, C.	
11371	" Lupton, T.	
16858	" Link, T.	
11169	" Leach, J.	
11399	" Meadows, J.H.	
11590	" Martin, J.T.	
15889	" Morgan, J.	
16974	" Markham, T.	
6741	" Murray, J.	
18343	" Mellor, M.	
17788	" Mitton, J.W.	
7033	" Morgan, T.	
11392	" Murray, J.	
6952	L/Cpl. Moran, D.	
16951	Pte, Maskery, W.	
~~7796~~	~~" Nicholls, H.~~	
16015	" Nash, J.	
17576	" Owens, D.	
6003	" Oliver, T.	
17673	" Owen, J.	
17464	" Oakley, F.	
5416	" Osborne, J.	
11200	" Oliver, J.	
11238	" Poyner, G.	
16840	" Prosser, R.	
17268	" Pugh, F.	
16493	" Powell, A.	
17065	" Ponting, H;	
18049	" Palmer, H.	
17740	" Parker, J.H.	
17988	" Powell, J.	
11375	" Passant, P.	
16347	" Parton, F.E.	
18870	" Parsons, C.	
18047	" Powell, F.	

"D" Company (Continued).

Regtl.No.	Rank and Name.	Remarks.
17087	Pte. Farmer, W.	
15001	" Pemberton, J.	
11034	" Roberts, T.	
18071	" Rogers, D.	
18302	" Roberts, G.	
11866	" Roberts, E.T.	Hospl
17827	" Rowlands, A.	
17838	" Ruscoe, H.	
6467	" Richards, E.	
17361	" Roberts, G.	
11216	" Richards, J.	
8313	" Rowlands, W.	
7816	" Sykes, G.	
18067	" Sankey, F.	
18120	" Staley, J.	
~~6945~~		
6648	" Shuker, A.	
6764	" Simcox, J.	
18130	" Stevenson, J.	
16864	" Tomkins, F.	
18254	" Treherne, A.	
16829	" Tomkinson, J.	
18087	" Twist, T.W.	
18040	" Thomas, T.J.	
16267	" Threadgold, J.	
6774	" Taylor, F.	
15012	" Vaughan, R.	
11751	" Vaughan, T.	
9073	" Vearnall, T.	
6456	" Vale, T.	
11293	" Weeks, G.	
17238	" Williams, P.	
11488	" Wright, H.	
6398	" Wedge, H.	
17784	" Whipp, J.	
6843	" Williams, W.	
11213	" Williams, J.	
17599	" Wedge, W.	
17955	" Williams, E.C.	
17920	" Whackett, F.	
5960	" Wood, J.	
11175	" Williams, W.	
11340	" Weale, F.	
11576	" Woodruff, H.	
8645	" Wortham, J.	
~~10362~~	" ~~Walsh, R.~~	
11391	" Wall, E.	
15030	" Whiteman, F.	
6596	" Weeks, G.	
18955	" Weston, H.A.	
11282	" Whitney, F.	
8653	" Winchester, W.	
9308	" Willington, R.	
16718	" Yates, G.	

CONFIDENTIAL

War Diary of

5th King's Shropshire L.I.

from 21.10.15 to 31.12.15.

(Volume 2.)

Army Form C. 2118.

WAR DIARY
or
INTELLIGENCE SUMMARY.
(Erase heading not required.)

Instructions regarding War Diaries and Intelligence Summaries are contained in F.S. Regs., Part II. and the Staff Manual respectively. Title pages will be prepared in manuscript.

Place	Date	Hour	Summary of Events and Information	Remarks and references to Appendices
YPRES	24/10/15		Battalion relieved by 1st LEICESTERS at POTIJZE. Entrained from YPRES to POPERINGHE and marched to Billets at HOUTKERQUE. Arrived in Billets at 5 a.m.	E.2.a.9.8. Sheet 27 (Belgium & France)
HOUTKERQUE	22/10/15		At rest in Billets at	E.2.a.9.8. Sheet 27 (Belgium & France)
Do.	23/10/15 to 26/10/15		Do.	Do. Reinforcements 10-O.R joined 26/10/15
Do.	27/10/15		The Army Commander inspected selected detachments of VI Corps at ABEELE. The detachment of 5th K.S.L.I. consisted of CAPT. N.T. PORTER and 25. O.R. several of whom had been recommended for Honours or Rewards as under: SGT. GITTINS, SGT. WILLIAMS, L.Cpl. WILSON, PARSONS, PTES LLOYD, CRAWSHAW, JORDAN, Cpl. KING, PTE. LLOYD. LT. COL. O.C. BORRETT, D.S.O. was in command of a composite Battalion. HIS MAJESTY THE KING was present at this Inspection.	Do.
Do.	28/10/15 to 6/11/15		In Billets at E.2.a.9.8.- Sheet 27.	(Belgium & France Map.)
Do.	7/11/15.		Presentation of Meritorious Cards by MAJOR-GEN. COUPER Commanding 14th Light Division. In Billets at E.2.a.9.8. Sheet 27.	Belgium & France.
Do.	8/11/15 & 19/11/15.		In Billets at E.2.a.9.8. Sheet 27. 22. O.R. Reinforcements arrived.	Belgium & France.

WAR DIARY
or
INTELLIGENCE SUMMARY.

(Erase heading not required.)

Army Form C. 2118.

Place	Date	Hour	Summary of Events and Information	Remarks and references to Appendices
YPRES	18/11/15		Battalion went to Trenches Relieved WEST YORKS. Occupied Trenches A.3. A.4. A.5. A.5 with supports at x3 & x2.	
Do.	19/11/15		In Trenches 2LT E.W. PARTRIDGE and 2LT V.B. HASKINS kill'd & 1 O.R killed 20 O.R. Reinforcements joined	
Do.	20/11/15		In Trenches No Casualties	
Do.	21/11/15		Do. Relieved by 5th Ox & Bucks L.I. - 5. O.R wounded.	
BRANDHOEK	22/11/15 & 23/11/15		Battalion at Rest. - B. HUTS - G.6.d. Sheet 28 - Belgium & France. -	
YPRES	24/11/15		Battalion to Trenches. occupying A3. A4. A5. A5B. x2. & x3.	
Do.	25/11/15 & 26/11/15		Do 6. O.R. Wounded	
BRANDHOEK	27/11/15 & 28/11/15 & 29/11/15		Battalion at Rest. 2 LT LESLIE A. JONES & 40 O.R. joined	
YPRES	30/11/15		To Trenches. occupying A3 A4 A5 A5b x3 & x2	
Do.	1/12/15		In Trenches - Relieved by 5th Ox & BUCKS. L.I. 3 O.R. Killed	
Do.	2/12/15 & 3/12/15		Battalion in Reserve at Canal Bank. KAAIE SALIENT - I.2.C. Sheet 28. - 6 O.R Wounded	
Do.	4/12/15		Battalion to Trenches. - Relieved 5th Ox & Bucks. L.I. {2 LT. R.A. BUTT 2 LT C.S. UNDERHILL joined	
Do.	5/12/15		Do. 2.LT. C.C. ABRAHAM. joined	

Army Form C. 2118.

WAR DIARY
or
INTELLIGENCE SUMMARY.
(Erase heading not required.)

Instructions regarding War Diaries and Intelligence Summaries are contained in F.S. Regs., Part II. and the Staff Manual respectively. Title pages will be prepared in manuscript.

Place	Date	Hour	Summary of Events and Information	Remarks and references to Appendices
YPRES	6/12/15		Battalion in Trenches. No casualties. (CAPT. H.E. MEASOR joined)	
Do	7/12/15 to 9/12/15		Do. 1 O.R. Killed - 7 O.R. Wounded. -	
Do	10/12/15		Battalion relieved in Trenches & arrived in Billets at ST. JAN-TER-BIEZEN. at 13 A.M. (F.27 Sheet 27 Belgium & France)	
ST. JAN TER-BIEZEN	11/12/15		Battalion at Rest in Billets at F.27 Sheet 27 ST. JAN-TER-BIEZEN.	
YPRES	12/12/15		Battalion to Trenches to occupy A.3.A.4: A.5: A.5b.x3 x2 Reinforcements 18. O.R. arrived.	
Do	13/12/15		Battalion in Trenches 2. O.R. Wounded	
Do	14/12/15		Do. No Casualties.	
Do	15/12/15		Battalion relieved by 2ND DURHAM. L.I. Returned to "A" Huts in A.30. Sheet 28.(Belgium & France) 3 O.R. Killed 16. O.R. Wounded.	
"A" HUTS	16/12/15		Battalion moved from "A" HUTS to Billets at HOUTKERQUE at E.2.a.9.8. Sheet 27 (Belgium & France)	
HOUTKERQUE	17/12/15 to 19/12/15		Battalion in Billets at HOUTKERQUE at E.2.a.9.8. Sheet 27. (Do.)	
Do	20/12/15.		The Army Commander presented ribbons for decorations recently awarded to Officers, N.C.O.s and men of 42ND INF. BDE. at HOUTKERQUE.	
Do	21/12/15.		Battalion in Billets at HOUTKERQUE. CAPT. O. SKULLY. joined (R.C. Chaplain)	

Army Form C. 2118.

WAR DIARY
or
INTELLIGENCE SUMMARY.
(Erase heading not required.)

Instructions regarding War Diaries and Intelligence Summaries are contained in F. S. Regs., Part II. and the Staff Manual respectively. Title pages will be prepared in manuscript.

Place	Date	Hour	Summary of Events and Information	Remarks and references to Appendices
HOUTKERQUE	22/12/15 to 24/12/15		Battalion at Rest in Billets at HOUTKERQUE - E.2.a.9.8. Sheet 27 Belgium & Maps France.	
Do.	25/12/15 to 29/12/15		Do. (2 LT. H.D.E. ELLIOTT rejoined from Hospital.) Do.	
BRANDHOEK	30/12/15		Battalion removed to B. HUTS in G.6.d - Sheet 28 · Belgium & France.	
Do.	31/12/15		Battalion in B. HUTS Do.	
Do.	1/1/16		Do.	
Do.	2/1/16		Do	

Moore N. Col.

CONFIDENTIAL

WAR DIARY

OF

5TH KING'S SHROPSHIRE L.I.

from January 1st to 31st 1916.

(Volume 3)

WAR DIARY
or
INTELLIGENCE SUMMARY
(Erase heading not required.)

Army Form C. 2118

Instructions regarding War Diaries and Intelligence Summaries are contained in F.S. Regs., Part II. and the Staff Manual respectively. Title Pages will be prepared in manuscript.

Place	Date	Hour	Summary of Events and Information	Remarks and references to Appendices
BRANDHOEK	1916 Jan.1,2,3.		Battalion in B. HUTS. G.6.d and G.12.b. Ref: Map Belgium. Sheet 28.	
Do.	Jan. 4th		Gas Demonstration by Chemical Advisor. 400 of Battalion present. and 400 of Remainder of Brigade. The Commander-in-Chief (SIR DOUGLAS HAIG) visited the Huts and was present at the above Gas Display.	
Do.	Jan 5,6+7		Battalion in B HUTS. G.6.d and G.12.b. Ref Map Belgium. Sheet 28. Left at 5.p.m. and proceeded to ELVERDINGHE. 2 LIEUT. G.P. BULMER joined.	
ELVERDINGHE	" 8th		Half Battalion proceeded to Trenches in right Sector; and other half to No. 2 REST CAMP, at A.16.c. (A+B Coys). C+D Coys relieved 7th RIFLE BRIGADE in Trenches E.28, E.29 + F.30. Casualty 1. O.R. killed.	
Do.	" 9th		C+D Coys in Trenches. A+B Coys at A.16.C. No 2 Rest Camp. 2.LIEUT. R.BROOKE. and 35.O.R.joined. 2.LIEUT. R.A.BUTT and 1.O.R. killed. (Sheet 28.) and 1.O.R. wounded.	
Do.	10-+11th		C+D Coys in Trenches. A+B Coys at A.16.a (Sheet 28) 2.O.R. Wounded.	
Do.	12th		A+B Coys relieved C+D Coys in Trenches. C+D Coys removed to A.16.C. 5 O.R. killed 10/1/16. 7. O.R. wounded	
Do.	13th + 14th		A+B Coys in Trenches. C+D Coys at A.16.C. (Sheet 28)	
Do.	15th		Do. CAPT. PALMER died in Hospital in England. 2.LIEUT: R.B.D.MALDEN. and 18. O.R. joined.	

WAR DIARY or INTELLIGENCE SUMMARY

Army Form C. 2118

Place	Date	Hour	Summary of Events and Information	Remarks and references to Appendices
ELVERDINGHE	16/1/16		Battalion moved to ELVERDINGHE.	
Do	17/1/16 18/1/16		Battalion at ELVERDINGHE. Working parties sent up each night. (2 O.R. wounded 17/1/16) 1 O.R. killed	
Do	19/1/16		Battalion went to Trenches in Left Sector	
Do	20/1/16		C & D Coys in Trenches. A & B Coys in Reserve. Back active with Machine Guns. Casualties 3 O.R. Killed, 2 LIEUT. C.S. UNDERHILL and 2 O.R. wounded.	
Do	21/1/16		C & D Coys in Trenches. A & B Coys in Reserve. Casualties 1 O.R. Killed 2 O.R. wounded. 2 LIEUT. UNDERHILL & 1 O.R. died of wounds.	—
Do	22/1/16		C & D Coys in Trenches. A & B at Malakoff Farm. Saragossa Farm & Pellissier Farm. Casualties 1 O.R. Killed 5 O.R. wounded.— Heard Aircraft at night which dropped Bombs on E. of Chateau.	—
Do	23/1/16		Battalion relieved by 5th OX & BUCKS L.I. and returned to B. HUTS at G.6.9 & G.12.5. Sheet 28. Casualties 2 O.R. wounded.	
BRADHOEK	24/1/16		Battalion in B. HUTS. Casualty 1 O.R. Machine Gun Section Killed	
Do	24 to 26/1/16	30	Do. Casualty 1 O.R. (Do) Killed	
ELVERDINGHE	27 to 30		Battalion moved to ELVERDINGHE and remained till 30th. Working parties provided each night.	
Do	31/1/16		A & B Coys moved to Trenches and relieved 9th K.R.R.s. C & D Coys moved to Farm at B.28.C.1.9.	

C.C. Snell Lieut Colonel
Commanding 7th Kings Shropshire L.I.

CONFIDENTIAL

War Diary

of

5th King's Shropshire L.I.

from February 1st to 29th 1916.

(Volume 3.)

Army Form C. 2118

WAR DIARY
or
INTELLIGENCE SUMMARY

(Erase heading not required.)

Instructions regarding War Diaries and Intelligence Summaries are contained in F.S. Regs., Part II. and the Staff Manual respectively. Title Pages will be prepared in manuscript.

Place	Date	Hour	Summary of Events and Information	Remarks and references to Appendices
ELVERDINGHE SHEET 28 BELGIUM	1/2/16		A + B Coys in Trenches. C + D Coys in Farm. B. 28. C.I.9. Shelling & Trench Mortaring. F.35. Trench Gun Bombers wounded enemy trench not worse. Body-strong side wire.	
Do	2/2/16		A + B Coys in Trenches. C + D Coys in Farm B. 28. C.I.9. Heavy Bombardment by Germans. Casualties 7. O.R. killed 13. O.R. wounded.	
Do	3/2/16		A + B Coys in Trenches. C + D in Farm B. 28. C.I.9.	
Do	4/2/16		A + B Coys in Trenches. C + D in Farm B. 28. C.I.9. 20th Division Officers visited Trenches. Relieved by 9th R.Bn. Canal Bank. Casualties 1. O.R. killed	
Do	5/2/16		Battalion arrived in "B" HUTS BRANDHOEK about 3. A.M. G.6.d and G.12.B.	
BRANDHOEK	6/2/16		Battalion in "B" HUTS. G.6.d and G.12.B. SHEET 28 BELGIUM.	
BRANDHOEK	7/2/16		Battalion "B" HUTS. G.6.d and G.12.B. Considerable Enemy Aircraft Activity. Bombs dropped on POPERINGHE.	
Do	8/2/16		Battalion moved to ELVERDINGHE B.14.15 Sheet 28. Belgium. 2 Platoons "A" Coy went to Trench Casualties 2. O.R wounded. L.2.	
ELVERDINGHE	9/2/16		Battalion went to Trenches in Left Sector. 9th K.R.R's on left. 9th R.B's on right. Shelling ELVERDINGHE in the evening. 2.Lt. W.F. SHEATHER joined	

WAR DIARY
or
INTELLIGENCE SUMMARY
(Erase heading not required.)

Army Form C. 2118

Instructions regarding War Diaries and Intelligence Summaries are contained in F.S. Regs., Part II. and the Staff Manual respectively. Title Pages will be prepared in manuscript.

Place	Date	Hour	Summary of Events and Information	Remarks and references to Appendices
ELVERDINGHE SHEET 28. BELGIUM	10/2/16		Battalion in Trenches. Germans bombard E.28 and SKIPTON RD. Casualties 2 O.R. killed. 3 O.R. wounded. MAJOR. G.A. DELME-MURRAY joined.	
Do.	11/2/16		"B" C° + "D" Coys in Trenches in E.24.25.26.27.28. "A" Coys at CANAL BANK. Battalion relieved by 6th K.S.L.I. - 62nd BDE- 20th DIV. at 10 p.m. and marched to POPERINGHE a/a billets there till morning. During relief about 2 a.m. SHEET 28. G.1. D.8.3. F.35 with Bombs, but were driven out by our Bombers. Our attacked our F.35 with Bombs, but were driven out by our Bombers. Our Machine Gunners were holding part of the line, and did splendid work. Three being recommended. Casualties 9. C.R. killed. 16 O.R. wounded. 1. O.R. Machine Gunners 3 missing	
POPERINGHE SHEET 28. G.1 D.8.5	12/2/16		Battalion marched to Billets at HOUTKERQUE. Arrived about 4 p.m. Belgium + France. SHEET. 27. E.14. D. BELGIUM and FRANCE.	
HOUTKERQUE SHEET 27. E.14.D	13/2/16		Battalion marched to Billets at WORMHOUDT. C.10.d.9.5 SHEET. 27. Belgium + France. and arrived about 12.30 p.m. 2 LTS T.E. BURKE. R.R. LAWRENCE. W.J.G. YEOMANS joined.	
WORMHOUDT C.10.d 9.5 SHEET 7.27	14/2/16		Battalion in Billets at WORMHOUDT. 38. O.R. joined. 3 Machine Gunners returned from Trenches who were reported missing, and believed killed, brought back with them their Machine Guns.	
Do	15/2/16		Battalion in Billets at WORMHOUDT. LT. F.W. RHODES. + 2 LT. R.G.W. STARK joined.	
Do	16/2/16		Do. 2LT. G.C. SHARP joined. 2 Officers and 33 O.R. Left Battalion to form BRIGADE. MACHINE GUN. COMPANY.	
Do	17/2/16		Battalion in Billets in WORMHOUDT. Inspection by C-in-C of 42nd Inf. Bde at 12.15 p.m.	

Army Form C. 2118

WAR DIARY
or
INTELLIGENCE SUMMARY
(Erase heading not required.)

Instructions regarding War Diaries and Intelligence Summaries are contained in F. S. Regs., Part II. and the Staff Manual respectively. Title Pages will be prepared in manuscript.

Place	Date	Hour	Summary of Events and Information	Remarks and references to Appendices
WORMHOUDT C.10.d.9.5 Sheet 27.	18/2/16		Battalion in Billets at WORMHOUDT.	
Do.	19/2/16 to 20/2/16		Do.	
Do	21/2/16		Battalion left WORMHOUDT and entrained at ESQUELBECQ STATION at 9 A.M. and arrived at LONGEAU via AMIENS at 8 p.m. and were conveyed by Motor Buses to BERTEAUCOURT LES DAMES which place was reached by about 11 p.m. Snow falling.	
BERTEAUCOURT LES DAMES.	22/2/16 to 24/2/16		Battalion in Billets at BERTEAUCOURT. Snow falling.	
Do	25/2/16		Battalion marched from BERTEAUCOURT to HEM. Arrived about 4 p.m. and stayed in Billets for the night.	
HEM	26/2/16		Battalion marched from HEM to GRAND RULLECOURT. SHEET 57c FRANCE. O.Q. Heavy snowstorm. Very bad travelling both for men & transport. arrived in Billets about 7.30 p.m.	
GRAND RULLECOURT.	27 + 28/2/16		Battalion in Billets at GRAND RULLECOURT. Snow. Freezing.	
GRAND RULLECOURT.	29/2/16		Battalion marched from GRAND RULLECOURT to SOMBRIN. O.23. SHEET 57c. FRANCE. Snow.	

O.C. Connell Lieut Col.
Commanding 5th K.S.L.I.

Report on relief on night of 11th – 12th February
of S31 & 32

There had been considerable shelling all day and the wires having been damaged & communication with S32 and F31 and 32 lost I went up to reconnoitre the route as soon as it was dusk. I found HELLGATE badly smashed in in five places. The way up along the trench boards between S32 and F32 had been severely shelled and trench mortared and in a number of places it was difficult to get round the holes. I found the garrison of F31 and 32 had suffered no casualties and then returned to Bn HQ to report. I reached HQ about 8 p.m. and it was decided after discussion that the best thing to do was for the guide to fetch the party up as arranged and that he should call for me at Company HQ in FARGATE

①

"to accompany" the relieving garrison.

The party was late and we did not leave FARGATE until 11.30 p.m. The men were all carrying packs and rations and were by no means fresh when they left FARGATE. By the time the relief reached S32 the moon had gone down and it was so dark that it was impossible to see 5 yards ahead. I found that the way along the trench boards had been shelled again since I last went up ~~and was~~ ~~broken~~. The men were very much exhausted and their packs were a severe handicap when it came to going through the mud and water to get round the shellholes. ~~The best~~ Very few of the trench boards were left and the last seventy yards where there are no trench boards was difficult to pass even without a pack. The relief proceeded at a snail's pace, and eventually at about 1.30 a.m. the first part of the relief reached F31 & 32. A few of the men were so exhausted that they had sat down and prevented the last part of the relief going on. Consequently connection was lost and it was necessary to go back from the trench time after time to assist the stragglers. Many of the men had lost their thigh boots and could only crawl on their hands and knees. My watch had become covered in the mud by this time, I should think we spent 2 hours in getting the stragglers we could find together. It was at the time when the bombardment began that the relieved garrison was ready to move out and at this time the way back between F31 and 32 and S32 was being very heavily shelled. I decided that it was useless to try to make back the way we had come and moved the relieved garrison to the right end of F31. From there we proceeded in the open behind the disused part of the trench to F30 and from F30 in the open ~~in our~~ ~~the trench to E29 and~~ ~~E28~~ until we struck into E28. Then we went down SKIPTON ROAD and by the time we reached the CANAL BANK it was daylight. ~~the open ground across which we had had come being very difficult~~ I should like to mention that A2004 Rfn BLACKWELL, the guide originally selected to take the party up, in my opinion deserves recognition for his services. He was invaluable in assisting the party up to the trench and indefatigable in fetching in stragglers. He left the trench again and again to fetch men in and it was entirely due to him that some of the weakest men ever reached the trench at all. Part of the time the ground behind F31 and 32 was being swept by heavy machine gun fire but still he went on ~~and returning~~ backwards and forwards to get men in

④

Before leaving F31 I suggested to the officer in charge of the relief that he should send a pistol to F30 to get into touch with ~~his~~ with his right and try to arrange for a relief of his party that way.

(sd). H. Dowson, Lieut
condg B. Coy.

CONFIDENTIAL

War Diary

of

5ᵗʰ King's Shropshire L.I.

from

March 1ˢᵗ to 31ˢᵗ 1916.

(Volume 4.)

WAR DIARY
or
INTELLIGENCE SUMMARY

(Erase heading not required.)

Army Form C. 2118

Instructions regarding War Diaries and Intelligence Summaries are contained in F.S. Regs., Part II. and the Staff Manual respectively. Title Pages will be prepared in manuscript.

Place	Date	Hour	Summary of Events and Information	Remarks and references to Appendices
SOMBRIN. G.23. Sheet 57.d. FRANCE.	1/3/16		Battalion in Billets at SOMBRIN. Marched to Billets at BERNEVILLE (R.I.C. Sheet 57.C) Transport moved to SIMENCOURT (Q.10.B. Sheet 57.d. FRANCE.)	
BERNEVILLE. R.I.C. 57.C Sheet. FRANCE.	2/3/16 to 4/3/16		Battalion in Billets at BERNEVILLE. Transport at SIMENCOURT.	
BERNEVILLE. R.I.C. Sheet 57.C FRANCE	5/3/16 & 6/3/16		Battalion in Billets at BERNEVILLE. Marched to ARRAS to Billets. ECOLE DES JEUNES FILLES. RUE GAMBETTA. (G.28.a. Sheet 51.B. FRANCE.) Snow.	
ARRAS G.28.a. Sheet 51.B FRANCE	6/3/16		Battalion in Billets. ARRAS. Snow.	
D°.	7/3/16		Battalion in Billets in ARRAS. Find. One Company now to take up line of defence from Bridge over Railway leading to RONVILLE (G.28.C. Sheet 51.B) to Level Crossing on ACHICOURT Road. (G.29.a.5.Sheet 57B/FRANCE.) Ten men were "accidentally wounded" while on carrying party, to 9th R.B.'s by the explosion of a French Bomb which was lying on the road over which the men marched. CAPT. E.V.E. TUNMER rejoined.	
D°.	8/3/16 & 9/3/16		3 Companies in Billets ARRAS. Working parties sent out at night, repairing and improving Trenches &c. One Company in Defence Line ARRAS (G.28.C. to G.33.a. Sheet 57B FRANCE)	
D°.	10/3/16 11/3/16		Snow falling. D°. D°. {Working & carrying parties sent out each night. 60 O.R. joined	
D°.	12/3/16		3 Companies in ARRAS, one in ARRAS Defence Line. A few Enemy Shells exploded near the Billets about mid-day. Working & carrying parties sent out at night.	

WAR DIARY or INTELLIGENCE SUMMARY

Army Form C. 2118

Place	Date	Hour	Summary of Events and Information	Remarks and references to Appendices
ARRAS G.28.a. Sheet 57B FRANCE	13/3/16		Battalion relieved 5th Ox & Bucks. L.I. in Trenches (H. Sector from M.H.8.2.2. to G.35.b.8. Sheet 57B FRANCE). One Company 9th R.B's relieved One Company 5th K.S.L.I. in ARRAS defence line, and this Company moved to Billets in RONVILLE (G.28.c. Sheet 57B FRANCE). 9th K.R.R.'s in Trenches on right flank. 8th R.B's on left.	
RONVILLE G.28.a. Sheet 57B FRANCE	14/3/16 15/3/16 16/3/16 17/3/16		One Company in Ronville (G.28.c.) Three Companies in Trenches as above. - Considerable Aeroplane activity on both sides. 1. O.R. wounded.	
Do.	18/3/16		One Company in RONVILLE, 3 Companies in Trenches. Heavy Artillery by Enemy Artillery on Front line Trenches doing considerable damage to Trench H.3y. (M.H.8. Sheet 57B.France) Casualties 3 O.R. killed. 9 O.R. wounded. 41. O.R. joined for duty.	
Do.	19/3/16		One Company in Billets in Ronville, remainder in Trenches. Our Artillery retaliated with heavies on Enemy front line Trenches. - Casualties 2.O.R. wounded.	
Do.	20/3/16		Distribution of Battalion same as yesterday.	
Do.	21/3/16		Battalion relieved by 5th Ox & Bucks. L.I. and moved to Billets at SIMENCOURT Relief of Trenches complete by 12 midnight, and all arrived in Billets by 3.30 a.m. (Q.10.d & Q.11.C Sheet 57C FRANCE) Casualties 1. O.R. wounded.	
SIMENCOURT Q.10.d-Q.11.C. Sheet 57C FRANCE	22/3/16		Battalion in Billets at SIMENCOURT	
	23/3/16		Do. -- CAPT. F. FORT rejoined.	
	24/3/16		Do. -- 2/LT. W.J. MILTON " Snow	
	25/3/16		Do. -- CAPT. N.T. PORTER " Rain	
	26/3/16		Do. -- CAPT. C.D. HARRIS joined for duty from CAMEROONS	

Army Form C. 2118

WAR DIARY
or
INTELLIGENCE SUMMARY
(Erase heading not required.)

Instructions regarding War Diaries and Intelligence Summaries are contained in F.S. Regs., Part II. and the Staff Manual respectively. Title Pages will be prepared in manuscript.

Place	Date	Hour	Summary of Events and Information	Remarks and references to Appendices
SIMENCOURT. G.10.d. Q.11.c. Sheet 51.c. FRANCE	27/3/16		Battalion in billets at SIMENCOURT. Shooting competition held on Rifle Range, open to Battalion, won by D Company. 30 O.R. Reinforcement arrived	
Do.	28/3/16		Battalion in billets at Simencourt.	
Do.	29/3/16		— Do. — Relieved 5th Ox & Bucks. L.I. in trenches (M. 4 & 2.2 to G.35.b.8.½. Sheet 57B. FRANCE.) 3 Companies. One Company in RONVILLE (G.28.c. Sheet 57B. FRANCE.) Unit in touch 9th K.R.R.'s right. 8th R.B.'s left.	
RONVILLE. G.28.c. Sheet 57.c. FRANCE	30/3/16		Distribution of Battalion same as yesterday. Considerable Aeroplane activity. One of ours brought down in flames, behind Enemy lines.	
Do.	31/3/16		Battalion distribution same as yesterday.	

O.C.
Lieut Colonel
Commanding 5th K.S.L.I.

CONFIDENTIAL

War Diary

of

5th King's Shropshire L.I.

from

April 1st to 30th 1916.

(Volume 5.)

WAR DIARY
or
INTELLIGENCE SUMMARY.
(Erase heading not required.)

Army Form C. 2118.

Place	Date	Hour	Summary of Events and Information	Remarks and references to Appendices
RONVILLE G.28.c. Sheet 51B FRANCE.	1/4/16		Battalion in Trenches (M.4. 6.2.2. to G.35.8.8.2. Sheet 51B FRANCE.) 2 Companies One Company in Ronville (G.28.c. Sheet 51B FRANCE.) Units in touch 9th KRR's on right. 8th RB's on left.	
Do	2/4/16		Distribution of Battalion same as yesterday. CAPT. S. CLARKE. R.C. CHAPLAIN joined for duty. 39 Other Ranks Reinforcements arrived from Base.	
Do	3/4/16		Distribution same as yesterday. 2 LIEUT. A. HYNDMAN joined for duty.	Casualties 2.O.R. Wounded
Do	4/4/16		Do.	
Do ARRAS G.28.a. Sheet 51B	5/4/16		Battalion relieved by 5th Ox Y Bucks. - 2 Companies to Billets in ARRAS (École des Jeunes Filles, Rue Gambetta) G.28.a. Sheet 51B FRANCE. One Company to Billets in RONVILLE (G.28.a. Sheet 51B FRANCE.) One Company to ACHICOURT. (G.32.a. and G.33.a Sheet 51B FRANCE)	
Do	6/4/16 to 11/4/16		Distribution of Battalion same as 5/4/16. CAPT. P.J. BELLASIS rejoined for duty 11/4/16	
Do.	12/4/16		Do.	Casualty – 1. O.R. Wounded
Do RONVILLE G.28.c. Sheet 51B FRANCE	13/4/16		Battalion relieved 5th Ox Y Bucks in Trenches (M.4. 6.2.2 to G.35. 6.8.2 Sheet 51B) 3 Companies One Company in RONVILLE (G.28.c. Sheet 51B FRANCE) 8th RB's on right. 9th KRRS on right. Leave cancelled. 3rd Army Order. All Officers and O.R. recalled.	
Do	14/4/16		Battalion distribution same as yesterday.	8. O.R Reinforcements joined
Do	15/4/16		Do	Casualty. 1.O.R. Accidentally Wounded

Army Form C. 2118.

WAR DIARY
or
INTELLIGENCE SUMMARY.
(Erase heading not required.)

Instructions regarding War Diaries and Intelligence Summaries are contained in F. S. Regs., Part II. and the Staff Manual respectively. Title pages will be prepared in manuscript.

Place	Date	Hour	Summary of Events and Information	Remarks and references to Appendices
RONVILLE. G.28.C. Sheet 57B FRANCE.	16/4/16 to 20/4/16		3 Companies in Trenches (M.4.b. 2.2 to G.25.b. 8.5. Sheet 57B. FRANCE.) 1 Company in RONVILLE (G.28.c. Sheet 57B. FRANCE.) LIEUT:- E.G.F. LLOYD rejoined. 18/4/16. 9th O.R. Reinforcements joined 20/4/16	
Do	21/4/16		Battalion relieved by 5th Ox & Bucks. Companies marched independently to Billets at SIMENCOURT (Q.10.d and Q.11.c Sheet 57C FRANCE.)	
SIMENCOURT Q.10.d and Q.11.C Sheet 57C FRANCE	22/4/16 to 28/4/16		Battalion in Billets at SIMENCOURT. CAPT. T.E. MOORE-LANE rejoined 23/4/16	
Do	29/4/16		Battalion relieved 5th Ox & Bucks in Trenches (M.4.b. 2.2.to G.35.b. 8.5. Sheet 57B. FRANCE.) 3 Companies in Trenches. One Company in RONVILLE (G.28.C. Sheet 57B. FRANCE) 9th R.Bs. & Capt. G.A.H.R.R's. night.	
RONVILLE	30/4/16		Disposition of Battalion same as yesterday.	

G. Helm L. Murray, Major.
Commanding 5th King's Shropshire L.I.

ORDERLY ROOM
No. 12/5/16
Date
5th KING'S SHROPSHIRE L.I.

CONFIDENTIAL

War Diary

of

5th Kings Shropshire L.I.

from

May 1st to 31st 1916.

(Volume 6.)

WAR DIARY
or
INTELLIGENCE SUMMARY.

(Erase heading not required.)

Army Form C. 2118.

Instructions regarding War Diaries and Intelligence Summaries are contained in F.S. Regs., Part II. and the Staff Manual respectively. Title pages will be prepared in manuscript.

Place	Date	Hour	Summary of Events and Information	Remarks and references to Appendices
RONVILLE G.28.c 51B FRANCE	17/5/16		Distribution of Battalion same. Our Artillery bombarded Enemy front line M.4.a.5.6 to M.4.b.7.0. and salient N.5.a.with H.E. Howitzers fired on Enemy second line M.4.d.7.6. to M.4.d.6.3.95. Medium Trench Mortars working in conjunction with J Stokes Guns shelled the circular work M.4.a.6.5. the result very satisfactory and much damage was done. After our bombardment finished the Enemy began to retaliate with Heavy Minen and a few shells but were silenced by our Guns. (Two upwards above Sht 51B. FRANCE)	
Do	18/19/5/16		Distribution same.	
Do	20/5/16		Do. Our Artillery bombarded Enemy front and patrol line.	
Do	21/5/16		Anniversary of Embarkation of Battalion from England. Distribution same Anniversary of Battalion landing in France.	
Do	22/5/16		Do.	
BERNEVILLE R.b.d Sht. ST.C. FRANCE	23/5/16		Battalion relieved by 5th Ox & Bucks L.I. and proceeded to BERNEVILLE.	
Do	24/5/16 to 30/5/16		Battalion in Billets at BERNEVILLE (R.b.a.& R.I.a. Sht. 51C FRANCE) Whilst Battalion there were held on 26th & 27th which included Foot race, tug of war, transport turnouts &c.	
Do ARRAS	31/5/16		Battalion relieved 5th Ox & Bucks L.I. in Trenches (M.4.& 2.2 & G.35. & 8. Sht. 51B.FRANCE.	

C.C. Onett Lieut Colonel
Commanding The Kings Shropshire L.I.

WAR DIARY
or
INTELLIGENCE SUMMARY.

(Erase heading not required.)

Army Form C. 2118.

Place	Date	Hour	Summary of Events and Information	Remarks and references to Appendices
RONVILLE. G.28.c Sheet 57B FRANCE.	1/5/16		Battalion in Trenches (M.H. 6.2.2 to G.35.b.8.5. Sheet 57B FRANCE) Distribution of 3 Companies in Trenches. One Company in RONVILLE (G.28.a. 57B FRANCE.)	
Do.	2/5/16 3/5/16 4/5/16		Distribution of Battalion same. 11 British Aeroplanes flew over sector on our left. (Casualties 1 O.R. Killed, 1 wounded	
Do.	5/5/16		Distribution same. Enemy shelled Trenches with Trench.	
Do.	6/5/16		Do. Anight. Our Bombers attempted a raid on an Enemy sap, but owing to the wire not having been sufficiently destroyed by our Artillery fire, they were unable to get through. There were no Casualties. LIEUT. J.C.B. FIRTH and 30 O.R. joined	
Do. ARRAS G.28.a Sheet 51B FRANCE	7/5/16		Battalion relieved by 5th Ox & Bucks L.I. Two Companies to ECOLE DES JEUNE FILLES ARRAS. (G.28.a Sheet 51B FRANCE.) One Company to ACHICOURT (G.32.d and G.33.c Sheet 51B FRANCE) One Company bivouac in RONVILLE (G.28.a)	
Do.	8/5/16 9/5/16		Distribution of Battalion same. Enemy shelled ARRAS near Station 8 p.m.	
Do.	10/5/16 to 14/5/16		Distribution same. Quiet.	
RONVILLE. G.28.c 57B FRANCE	15/5/16		Battalion relieved 5th Ox & Bucks L.I. in Trenches (M.H. 6.2.2 & G.35.b.8.5. Sheet 57B FRANCE) 3 Companies in Trenches. One Company RONVILLE	
Do.	16/5/16		Distribution same. Our Aeroplanes active over Enemy lines in morning. Enemy shelled Communication Trench in afternoon. 2 LIEUT. J.H. QUIRK and 2 LIEUT. H.W. MENDELL	

Confidential

WAR DIARY.

OF

5TH KING'S SHROPSHIRE L.I.

FROM

JUNE 1ST to 30TH 1916.

(VOLUME 7)

Army Form C. 2118

WAR DIARY
or
INTELLIGENCE SUMMARY

(Erase heading not required.)

Instructions regarding War Diaries and Intelligence Summaries are contained in F. S. Regs., Part II. and the Staff Manual respectively. Title Pages will be prepared in manuscript.

Place	Date	Hour	Summary of Events and Information	Remarks and references to Appendices
RONVILLE G.28.c 57B.FRANCE.	1/6/16		Battalion in Trenches (M.4.B.2.2 to G.35 & 8.2.2 Sheet 57B.FRANCE.) Bn. Company in RONVILLE (G.28.c 57B FRANCE)	
Do.	2/6/16 3/6/16		Casualties 2 O.R. killed; 1 wounded – 8 O.R. joined	
Do.	4/6/16		Distribution same. Enemy shelled Battalion head quarters which were vacated.	
Do.	5/6/16 6/6/16 7/6/16		Distribution same.	
Do.	8/6/16		Battalion relieved by 5th OX.&BUCKS.L.I. Two Companies to ECOLE DES JEUNES FILLES ARRAS(G.28.a. 57B FRANCE) One Company to ACHICOURT.(G.32.d and G.33.c) 57B FRANCE. One Company remaining in RONVILLE (G.28.c)	
ARRAS SHEET 57B.	9/6/16		2 Companies in ARRAS. One in ACHICOURT. One in RONVILLE. Enemy Aeroplane dropped Bombs on ACHICOURT and RONVILLE at night. Casualties 3 O.R. wounded.	
Do.	10/6/16 to 13/6/16		Distribution of Battalion same as 9/6/16.	
Do.	14/6/16		Time advanced One hour at 11 p.m.	
Do.	15/6/16 16/6/16 17/6/16 18/6/16		Do. Do. Do. Do. 2/Lieut. H.T. HUGHES, joined 2/Lieut. C.V. HOLDER joined	

WAR DIARY
or
INTELLIGENCE SUMMARY
(Erase heading not required.)

Army Form C. 2118

Instructions regarding War Diaries and Intelligence Summaries are contained in F.S. Regs., Part II. and the Staff Manual respectively. Title Pages will be prepared in manuscript.

Place	Date	Hour	Summary of Events and Information	Remarks and references to Appendices
ARRAS SHEET 51B FRANCE	19/6/16		Battalion relieved 10th GLOUCESTERS in ISUB-SECTOR Right. 2 Companies in the line G.35.b.8.5. 5 to G.30.a. 7.5.4.5. 51B FRANCE. 1 Company RUE DE ST QUENTIN. One Company ST SAUVEUR (G.29.)	
ST SAUVEUR SHEET 51B. FRANCE	20/6/16		Distribution of Battalion same. 2 Lieut N.L. MACHELL joined. 1 O.R. wounded	
Do.	21/6/16 22/6/16		Distribution same. Enemy shelled station & vicinity. 1 O.R. wounded.	
Do.	23/6/16		Do. 3 Company 4th KINGS LIVERPOOLS (PIONEERS) relieved D Company as permanent Garrison of ST SAUVEUR DEFENCES	
Do.	24/6/16 25/6/16		Distribution same. Bombardment in afternoon of Enemy trenches and TILLOY Do. Do. Bombardment in afternoon of Enemy front line & Tilloy 2 Companies in Reserve relieved 2 Companies in trenches. Enemy retaliated. Balloon brought down.	
Do.	26/6/16 27/6/16			
Do.	28/6/16		Distribution same. Night bombardment on Enemy trenches also trumps of Roads in rear of Enemy's lines. LIEUT. J.C.B. FIRTH and One O.R. wounded	
Do.	29/6/16		Enemy Artillery retaliated in the early hours of the morning. Bombardment of Enemy wire in the afternoon. One of our Aeroplanes dropped bombs on Enemy front line.	
Do.	30/6/16		Distribution of Battalion same. Enemy shelled ARRAS.	

O.C. Orwell Lieut Col
Commanding 5th King's Shropshire L.I.

Confidential

War Diary

of

5th King's Shropshire L.I.

from

July 1st to 31st 1916

(Volume 8)

WAR DIARY
or
INTELLIGENCE SUMMARY
(Erase heading not required.)

Instructions regarding War Diaries and Intelligence Summaries are contained in F.S. Regs., Part II. and the Staff Manual respectively. Title Pages will be prepared in manuscript.

Place	Date	Hour	Summary of Events and Information	Remarks and references to Appendices
ST SAUVEUR. SHEET. 51.B FRANCE.	1.7.16		Battalion in trenches in I SUB-SECTOR RIGHT. (2 Companies in the line G.35.b.8½. to G.30.a.7½. 51ᴮ FRANCE. 1 Company RUE DE SᵗQUENTIN. One Company ST SAUVEUR. (G.29)	G.28.d.
Do	2.7.16		Distribution same. 2nd LIEUT R.C.M ELLIOTT joined.	
Do	3.7.16		Distribution same. One of our aeroplanes was observed to fall behind the enemy's line.	
Do	4.7.16		Distribution same.	
Do	5.7.16		Distribution same	
Do	6.7.16		The 2 Companies in Beaure relieved the 2 Companies in the line	
Do	7.7.16 8.7.16		Distribution same. Casualties 3 O.R. wounded.	
Do	9.7.16		Battalion relieved by the Rifle Brigade, and afterwards proceeded to billets in ARRAS. (2 Companies in the ECOLE DES JEUNE FILLES. (G.28.a.51ᴮ FRANCE) remaining Companies in HOTEL DU COMMERCE.) G.28.a.51ᴮ FRANCE	
ARRAS (G.28.a.51ᴮ)	10.7.16 & 11.7.16		Distribution of Battalion the same. Our aeroplanes very active in afternoon of 11 inst	

INTELLIGENCE SUMMARY

(Erase heading not required.)

Instructions regarding War Diaries and Intelligence Summaries are contained in F.S. Regs., Part II. and the Staff Manual respectively. Title Pages will be prepared in manuscript.

Place	Date	Hour	Summary of Events and Information	Remarks and references to Appendices
ARRAS (G 28 a 5.1) FRANCE	12.7.16		The Battalion relieved the 5th D. of 9 Bn. obo. L.I. in H RIGHT SECTOR. 2nd Lieuts. Y.J. Simpson, 2nd Lieut. A. Atkinson, 2nd Lieut. N. R. Cosgrove & 2nd Lieut. A.W. Parsons joined the 1st Battalion	
ACHICOURT H Right Sector (SHEET 51 FRANCE)	13.7.16		Battalion in trenches. H RIGHT SECTOR. Enemy's trench Mortars very active on B Coy's front, causing considerable damage to H28 & H30. Our Artillery retaliated in the afternoon.	
Do	14.7.16		Battalion in trenches. H RIGHT SECTOR. A smoke screen was made by the 55th Division on our right. Immediately the smoke was opened by the enemy, he opened fire only for a short time. Casualties 3 killed 20 wounded	
Do	15.7.16		Battalion in trenches. H RIGHT SECTOR. Lieut. Col. O.C. Borrett, D.S.O. relinquishes command of the Battalion this day, on being transferred to take command of the 1st Battn. The King's Own (Royal Lancaster) Regt. & hands over command of 5th King's Shropshire L.I. to Major G.A. DeLisle Murray	
Do	16.7.16		Battalion in Trenches. H RIGHT SECTOR. Casualties 11 O.R. wounded. Telegram received announcing that His Majesty the King had graciously awarded the Military Cross to Company Sergt. Major Morris	
Do	17.7.16		Battalion in trenches. H RIGHT SECTOR.	
Do	18.7.16		Battalion relieved by 9th King's Royal Rifle Corps, and afterwards proceeded to billets in ARRAS (2 Companies in ECOLE DES JEUNE FILLES and 2 Companies in RUE DE AMIENS)	

INTELLIGENCE SUMMARY

(Erase heading not required.)

Instructions regarding War Diaries and Intelligence Summaries are contained in F.S. Regs, Part II. and the Staff Manual respectively. Title Pages will be prepared in manuscript.

Place	Date	Hour	Summary of Events and Information	Remarks and references to Appendices
ARRAS (SHEET 51B) FRANCE	19.7.16		Distribution of Battalion the same.	
Do	20.7.16		Do	
Do	21.7.16		Distribution of Battalion the same. The Battalion paraded at 11 am today for presentation by the commanding officer, of meritorious ribbons awarded for gallant & meritorious conduct to the following N.C.O.'s and Men. 11495 Sgt KING 20157, Sgt E.J. DAVIES, 8078 Sgt I. POPE, 10620 L/Cpl W.R. CHORLEY. 10981 Pte J. LLOYD, 15891 Pte S. BUTTERWORTH, 5486 Pte J. GOULDING, 17003 Pte C. HERRING	
BLANGY 22.7.16 (G 23. SHEET 51B FRANCE)			The Battalion relieved the 6th Batt Somerset Light Infantry in trenches in I LEFT SECTOR. (3 Companies in the line, 2 Platoons in CEMETERY DEFENCES and 2 Platoons in ARRAS)	
Do	23.7.16		Distribution of Battalion the same. Casualties 1 O.R. wounded.	
Do	24.7.16		Do Casualties 7 O.R. wounded. Enemy attempted a raid on trenches on extreme left of A Coy. (covered by 43rd Infantry Brigade), about 11 pm but met with no success. 2 Lieut W.H. JONES joined the Battalion.	
Do	25.7.16		Distribution of Battalion the same. 2nd Lieut N.P. D'ALBUQUERQUE joined	

INTELLIGENCE SUMMARY

(Erase heading not required.)

Instructions regarding War Diaries and Intelligence Summaries are contained in F.S. Regs., Part II. and the Staff Manual respectively. Title Pages will be prepared in manuscript.

Place	Date	Hour	Summary of Events and Information	Remarks and references to Appendices
BLANGY (G.28 SHEET 51B)	26.7.16		Distribution of Battalion the same.	
Do & AGNEZ-LES-DUISANS (K.12 SHEET 51c FRANCE)	27.7.16		Battalion was relieved by 9th Batt. Lancashire Fusiliers in I LEFT SECTOR and afterwards marched to billets at AGNEZ-LES-DUISANS. (SHEET 51c FRANCE) LIEUT. W.R. FABER joins the Battalion.	
AGNEZ-LES-DUISANS & GRAND ROULLECOURT (O.9 SHEET 51c FRANCE)	28.7.16		Battalion marched from AGNES-LES-DUISANS to billets at GRAND ROULLECOURT, which place was reached about 3 p.m. Length of march about 9 miles. 2nd LIEUT J.C. THOMPSON and 2nd LIEUT J.A. LEE joined the Battn.	
GRAND ROULLECOURT (O.9 SHEET 51 C.2 FRANCE)	29.7.16		Battalion marched from GRAND ROULLECOURT at 11.10 A.M. to billets at BARLY, which place was reached about 3.20 p.m. Weather hot.	
BARLY (LENS 11) 1/100,000	30.7.16		Battalion in billets at BARLY. 2nd Lieut. J.Y. JACKSON joined the Battalion. Hot weather.	
BARLY & CANDAS (LENS 11) 1/100,000	31.7.16		Battalion marched from BARLY to CANDAS, a distance of about 7½ miles. Hot weather.	

G.A.J.L.M.E. Murray. Major
Commanding 5th King's Shropshire L.I.

42nd Brigade.
14th Division.

1/5th BATTALION

KING'S SHROPSHIRE LIGHT INFANTRY

AUGUST 1916

Appendices attached :- Congratulatory Messages.

CONFIDENTIAL.

War Diary of

5th King's Shropshire. L.I.

from

August 1st to 31st 1916

(Volume 9)

WAR DIARY
or
INTELLIGENCE SUMMARY.

(Erase heading not required.)

Army Form C. 2118.

Instructions regarding War Diaries and Intelligence Summaries are contained in F. S. Regs., Part II. and the Staff Manual respectively. Title pages will be prepared in manuscript.

Place	Date	Hour	Summary of Events and Information	Remarks and references to Appendices
CANDAS (LENS 11)	1/8/16		Battalion in billets at CANDAS. 2nd LIEUT. HIGGINSON takes over duties of Assistant Adjt. Weather hot.	
Do (LENS 11)	2/8/16		Battalion in billets at CANDAS. A Concert was held in the evening, in which members of the R.F.C. greatly assisted.	
Do (LENS 11)	3/8/16 to 6/8/16		Battalion in billets at CANDAS. Weather hot.	
Do (SHEET 62 D) FRANCE	7.8.16		Battalion entrained at CANDAS STATION at 11 a.m., and after long train journey, arrived at MERICOURT (J.H.a. SHEET. 62 D FRANCE) detrained there, & marched to billets at BUIRE-SUR-L'ANCRE, (distance of about 2 miles) which was reached about 6 p.m.	
BUIRE-SUR-L'ANCRE (SHEET 62 D FRANCE)	8.8.16		Battalion in billets at BUIRE-SUR-L'ANCRE. (SHEET. 62.D. FRANCE). D.29.6. Weather hot.	
Do (SHEET 62 D) FRANCE	9.8.16		Battalion in billets at BUIRE-SUR-L'ANCRE. (SHEET. 62.D. FRANCE). The Battalion paraded at 9.30 p.m. to practice night operations. D.29.6.	
Do (SHEET 62 D) FRANCE	10.8.16		Battalion in billets at BUIRE-SUR-L'ANCRE (D.29.6. Sheet 62. D. FRANCE)	
Do (SHEET 62 D) FRANCE	11.8.16		Battalion in billets at BUIRE-SUR-L'ANCRE (D.29.6. SHEET 62.D. FRANCE). The Battalion paraded at 9 A.M., to listen to address by the G.O.C. 42nd Infantry Brigade	

WAR DIARY
or
INTELLIGENCE SUMMARY

(Erase heading not required.)

Army Form C. 2118

Place	Date	Hour	Summary of Events and Information	Remarks and references to Appendices
BUIRE-SUR-L'ANCRE (SHEET 62D FRANCE)	12/6/16		Battalion marched from BUIRE-SUR-L'ANCRE to F.14.a. (SHEET 62D FRANCE) near FRICOURT, & bivouaced there. Weather hot.	
F.14.a. (SHEET 62D)	13/6/16		Battalion in bivouac at F.14.a. SHEET 62D FRANCE. Reinforcement of 52 O.R. joined today. The following N.C.Os & men attended at 14th Div. H.Q. for presentation of Medal Ribbon by Major General RAWLINSON. COMMDG. 4TH ARMY :- 11495 SGT. A KING. 8078 CORPL. J POPE. 17003 PTE. C HERRING. 5496 PTE. J GOULDING.	
Do	14/6/16		Battalion in bivouac at F.14.a. Batt. found working party of 1 Officer and 150 O.R. Our Artillery continuously bombarding enemies lines. Weather - showery.	
Do	15/6/16		Battalion in bivouac at F.14.a. Heavy night bombardment by our Artillery.	
Do	16/6/16		Battalion in bivouac at F.14.a. Our aeroplanes very active during the day. Weather - fine.	
Do	17/6/16		Do. German aeroplane observed to descend entirely in flames.	
Do	18/6/16		29 O.R. joined today. At 10.45 a.m. the Battalion proceeded to POMMIER REDOUBT. (Ref. ALBERT (COMBINED SHEET) MAP) as Reserve Battn to 43rd Inf. Bde who made an attack. 11 Officers and 131 O.R. did not proceed with Batt., and remained behind at Details Camp situate at F.14.a. (SHEET 62D)	
Ref. ALBERT (COMBINED SHEET)	19/6/16		A & B Coys C & D Coy left POMMIER REDOUBT at 5 a.m. & 9 a.m. respectively, and under orders of 43rd Inf Bde proceeded to MONTAUBAN ALLEY. Casualties 5 O.R. wounded. Heavy artillery bombardment by our guns. 2/Lt. J. REYNOLDS joined.	

WAR DIARY
or
INTELLIGENCE SUMMARY.

Army Form C. 2118.

Place	Date	Hour	Summary of Events and Information	Remarks and references to Appendices
ALBERT TRENCH (COMBINED SHEET)	20/8/16		The Battalion left MONTAUBAN ALLEY on night of 19 inst and took up position in CRUCIFIX ALLEY, and worked on deepening trenches and collecting salvage	
Do	21/8/16		Weather fine. Battalion left CRUCIFIX ALLEY and proceeded to bomb line trenches, occupying portion of DEVIL'S TRENCH (S.11.12.d.ALBERT.) in vicinity of DELVILLE WOOD (S.11.12. d. ALBERT.) COMBINED SHEET). Enemy aeroplanes dropped bombs on Brigade Transport Camp.	
DELVILLE WOOD (S.12.c+d) ALBERT (COMBINED SHEET)	22/8/16		Battalion occupying DEVIL'S TRENCH. Continuous Artillery fire.	
Do	23/8/16		Do	
Do	24/8/16		Do. Weather fine. Our Artillery kept up a severe bombardment of enemy's lines. At 5.45 pm today the 42nd Inf. Bde made an attack, with BEER TRENCH as its final Objective. 5th Dt Y/Bucks & 9th K.R.R. Corps on our right. The Battalion gained the objective, but owing to right flank being unsupported, was obliged to retire on EDGE TRENCH and finally on INNER TRENCH. In the course of the action, the Battalion captured 2 Machine Guns.	Casualties 11 Officers 194 O.R.
Do	25/8/16		The Battalion was relieved by 6th K.O.Y.L.I. and afterwards marched to camp at F.14.a. (NEAR FRICOURT) (SHEET 62.D FRANCE)	2 Officers & 115 O.R.
SHEET 62.D FRANCE	26/8/16		Battalion in bivouac camp at F.14.a.	

WAR DIARY
or
INTELLIGENCE SUMMARY.
(Erase heading not required.)

Army Form C. 2118.

Instructions regarding War Diaries and Intelligence Summaries are contained in F. S. Regs., Part II. and the Staff Manual respectively. Title pages will be prepared in manuscript.

Place	Date	Hour	Summary of Events and Information	Remarks and references to Appendices
I M A. (SHEET 62 D FRANCE)	27/6/16		Battalion in bivouac at I M A	
Do	28/6/16		Battalion proceeded to POMMIER REDOUBT at 4 p.m. today. A halt was made at this place until 9.15 p.m. when Companies marched off independently to relieve 6 K.O.Y.L.I. in & in front of DELVILLE WOOD. On our immediate right 9 R.B. relieved the Regt. on the night. Owing to heavy rains & severe shelling, the trenches were in a very bad state	
(ALBERT COMBINED SHEET)	29/6/16		Battalion in DELVILLE WOOD. Trenches. The Enemy shelled the Wood incessantly with heavies. Front line trenches received very little shelling. Weather - Heavy rain.	
Do	30/6/16		Battalion in DELVILLE WOOD. Trenches. German Rifle shelled DELVILLE OR Bazentin. WOOD very heavily from 2 p.m. to 5 p.m. Casualties. 8 killed 4 missing	
Do	31/6/16		Battalion relieved by 6th R. West Kents in early hours of this morning, and afterwards proceeded to camp at I M A. After a short interval for rations the Battalion was conveyed by motor Buses to MERICOURT STATION (J H 62 D FRANCE) when they entrained about 6 p.m. and were conveyed by rail to AIRAINES which place was reached about 10.15 p.m. Detrained here and marched to billets at YERGIES, (a distance of about 5 miles) & arrived here about 2.30 a.m.	APPENDICES No 1. 2 3 (SUBJECT) Congratulatory Messages Attached at back
AIRAINES 9 26/65 (Map) (DIEPPE) 10.				

G. Helme Murray Major
Commanding 5 King's Shropshire L.I.

APPENDIX I

WAR DIARY
or
INTELLIGENCE SUMMARY.

(SUBJECT) CONGRATULATORY MESSAGES

Army Form C. 2118.

Place	Date	Hour	Summary of Events and Information	Remarks and references to Appendices
			Reference to Operations of 24th August 1916	
			The following messages and letters have been received from 4th Army, 11th Division, 9 & 2nd Infantry Brigade, and copies are herewith given:—	
			From 4th Army on 26/8/16:- "The Army Commander congratulates all ranks on their gallant attack on 24th inst."	
			From 11th Division on 1/9/16:-	
			11th (Light) Division. Special Order.	
			"On completing our first tour of duty in the Battle of the Somme, the G.O.C. wishes to express to all units and all ranks his great appreciation of the discipline, hard work, and cheeriness shown by the officers, N.C.O's and men of the 11th (Light) Division."	
			"After a prolonged tour of duty in the trenches the Division was called on at short notice and without any opportunity for special training, to take part in what will probably be the Decisive Battle of the War."	
			"The Division has carried out its task so as to earn the special thanks of the Corps Commander on all occasions when called upon to attack."	
			"The many objectives allotted to the Division have been secured, heavy casualties inflicted on the enemy and in addition, over 400 prisoners and 16 machine guns have been captured."	
			"To those who have fallen in the Battle a special tribute is due the Division has to mourn the loss of many brave men and good comrades; at the same time it has the satisfaction of knowing that	

APPENDIX N

Subject: (CONGRATULATORY MESSAGES)

"by its steadiness and soldierly qualities, it has maintained all the "advantages, to gain which their brave men gave their lives."

"The recent exploits of the Division are to be carefully explained to all drafts, so that they may know the high standard the 1st (Highld) Division has set them to live up to."

"In all probability the Division will, after a period of rest from fighting be called upon to take a further part in the battle. When this call comes, the G.O.C. is confident that the Division will be found ready to emulate, and surpass its recent successes."

(Signed) C.D. Bruce, Lieut-Col
G. Staff
1st (Highld) Division.

From W: 1st Inf. Bde., on 29 August 16.

"Dear Dudgeon,
I appreciate your kind letter and how much it will be appreciated by the 2nd Worcesters to whom I am forwarding it at the same time I should like to say that it was due to the very gallant way in which your fellows cleared our flank in DELVILLE WOOD, water and artillery barrage (which I saw myself and which appeared to me to be too heavy to make any advance possible, that the Worcesters were able to push on to their objective. The way your fellows advanced through DELVILLE WOOD through that German barrage was the admiration of all of us who saw it."

Yours sincerely,
(Sd) Walter Braith.

APPENDIX D

WAR DIARY
INTELLIGENCE SUMMARY (SUBJECT CONGRATULATORY MESSAGES)

Army Form C. 2118

Place	Date	Hour	Summary of Events and Information	Remarks and references to Appendices

H.Q.n Inf. Bde. B.M. 14559

"The above copy of a letter received from Brigadier General BAIRD, C.M.G., D.S.O. Commanding 100th Inf Bde on an left on 24th August is forwarded to you. It is a source of great gratification to the Brigadier that this letter has been written about the Brigade, and he takes this opportunity of again congratulating all ranks on their gallant attack."

(Sd) B Paget Capt
Bde Major.
His Infantry Bde

5th Shrops L.I. 42nd Inf Bde.
==*=*=*=*=*=* B.M. 19/201.

With reference to the operations of the 24th inst. from reports it appears -
(a) that your Battalion gained and occupied BEER Trench from the right of the 5th Oxf & Bucks L.I. as far as its junction with COCOA LANE, where a machine of the Bde Machine Gun Company came into action.
(b) that during the night by order of one of your officers the men of the 5th Shrops L.I. holding BEER Trench fell back to the edge of the Wood leaving the right flank of the 5th Oxf & Bucks L.I. "in the air".
(c) that on finding out what had happened an officer of the 5th Oxf & Bucks L.I. restored the line by forming a defensive flank with some men of the 5th Shrops L.I. brought forward for the purpose from the edge of the Wood.
(d) you state in your report that you gave Captain TURNER orders to establish a strong post at the junction of BEER Trench and COCOA Lane, and that Colonel MORRIS, 9th Rif Brig., gave you the same order on your return to Battalion H.Q. and that this was effected by 5.30 am. on 25th instant.
(e) you also state in your report that as far as you could judge the enemy had retired at least 600 yards, that there was very little machine gun fire, but that there was intermittent shelling.

Please report for the information of the G.O.C. on the following points after very careful investigation :-

I. On whose order was your line retired from BEER Trench to the edge of the Wood.
II. Why was this done, and no attempt made to hold the ground gained and form a defensive flank from the junction of BEER Trench and COCOA LANE, especially in view of para (e) above.
III. Why was the strong point ordered to be made at the junction of BEER Trench and COCOA LANE both by you and by Colonel MORRIS, 9th Rif Brig., not made and held.
IV. On what evidence do you base the statement in your report that this strong point was completed by 5.30 am. on the 25th. inst, and if this was the case, why was it not occupied.
V. What steps did you take to ensure that the order regarding the construction of this strong point, twice given, was carried out.

Please report by 6 pm. tomorrow on the above.

27th August 1916.

Paget
Capt,
Bde Major,
42nd Inf Bde.

CONFIDENTIAL

War Diary

of

5th King's Shropshire L.I.

from

September 1st to 30th 1916

Volume 10

WAR DIARY
or
INTELLIGENCE SUMMARY

Army Form C. 2118

Place	Date	Hour	Summary of Events and Information	Remarks and references to Appendices
VERGIES (Map Dieppe 16)	1.9.16		Battalion in Billets at VERGIES. (MAP DIEPPE 16)	
Do	2/9/16 10 5.9.16		Do Weather fine	
Do	6.9.16		Do A draft of 150 O.R. joined the Battalion today. This draft was composed chiefly of men transferred from 16th & 17th (D.T.) Notts & Derby Regt. No section, who, owing to their relief not being carried out promptly, did not leave the trenches which the Battalion on August 30th reformed the Battalion today. An Appendix No.1, under heading of this Summary is attached to this Diary, shewing copies of correspondence passing between O.C's 2nd & 11th Divsn. 12th, 43rd, 44th Inf Bdes, giving reasons for the delay in relief, & recording the good work, assistance given in repelling a German attack on 31/8/16, and appreciation of the fine spirit shewn throughout.	
Do	7.9.16		Battalion in Billets at VERGIES (MAP. DIEPPE 16). Weather fine. Commanding Officer inspected the drafts joining yesterday. A draft of 115 O.R. joined today.	
Do	8.9.16 10/9/16		Battalion in Billets at VERGIES (MAP DIEPPE 16) During the time the Baton was in VERGIES 48 hours leave was granted to several parties in order to proceed to AULT (situated beach resort)	
Do	11.9.16		Battalion left VERGIES at 3-30 A.M. & marched to AIRAINES, where it entrained at 8 am, and after a slow railway journey, detrained at MERICOURT (J.4. 62. FRANCE) and afterwards marched to camp in E.15.a. arriving here at 6.45 pm	
Do	Do		2 Lieut H. NAYLOR & Lieut J. CHAPMAN joined the Battalion today.	

WAR DIARY
or
INTELLIGENCE SUMMARY

Army Form C. 2118

Place	Date	Hour	Summary of Events and Information	Remarks and references to Appendices
F.13.C. SOUTH. (62. D. FRANCE)	12/9/16		Battalion moved to tents situate on F.13.C. SOUTH. at 1 p.m. Weather fine	
Do	13.9.16		Battalion in tents at F.13.C. (62. D. FRANCE). Weather fine. Lieut. T.G. BONNYMAN joins the Battalion today. Great artillery activity.	
Do	14.9.16		At 6.30 p.m. the Battalion proceeded to POMMIER REDOUBT. (A.1.b. ALBERT combined sheet) and halted there until 1 am when it moved up to YORK ALLEY. (S.16.C. FRANCE 57, 0.5.W) An advanced Transport & Detail Camp was formed in Square A.2. & Central.	
SHEET.FRANCE 57 C.S.W.	15.9.16		Weather fine but cold evenings. At 6.20 a.m. today the Battalion moved forward from YORK ALLEY (S.18.a.57)(in FRANCE), C & D Coys leading, followed by B & A Coys. Our objective was GIRD TRENCH. (from N.32.b.3½.8 to N.26.c.6.9. SHEET. 57.C.S.W. FRANCE). which, owing to both flanks of leading boys' being "left in the air" we failed to get. Our final position was, however, just behind this trench. During the action we captured 4 field guns and 1 machine gun, (at a point about between N.31.D.10.B and N.31.0.6.9.) but were unable to remove these at the time, these guns had previously caused us serious trouble. Also 08 prisoners also, to the number of 50 fell into our hands. Casualties 1 Offr. 34 killed. O.R. = 18 Wounded. O.R. = 2 OR = 34 missing. A new engine of war a petrol-driven armoured car, termed "The Tank", was used for the first time. Four of these machines were allotted to the Division during this operation, and are considered to have done splendid work.	

Army Form C. 2118

WAR DIARY
or
INTELLIGENCE SUMMARY
(Erase heading not required.)

Place	Date	Hour	Summary of Events and Information	Remarks and references to Appendices
SHEET. 57.C.S.W.	16.9.16		The Battalion was relieved by 6th D.C.L.I. & moved down to MONTAUBAN AREA. (S.28.6. (57.C.S.W. FRANCE) and after about 11 hours rest moved up to SWITCH TRENCH (T.8.N.35. 57.CSW. FRANCE) in relief of 8th K.R.R. Corps. & A/B coys moved forward to GAP TRENCH (T.2.d.25 to north at T.1.6.17) much annoyed by Blake GEUDECOURT. (N.26. B) which was afterwards cancelled. The Battn. was	
Do 62.D.FRANCE	17.9.16		relieved at about 5 p.m. by the 6/7th Int. Bde. & marched back to POMMIER REDOUBT. (A.1.6. ALBERT. COMBINED SHEET.) were joined here by the details from A.S.D. Centrale, and after short interval for breakfast proceeded to camp in F.13.C. (SHEET. 62.D.) Casualties Officers 1, 2 OR killed. 8 OR wounded.	
62.D. FRANCE	18.9.16		Battalion in camp in F. 13.C. until 10.30 p.m. when it proceeded to camp in D.18.a. (62.D. FRANCE) Raining.	
Do	19.9.16		Battalion in tents at Camp D.18.a. Do	
Do	20.9.16		Do. Notification received by Owl Routine Orders of 20/9/16, that under authority of H.M. The King that the Award of the Military Cross has been conferred on the following officers of this Battn. - Lieut. G.P. BULMER, 2/Lieut. J.C. JINKS, also Divisional Routine Orders of 16/9/16 state-"under authority granted by H.M. The King, Military Medals have been awarded to the following N.C.O's & Men. 5 K.S.L.I. 11849. Sgt. Y. MALT. 17729. Sgt. H. BUTTON. 9444. Corpl. D. JONES. 19046. L/Cpl. E. PARRY. 20056. Pte. W. BUCKLEY. 10695. Pte. W.H. ASHTON. 17707. Pte. W. LONGWORTH. 18183. Pte. F. STEPHENSON. 20025. Pte. E. BARBER. Notification of these awards were re-published in Batton orders of today, together with the congratulations of the commanding officer.	

WAR DIARY or INTELLIGENCE SUMMARY

Army Form C. 2118

(Erase heading not required.)

Place	Date	Hour	Summary of Events and Information	Remarks and references to Appendices
SHEET 62D FRANCE	21.9.16		Battalion in Camp in D.19.A. (SHEET. 62.D. FRANCE) The transport moved off at 12.40 a.m. & proceeded by road to GRAND ROULLECOURT. (O.g.b. SHEET 51.C. FRANCE)	
Do GRAND ROULLECOURT (O.g.b 51.c FRANCE)	22.9.16		Battalion entrained about 10 a.m. on the ALBERT-AMIENS ROAD (D.16.c. central) & moved off to GRAND ROULLECOURT (O.g.b SHEET. 51.C. FRANCE) 62.D FRANCE which place was reached about 5 p.m.	
GRAND ROULLECOURT (O.g.b.) SHEET. 51.C FRANCE	23.9.16		Battalion in billets at GRAND ROULLECOURT. (O.g.b. SHEET. 51.C. FRANCE). Re-inforcements of 33 O.R. joined today.	
Do	24.9.16		Battalion in billets at GRAND ROULLECOURT.	
Do & K.28.D & K.36.D.SC	25.9.16		Battalion en-bussed at 9 a.m today from GRAND ROULLECOURT SQUARE and were conveyed to K.28.d., from there marched to billets in WARLUS. (K.36.D. 51.C. FRANCE)	
WARLUS (K.36.D.) 51.C FRANCE	26.9.16		Battalion in billets at WARLUS. (K.36.d. 51.C. FRANCE) At 8.30 p.m the Battalion relieved the 8th Royal Fusiliers in Brigade Reserve at AGNY. (M&d. SHEET, 51.B.S.W)	
AGNY M&d (SHEET 51.B.S.W)	27.9.16		Battalion in billets in AGNY. (M&d. SHEET 51.B.S.W) The transport moved to BERNEVILLE. (Q.6.b. SHEET. 51.C FRANCE	

Army Form C. 2118

WAR DIARY
or
INTELLIGENCE SUMMARY
(Erase heading not required.)

Place	Date	Hour	Summary of Events and Information	Remarks and references to Appendices
AGNY M&A (SHEET 51 SW)	28/9/16		Battalion in billets at AGNY. 7 ORs joined the Battn. today	
Do	29/9/16		Trench Fire	
Do	30/9/16		Do.	APPENDIX I (Subject [cwm/wmm] is attached to back of Diary)

T. M. Kane Capt.
Commdg. 5 King Shropshire L.I.

14th Division.   24th Divn.
                                                       G.X. 641.
_____

      Three Lewis gun detachments of the 5th K. S. L. I. were returned by motor bus to-day.

      General MITFORD, 72nd Inf. Bde. is, I believe, writing to the G. O. C. 43rd Infantry Brigade, to express his appreciation of their services ; I hope you will also express to their commanding officer and the detachments themselves my thanks for their valuable help in repelling a German attack on the afternoon of the 31st August, and for their spirit throughout.

      I regret the delay in returning them.

                            sd/ J. C. CAPPER, Major-General,
3rd Sept., 1916.   Commanding 24th Division.

(2)

G. O. C.
    43rd Inf Bde   A. B. 64

      I much regret that it was not found possible to relieve the three Lewis guns and teams of 5th K. S. L. I. in the early morning of the 31st August, owing to the delay caused on the road up from FRICOURT. Lewis gun sections of R. W. Kents thereby becoming detached.

      At 8.15 a.m. an intense bombardment of the Wood was commenced by the enemy, and fire did not slacken until 4.30 p.m., shortly after which hour the teams of 5th Shrops L. I. were able to leave.

      Would you please express to O. C. 5th K. S. L. I. my appreciation of the able assistance and good work done by his teams during to-day. They got some good targets, and availed themselves of them ; I think the men enjoyed themselves.

      I much regret that the teams suffered some casualties during to-day's operations.

                            sd/ B. MITFORD, Br. General
3rd Sept., 1916.   Com'g 72nd Inf Bde.

(3)

5th Shrops L. I.   42nd Inf Bde
_____   B.M. 14/565

      Reference the above letters from G. O. C. 24th Division and G. O. C. 72nd Inf Bde, please convey to these men the congratulations of the G. O. C. 42nd Inf Bde on their good work and his high appreciation of their services.

                            (Sgd) B. PAGET.

                                 Capt.
                              Bde Major,
6th Sept. 1916.   42nd Inf Bde

(Roll of above-mentioned (Lewis Gunners) is attached herewith.

2/Lieut J.C. Jinks.

8782	Pte	McCawley J
17952	"	Hoard C.J.A.
6141	"	Evans W
17020	"	Butler W
17918	"	Hughes M
19394	"	Chetwynd W
6377	"	Kirkham W
2007	"	Buzzard G
1736	"	Roberts C
11371	"	Lupton D
17412	"	Evans W.A.
17469	"	Lewis W
11508	"	Lawley J
18914	"	Morris W
5594	"	Walters W

Vol 12

12.S.

CONFIDENTIAL

WAR DIARY

of

5th King's Shropshire L.I.

from

October 1st to 31st 1916

(Volume 11)

WAR DIARY
or
INTELLIGENCE SUMMARY.
(Erase heading not required.)

Army Form C. 2118.

Place	Date	Hour	Summary of Events and Information	Remarks and references to Appendices
AGNY (M.8.D) SHEET 51B S.W. (FRANCE)	1/10/16		Battalion in billets, in Brigade Reserve, at AGNY (M8.D. SHEET 51B S.W.) LIEUT. S.G. BUDGETT and 2 LIEUT G.P. BULMER proceeded to DOULLENS for interview with R.F.C. officer. The following is an extract from 1st Devon Routine Orders of Oct. 1: 1916.— Honours & Awards.— Notice Authority of H.M. THE KING, MILITARY MEDALS are awarded to the undermentioned N.C.O's and men. 5th K.S.L.I. No. 11512. PTE. W. THOMAS, No. 10773. SERGT. J. MADDOX, No. 11088. SERGT. T. TOMKINS, No. 10677. CPL. J. ROGERS, No. 16360. PTE. J. CHALLINOR, No. 18170. PTE. T. BITHELL, No. 11508. PTE. J. LAWLEY, No. 17489. PTE. W. LEWIS, No. 17488. PTE. J. HOPWOOD, No. 7133. SERGT. F. LANGFORD, No. 6483. PTE. J. MCKEON, No. 11064. PTE. C. JAMES. This extract was published in Battalion orders of 2nd inst. together with the Commanding officer's congratulations.	
Do	2/10/16		Battalion relieved in Brigade Reserve by 5th Ox. & Bucks (L.I.) and afterwards proceeded to relieve 9th K.R.R. Corps in trenches in O.P. left Sector. (A Coy. trenches G.24. to 24) (C Coy. trenches G.16.to.20) M.10.C.5.6 to M.15.a.9.8) M.15.a.7.8 to M.15.a.8.4 SHEET 51.B.S.W. (D Coy. trenches G.17. to G.16) SHEET 51.B.S.W. M.15.a.8.4. to M.15.C.1.8. B. Coy in reserve (M.9.b.9.0 to M.9.b.1.1.) SHEET 51.B.S.W. 9th Rifle Brigade on right, a Battalion of 40th Inf. Bde. on our left.	
Do	3/10/16		Battn. in trenches of left Sector. (G.17. to 24. (M.15.a.8.4. to M.10.c.5.6) AGNY was slightly shelled in afternoon. LIEUT. BUDGETT & 2/LIEUT BULMER rejoined today from interview by R.F.C. Officer. M. PIERRE DURNERIN (interpreter) joined the Battn. today. 51B FRANCE	
Do	4/10/16		Battn. in trenches. of left Sector. (G.17. to 24) (M.15.a.8.4. to M.10.c.5.6)	

1377 Wt.W10791/1773 500,000 1/15 D.D.&L. A.D.S.S./Forms/C. 2118.

WAR DIARY
or
INTELLIGENCE SUMMARY.
(Erase heading not required.)

Army Form C. 2118.

Place	Date	Hour	Summary of Events and Information	Remarks and references to Appendices
AGNY (SHEET 51B) FRANCE	5.10.16		Battalion in Trenches in G Left Sector. Enemy's machine guns active about 8 p.m. firing on roads in vicinity of AGNY.	
Do	6.10.16		Battalion in Trenches in G Left Sector. Rainy weather. Enemy machine gun fire swept parapets of GOAT POST (B Coy) at intervals during the night.	
Do (SHEET 51B) FRANCE ↓ DAINVILLE (L.29.C. SHEET 51C FRANCE)	7.10.16		Enemy's Trench Mortars were busy on D Coy's front about 4 p.m., they, however, did not cause any serious damage. The Battalion was relieved during the afternoon by the 9 K.R.R. Corps, afterwards proceeded to rest billets at DAINVILLE. (L.29.C. SHEET 51C FRANCE) Casualties during this tour. NIL. Notification received tonight, (by 42nd Inf Bde Message No. 84/1 d. 7.10.16), that, under Authority of H.M. THE KING, the following Officers and N.C.O's of 5th K.S.L.I had been granted the undermentioned awards:— MILITARY CROSS.— CAPT. G. TURNER. CAPT. J.T. SMEALL. (R.A.M.C. Attached 5 K.S.L.I) D.C.M. No. 9714. Sgt. H. BEESTON. No. 11089. Sgt. J. MORGAN. No. 9406. C.S.M. G.C. FURBER. These awards were re-published in Battn Orders of 8 inst, together with the Commanding Officers congratulations	
DAINVILLE (L.29.C. SHEET 51C FRANCE)	8.10.16		Battalion in rest at DAINVILLE. (L.29.C. SHEET 51C FRANCE)	

WAR DIARY or INTELLIGENCE SUMMARY

Army Form C. 2118

Place	Date	Hour	Summary of Events and Information	Remarks and references to Appendices
DAINVILLE (h.29.C) SHEET 51.C (FRANCE)	9.10.16		Battalion in billets at DAINVILLE (h.29.C 51° FRANCE.) Weather fine. A class (Physical Training, Bayonet fighting etc) consisting of 4 Officers & 16 N.C.O's was taken by Staff Sergt. Mc HALE, Army Gymnastic Staff, daily during the period the Battn was in DAINVILLE	
Do	10.10.16 & 11.10.16		Battalion in billets at DAINVILLE (h.29.C 51° FRANCE). On 11" inst, Officers of the Battalion attended a demonstration given by the Officer Commanding 11th Divl Signal Coy, of the method of handling Carrier Pigeons, sending & affixing messages etc. A successful concert was held in the Y.M.C.A. HUT on the evening of 11th inst.	
Do	12.10.16		Battalion in billets at DAINVILLE. Battalion found 2 working parties of 100 each (13) working on burying cables etc. Capt. G. TURNER proceeded to England today on mining instructions to report at Brigade Majors House, MARLBOROUGH LINES, ALDERSHOT, prior to assembly a Course, intended to prepare selected regimental officers in the duties which devolve upon the command of a Battalion. Capt. T.C. TANNER joined the Battn today.	
Do & Gfs/left sector	13.10.16		Battalion relieved 9th K.R.R. CORPS in G/s Left sector. A Coy occupying trenches G.21 to 24. (M.10.C.5.6. to M.15.B.9.8.) & C Coy in trenches (G.16 to G.6) (M.15.B.9.8 to D Coy in trenches. G.17 to G.16 (M.15.a.8.4 to M.15.d.1.8.) M.15.a.8.H) B Coy in Reserve. (M.9.C.9.9 to M.9.C.1.1) Our Artillery fired on BEURAINS (M.11.A. 51 SW B FRANCE) from 4 to 5.30pm, enemy retaliated with trench mortars, but did not touch G/s sector.	

WAR DIARY
or
INTELLIGENCE SUMMARY.

(Erase heading not required.)

Army Form C. 2118.

Place	Date	Hour	Summary of Events and Information	Remarks and references to Appendices
AGNY (M.8.d. SHEET 51 B.S.W.)	14/10/16		Battalion in trenches in G. Left Sector. (Trenches G.12 to G.24) Slightly shelling in morning. A large fire broke out behind the enemy's lines about 7-30 pm & continued to burn for two hours or so, it appeared to be in the village of BAILLEUL. (B.27.c. SHEET 51 B.N.W.)	(M.15.a.8.H. to M.10.c.5.6. SHEET 51 S.W. FRANCE)
Do	15/10/16		Battalion in trenches. G. Left Sector (Trenches G.12 to G.24) Our Artillery shelled 2nd & 3rd German lines, 16 of the shells were observed by the Battn observer, to burst very low & appeared to be effective. In the course of the day, five enemy observation balloons ascended in front of this sector, they were pulled down about 5 pm.	8 O.R. joined today.
Do	16/10/16		Battalion in trenches G. Left Sector. Our trench mortars were active during the day.	
Do	17/10/16 & 18/10/16		Battalion in trenches G. Left Sector. Casualties 2 O.R. wounded.	
Do	19/10/16		Battalion relieved by 9th K.R.R. CORPS, & afterwards moved to AGNY. (M.8.d. SHEET (51.B.S.W FRANCE)) in Brigade Reserve. (A Coy in SUNKEN ROAD) B Coy. (2 platoons in SUNKEN ROAD, 1 Platoon in GOAT POST, 1 Platoon in MILL POST). C & D Coy in AGNY.	

Army Form C. 2118

WAR DIARY
or
INTELLIGENCE SUMMARY
(Erase heading not required.)

Instructions regarding War Diaries and Intelligence Summaries are contained in F.S. Regs., Part II. and the Staff Manual respectively. Title Pages will be prepared in manuscript.

Place	Date	Hour	Summary of Events and Information	Remarks and references to Appendices
AGNY. M.&D. SHEET 51.S.W. (FRANCE)	20/10/16		Battalion in Brigade Reserve at AGNY. (M.&D. SHEET. 51.S.W. FRANCE) One of our aeroplanes brought down near AGNY, by machine gun from enemy aeroplane. Enemy machine guns active from 8 & 10 p.m. firing on roads about AGNY. The following is an extract from 1st Divisional Routine orders of 19/10/16:- Under authority granted by H.M. THE KING, the General Officer Commanding-in-Chief has awarded the following Decorations:- S.K.S.L.I. LIEUT. F.W. RHODES. DISTINGUISHED SERVICE ORDER. This announcement was published in Battalion orders of 19/10/16.	
Do	21/10/16		Distribution of Battalion the same. Weather frosty.	
Do	22/10/16		Do. Our aeroplanes very active throughout the day.	
Do	23/10/16		Battalion in Brigade Reserve in AGNY. (M.&D. SHEET 51.S.W. FRANCE) Considerable aeroplane activity about 4 p.m.	
Do	24/10/16		Battalion in Brigade Reserve AGNY. (M.&D. SHEET 51.S.W. FRANCE) The following officers joined the Battalion today:- MAJOR. C.R.B. WINGFIELD, 2/LIEUT. A.P. WEBB, 2/LIEUT. H.T. CLARKE, 2/LIEUT. G.R. MATHER, 2/LIEUT. A.W. KEIGHT.	
Do	25/10/16		Battalion in Brigade Reserve. AGNY. (M.&D. SHEET. 51.S.W. FRANCE) Weather wet.	

WAR DIARY
or
INTELLIGENCE SUMMARY.
(Erase heading not required.)

Army Form C. 2118.

Instructions regarding War Diaries and Intelligence Summaries are contained in F. S. Regs., Part II. and the Staff Manual respectively. Title pages will be prepared in manuscript.

Place	Date	Hour	Summary of Events and Information	Remarks and references to Appendices
AGNY (51c. S.W. 51c.FRANCE) WANQUETIN (51c.FRANCE)	26/10/16		The Battalion was relieved at 10.50 p.m. by the 11th Batt'n MIDDLESEX REGT. and afterwards proceded to CROSS/ROADS at K.35 t.5.7. (51c.FRANCE) where it em-bused and was conveyed to billets at WANQUETIN (K.32. SHEET. 51c.FRANCE), which place was reached at 2.45 A.M. 27 inst.	
WANQUETIN (51c.FRANCE) BLAYINCOURT to LIGNEREUIL (51c.FRANCE)	27.10.16		Batt'n in billets at WANQUETIN. (51 c. FRANCE) The Battalion moved off from here at 1.35 p.m. & marched to billets at BLAYINCOURT (I.28.c) & LIGNEREUIL. (I.21.b. (SHEET 51c.FRANCE)), the last-named place was reached about 5.20 p.m. Distance of march was about 8 miles. Distribution of Batt'n as follows:- A Coy in BLAYINCOURT, B, C, D, Coys in LIGNEREUIL (I.21. b 51c. FRANCE)	
LIGNEREUIL BLAYINCOURT (51c. FRANCE)	28.10.16		A Coy in BLAYINCOURT (I.28.c. 51c.FRANCE) B.C.D. Coys and Transport in LIGNEREUIL (I.21.b. 51c.FRANCE). Notification received by wire Polo S.C. No 924 d/26.10.16 9th Rnd Routine Order d/26/10/16 that the following N.C.O's had been awarded the MILITARY MEDAL:- No 11498. SGT. A.T. SMITH. No 10024. SGT. W. BULLOCK. Notifications of these awards were published in Batt'n orders of 29th inst., together with the commanding officers congratulations.	
Do	29.10.16		A Coy in BLAYINCOURT (I.28.c. 51 B.FRANCE) B.C.D. Coys & Transport in LIGNEREUIL (I.21.F.) The commanding officer inspected the Regimental Transport today.	
Do	30.10.16		Do Do Parade today.	
Do	31.10.16		Do (In accordance with the Programme of Training the to be done by the Battalion whilst in this Area) were carried out yesterday & also today.	

G. H. Selwyn-Murray. Lieut. Col.
Commanding 1st King's Shropshire L.I.

CONFIDENTIAL

Vol 13   del 13.8. 6 sheet

WAR DIARY

of

5th King's Shropshire L.I.

from

November 1st to 30th 1916

(VOLUME ~~12~~)

WAR DIARY
or
INTELLIGENCE SUMMARY.

(Erase heading not required.)

Army Form C. 2118.

Place	Date	Hour	Summary of Events and Information	Remarks and references to Appendices
BLAYINCOURT (I.27.d. & I.26.c.) LIGNEREUIL (I.M.t. SIC FRANCE)	1/11/16		A Coy in BLAYINCOURT. (I.27.d. & I.26.c.) B.C.D. Coy's Transport in LIGNEREUIL (I.M. 51c FRANCE) (Training Area)	
Do	2/11/16		Disposition of Battn same as 1st inst. The following programme of work was carried out today:— 9-9.30 A.M. Physical exercises. 9.30 to 10-15 A.M. Rifle Exercises. 10.30 to 11-15 A.M. Extended order drill. 11-15 A.M. to 12 Noon. Platoon Drill. 2 to 3 P.M. Short route march by Coy's.	
Do	3/11/16		Distribution of Battn the same as 2nd inst.	
Do	4/11/16		Battalion Route March:— Route — DENIER-SARS-LEZ-BOIS — MAGNICOURT-SUR-CANCHE — thence along main Road to AMBRINES, & back to billets. (SIC FRANCE)	
Do	5/11/16		Distribution of Battn the same as 4th inst.	
Do	6/11/16		Do. The following work was carried out today:— 9. A.M to 11 A.M. Elementary Outposts. 11-15 A.M. to 12 noon. Bayonet fighting & Physical exercises. one Coy shooting on range. 2 to 3 P.M. Battn Drill under Regtl. Sgt Major.	
Do	7/11/16		The Battn moved off from LIGNEREUIL at 9 A.M. & marched to billets at IVERGNY (N.21) 51c FRANCE) which were reached about 12 noon. Length of March about 5½ miles. Not weather.	
IVERGNY (N.21)c 51c FRANCE	8/11/16		Battn in Training Area, at IVERGNY. (N.21.) 51c FRANCE) Marching Wet	
IVERGNY (N.21) SIC FRANCE.			Do.	
Do	9/11/16		Work was carried out today in accordance with following programme:— 9 to 11 A.M. Elementary Outposts, 1 Coy shooting on range. 11-15 P.M. to 12 noon Coy Drill. 2 to 3 P.M. Short Route march by Coy's. Battalion Parade Mounted at N.10 to 3.4. (SIC FRANCE). Rifle Range situate at about (N.15.c.7.5) 51c.	

WAR DIARY
or
INTELLIGENCE SUMMARY.
(Erase heading not required.)

Army Form C. 2118.

Place	Date	Hour	Summary of Events and Information	Remarks and references to Appendices
IVERGNY (N.21) (51°C. FRANCE)	10/11/16		Battalion in Billets at IVERGNY (N.21 (51°C. FRANCE). Work was carried out in accordance with the following programme:- 9- to 9.30 A.M. Musketry (training), 9.30 to 10.30 A.M. extended order Drill 10.45 A.M. to 11.15 A.M, Company Drill, 11-15 to 12 Noon Bayonet Sighting. 2 to 3 pm Short Route March by Coys	
Do	11/11/16		Battalion in Billets at IVERGNY (N21. (51°C. FRANCE). The programme of work carried out today is as follows:- 9.10 A.M. Battn Route March, 1oo, Coy firing. 2nd Lt M. CUTLER joins today	
Do	12/11/16		Battn in Billets at IVERGNY. (N.21 51°F. FRANCE)	
Do	13/11/16		Do. Today is as follows:- 9-9.30 A.M. Physical Exercises, 9.30 to 10 A.M Bayonet fighting 10-15 to 12 Noon Elementary Night Work. LIEUT. T. G. BONNYMAN takes over duties of Town Major, IVERGNY, from 2/Lt F. RITCHIE R.E.	
Do	14/11/16		Battn in Billets at IVERGNY (N.21 51°C. FRANCE). STAFF. SERGT. LOVELAND, ARMY GYMNASTIC STAFF visits the Battn today, and took a class, composed of Junior Officers, q also N.C.O's in Bayonet fighting q Physical Drawing.	
Do	15/11/16		Battn at IVERGNY (N.21 51°C. FRANCE), G.O.C. H.'s Inf'. Bde gave a lecture to all officers and N.C.O's (at 9 am in the Recreation Room) on the following subject: MUSKETRY. Work was carried out today as follows:- 9 to 9.20 A.M. Physical Drawing under Reg'l Serg't Major. 9-45 to 12 Noon Artillery Formations, 2 to 3 pm Elementary Night Work.	
Do	16/11/16		Battn at IVERGNY. (N.21 51°C. FRANCE) The programme of work carried out during the day, is as follows:- 9 to 12 Noon, Advance Guards, A q B Coys firing, 5 to 7 pm Night Outposts.	

Army Form C. 2118.

WAR DIARY
or
INTELLIGENCE SUMMARY.
(Erase heading not required.)

Instructions regarding War Diaries and Intelligence Summaries are contained in F. S. Regs., Part II. and the Staff Manual respectively. Title pages will be prepared in manuscript.

Place	Date	Hour	Summary of Events and Information	Remarks and references to Appendices
IVERGNY (N.21.S¹⁰ FRANCE)	17/11/16		Battn in billets at IVERGNY. (N.21.S¹⁰ FRANCE). G.O.C. H.Q. infantry inspected the transport today.	
Do	18/11/16		Battn in billets at IVERGNY (N.21.S¹⁰ FRANCE). Battalion Route march. Route :- VIA LUCHEUX - BREVILLERS-LE-SOUICHE & back to billets	
Do	19/11/16		Battn in billets at IVERGNY (N.21.S¹⁰ FRANCE). Sgt. WHITNEY, 142ⁿᵈ INF. BDE GAS N.C.O gave a demonstration of the setting on of Box Respirators, to all officers & N.C.O's of the Battalion.	
Do	20/11/16		Battn in billets at IVERGNY. (N.21.S¹⁰ FRANCE). Programme of work carried out today is as follows, 9 A.M to 12 noon Advance Guards, 9 - 2 Coy firing.	
Do	21/11/16		Battn in billets at IVERGNY (N.21 S¹⁰ FRANCE) 2 Coys were firing on the range in morning & 1 Coy of gunners in the afternoon	
Do	22/11/16		Battn in billets at IVERGNY. (N.21.S¹⁰ FRANCE). During the period the Battn are in IVERGNY; horses & men were lent to the inhabitants to assist them in Farm Work, thrashing etc.	
Do & DAINVILLE. (L.29.C) S¹⁰ FRANCE	23/11/16		The Battalion moved off from IVERGNY. (N.21 S¹⁰ FRANCE) at 9.45 A.M 9 marched to Q.13.6.9.1. (East end of GOUY-EN-ARTOIS), dinners were served here, and at 3 P.M the Battalion moved off & proceeded to billets at DAINVILLE, (L.29.C.S¹⁰FRANCE). This place was reached about 15ᵗ Mill.6. length of march about 15ᵗ Mill.6.	
DAINVILLE (L.29.C) S¹⁰ FRANCE	24/11/16		Battalion in Billets at DAINVILLE. (L.29.C. S¹⁰ FRANCE)	

Army Form C. 2118.

WAR DIARY
or
INTELLIGENCE SUMMARY.
(Erase heading not required.)

Instructions regarding War Diaries and Intelligence Summaries are contained in F. S. Regs., Part II. and the Staff Manual respectively. Title pages will be prepared in manuscript.

Place	Date	Hour	Summary of Events and Information	Remarks and references to Appendices
DAINVILLE. (L.29.C 51° FRANCE)	25/11/16 to 29/11/16		Battalion in Billets at DAINVILLE (L.29.C. 51°FRANCE). The Battalion furnished working parties daily, to the number of 400. N.C.O's & men, for work on Corps Line etc, under the direction of Officer-in-Charge Details, 144th Coy R.E. 2/Lieuts W.R. PRESHOWE. T. ONSLOW. & F. BUCKLEY joined the Battn. 29/11/16	
Do	30/11/16		Battalion in Billets at DAINVILLE. (L.29.C 51° FRANCE), Working Parties found by Battn, same as 29 inst.	

G. O. M. S. - Murray Nicext Pool.
Comndg 5th King's Shropshire L.I.

Vol 14

14.S.
11 sheets

WAR DIARY.

CONFIDENTIAL.

UNIT.— 5th King's Shropshire L.I.

PERIOD. From 1st December 1916 To 31st December 1916.

VOLUME NO. 13

WAR DIARY
or
INTELLIGENCE SUMMARY
(Erase heading not required.)

Army Form C. 2118

Instructions regarding War Diaries and Intelligence Summaries are contained in F.S. Regs., Part II. and the Staff Manual respectively. Title Pages will be prepared in manuscript.

Place	Date	Hour	Summary of Events and Information	Remarks and references to Appendices
DAINVILLE (L.29.C.) SIC. FRANCE	1/17/16		Battalion in billets at DAINVILLE (L.29.C.SIC FRANCE) and found working parties, under the supervision of O/C. 144 Coy. D/ark. R.E.	
Do	2/17/16		Usual working parties found.	
Do	3/17/16 & 4/17/16		Do. Do. Time chiefly spent in fitting & testing of the New Bat. Respirator. Our aeroplanes active during the afternoon & the H. a flock of IV bearing over the enemy lines about 9.30 A.M. Enemy fired two shells into DAINVILLE about 2.30 p.m. H.	
Do	5/17/16 & 6/17/16		Battalion in Billets at DAINVILLE. (L.29.C. SIC FRANCE)	
Do	7/17/16		Do	
Do	8/17/16		Battalion moved off from DAINVILLE at 5-50 A.M this morning' and marched to AVESNES-LE-COMTE (J.75.d. SIC. FRANCE) where breakfast was served at 10 A.M the Baton resumed the march, & proceeded to billets at GOUY-EN-TERNOIS. (B.28.d. SIC. FRANCE), which place was reached at about 3pm. Length of march, 15 miles.	
GOUY-EN-TERNOIS (B.29.d.) SIC FRANCE	9/17/16		Battalion in billets at GOUY-EN-TERNOIS. (B.29 d. SIC. FRANCE) Weather, wet.	

WAR DIARY or INTELLIGENCE SUMMARY

Army Form C. 2118

(Erase heading not required.)

Instructions regarding War Diaries and Intelligence Summaries are contained in F.S. Regs., Part II. and the Staff Manual respectively. Title Pages will be prepared in manuscript.

Place	Date	Hour	Summary of Events and Information	Remarks and references to Appendices
GOUY-EN-TERNOIS (B.78.d.51c)	10/12/16		Battalion in billets at GOUY-EN-TERNOIS. (B.78.d.51c.FRANCE) No. 13. Platoon, D Coy, under charge of 2/Lieut. A.P.WEBB, takes part in 1st Divisional Musketry Competition and wins the first prize. (£10) offered. A Draft of 7. O.R. joined today.	
Do	11/12/16		Battalion in billets at GOUY-EN-TERNOIS. (B.78.d.51c.FRANCE) Wet weather. Major LOVEBAND, Army Gymnastic Staff, visited the Battn today, & instructed N.C.O.'s in Physical Training and Bayonet Fighting. A draft of 175 O.R. joined today.	
Do	12/12/16		Battalion in billets at GOUY-EN-TERNOIS. (B.78.d.51c.FRANCE)	
Do	13/12/16		Do Brigade Inter-Coy. Rifle Competition, in which D Coy takes part & gains 3rd Prize, took place today.	
Do	14/12/16		Battn at GOUY-EN-TERNOIS (B.78.d.51c.FRANCE)	
Do	15/12/16		The Battalion moved off from GOUY-EN-TERNOIS. (B.78.d.51c.FRANCE) at 8.45 A.M. today, and marched to billets at GOUVES (K.16.d) and MONTENESCOURT (K.21.A), reaching there place about 2pm. length of march about 12 Miles.	
GOUVES, (K.16.d) MONTENESCOURT (K.21.A) AGNY (M.9.d.5.1B.S.W)	16/12/16		The Battalion marched at 1pm & proceeded to relieve the 11th Battn. MIDDLESEX REGT. in Brigade Reserve at AGNY. (M.9.d.51B.S.W.FRANCE)	

WAR DIARY or INTELLIGENCE SUMMARY

Army Form C. 2118

(Erase heading not required.)

Place	Date	Hour	Summary of Events and Information	Remarks and references to Appendices
AGNY (M.8.D.) SHEET 51 B.S.W.	19/12/16 to 20/12/16 21/12/16		Battalion in Brigade Reserve at AGNY. (M.8.d.) 51B.S.W. FRANCE)	
Do	22/12/16		Battn was relieved in the afternoon, by 5th Ox & Bucks L.I., and afterwards proceeded to relieve 9th K.R.R. CORPS in trenches G.12 to G.7H in G. LEFT SECTOR. Disposition at left as follows:- A Coy in trenches G.21 to M. (M.10.c.5.6 & M.15.b.g.9. 51B SW. FRANCE & g.9) B Coy in trenches G.16 to G.20. (M.15.b.g.g. to M.15.a.8.4). C Coy in reserve (M.g.b.9.0 & M.g.6.1.1) 51 B SW FRANCE D Coy in trenches G.12 to G.16. (M.15.a.8.4 to M.15.C.1.8)	
G. LEFT SECTOR (M.8.d.) 51 B SW	23/12/16		Battalion in trenches in G left sector. Situation quiet a few 77 m.m shells fell between G.R. & G.S. LINE. Enemy searchlight busy at night.	
Do	24/12/16		Battalion in trenches in G left sector. (M.8.d. 51B SW) Our artillery bombarded shef enemy line, in the afternoon.	
Do	25/12/16		Disposition of Battn the same as 24th. Situation normal. Trenches in a v. bad condition, owing to heavy weather.	
Do	26/12/16		Do. Our 18-pounder fired 10 rounds at enemy lines opposite G.22 & G.23 during the afternoon, and also fired at enemy searchlights at night. Casualties. 1 O.R. wounded	

Army Form C. 2118

WAR DIARY
or
INTELLIGENCE SUMMARY
(Erase heading not required.)

Instructions regarding War Diaries and Intelligence Summaries are contained in F.S. Regs., Part II. and the Staff Manual respectively. Title Pages will be prepared in manuscript.

Place	Date	Hour	Summary of Events and Information	Remarks and references to Appendices
(LEFT SECTOR)	27/1/16		Disposition of Battn same as 26th. Our Heavy Field Artillery carried out, what appeared to be an effective bombardment of the enemy trenches in g SECTOR on our right, during the afternoon. Enemy retaliation was weak. One light shell fell near Battn HdQrs about 4 p.m. The Battalion was relieved at about 5 p.m. by the 9th K.R.R. CORPS, and made proceeded to billets at DAINVILLE.	
DAINVILLE (L.29.C) S'IC. FRANCE	28/1/16 29/1/16		Battalion in billets at DAINVILLE. (L.29.C.S'IC) During the night of 29th, our Heavy Artillery fired on enemy back areas, at irregular intervals.	
Do	30/1/16 31/1/16		Battalion in billets at DAINVILLE. (L.29.C. S'IC. FRANCE)	

C R Wingfield Major
Commdg 5th Kings Shropshire L.I.

WAR DIARY.

CONFIDENTIAL.

UNIT,   5th King's Shropshire Light Infantry.

PERIOD. From   Jan 1st 1917   To   Jan 31st 1917.

VOLUME NO. 14

WAR DIARY
or
INTELLIGENCE SUMMARY.

Army Form C. 2118.

Place	Date	Hour	Summary of Events and Information	Remarks and references to Appendices
DAINVILLE (L.29.C.5.) 51C. FRANCE	1/1/17		Battalion in billets at DAINVILLE (L.29.C.FRANCE). At 1 pm the A Coy in reserve. Batn proceeded to relieve the 9th K.R.R. Corps in trenches in G. Left Sector. (B.6 & D Coy in front line trenches G.12 to G.17).	(M.9 & 9.0.51BSW) (M.15 & 8 & 6.71.15. & 9.B) 51 BSW FRANCE
G. Left Sector I9GNY. 51BSW	2/1/17		Battalion in trenches G. Left Sector. AGNY. (51BSW) Our 18 pdrs fired on enemy front line, opposite I/13, from 9.30 am to 10.30am at 11 pm our Lewis gunners fired on, and dispersed enemy patrol in front of G.16	
G. Left Sector AGNY 51 B.S.W.	3/1/17		Battalion in trenches. G. Left heat of AGNY. (51BSW). Our Artillery fired about 30 S.9 & 12 4.5 on enemy wire in front of I/A late G.15. Two enemy heavy trench mortars fell on railway just behind front line trench, at 1.50 pm.	In "It" mot-
	4/1/17			
Do	5/1/17		Battalion in trenches G. left heat of AGNY. (51.B.S.W)	
Do	6/1/17		Raiding operations taking place on our left (by the 43rd Inf Bde) a smoke screen was made by this Battalion in the afternoon commencing at 3.10 pm. Reports received from boys are given herewith:- A Coy. (M9 & 9.0) "The G.F. line is not damaged. No shells struck the trench." B Coy. (Centre Coy) (M.15 & 9B) "Smoke Bombs were thrown at 3.6 pm, 3.24 pm, and 3.40 pm. Retaliation to our bombardment was very slight, consisting only of a few 77mm shells. On the smoke clouds starting the enemy immediately sent up rockets breaking into two pale pink stars. The enemy Barrage was very feeble, consisting of only few 77 mm shells and slight Trench Mortars. A very slight Barrage of 77 mm fell on the line trench and occasional shells on seldoms line. Damage to trenches & wire slight."	

Army Form C. 2118.

WAR DIARY
or
INTELLIGENCE SUMMARY.
(Erase heading not required.)

Instructions regarding War Diaries and Intelligence Summaries are contained in F. S. Regs., Part II. and the Staff Manual respectively. Title pages will be prepared in manuscript.

Place	Date	Hour	Summary of Events and Information	Remarks and references to Appendices
G.Left Sector AGNY (151 BSN)	6/1/17		B Coys Reports (continues) "Enemy M/Guns were very active, and seemed to cover the whole bay front." When the smoke was sent off, there was no retaliation. C.Coys. (Left Coy):- (M.10.c.5.9 to M.15.6.9.8) "About 5 minutes. Enemy then opened with 77 mm shells & rare bombs, most of the latter were directed at our Stokes Gun Emplacement. The front line trench has been knocked in, in one or two places, otherwise no damage has been done." (Signals) As soon as smoke was sent off, enemy sent up two & red lights from a sap in front of G.31." D.Coy (Right Coy) (M.15.a.9.4 to M.15.c.1.9) "The 3 smoke screens were put up as per instructions. To the first one being put up the enemy sent up a rocket which burst into 2 red lights, and his light field guns sent over two shells. On the second (i.e at 3-16 pm) he commenced shelling support line with light shells. On the third screen, (at 3-46 pm) being made, he increased his fire and shelled the front line and support line with light shells, also sending over several Heavy Trench Mortars, and opening out heavy Machine Gun fire. This continued to 4-15 pm. Damage to trenches quite slight." Casualties. 2/Lt. TONSLOW & 2 O.R. Killed. The following extract from Hyne's letter BM 2/31/17 (received in connection with the operation), is given herewith :- "The G.O.C #3" Infde wishes to thank all ranks of 5" Kalps on behalf of himself and his role for the very effective co-operation they provided."	

A 5834 Wt. W4973 M687 750,000 8/16 D. D. & L. Ltd. Forms/C.2118/13.

WAR DIARY
or
INTELLIGENCE SUMMARY.
(Erase heading not required.)

Army Form C. 2118.

Place	Date	Hour	Summary of Events and Information	Remarks and references to Appendices
G. Leftwelos AGNY.	7/1/17		The Battalion was relieved by 9th K.R.R. Corps & moved into Brigade Reserve at AGNY. (M 8 d 51 B SW FRANCE)	
AGNY (M.8.d) (51 B SW)	8/1/17		Battalion in Brigade Reserve at AGNY. (M 8 d) 51 B SW FRANCE) Found working parties for R.E's, 11th Kings Regt, & left Battalion.	
Do	9/1/17		Do The following notice appears in D.R.O's of 5th inst:- "His Majesty the King has been graciously pleased to award the undermentioned Officers, N.C.O's & men the distinguishes service in the field. The notification appeared in the London Gazette of Jany 1st and 2nd 1917." - 5th K.S.L.I MILITARY CROSS. No 9135 R.S.M J.A. PITT. D.C.M. No 11470 Sergt J. BUTLER. No 18336 L/Cpl P. BROADHURST.	Capt C.S. SMITH & 2/Lt H.T. COLBOURN joined today
Do	10/1/17		Battalion in Brigade Reserve at AGNY (M.8.d. 51 B SW FRANCE) Enemy aeroplane flew very low over SUNKEN ROAD in the afternoon Usual Working Parties found. Capt G. TURNER M.C. rejoined the Baton today from service Officers Class ALDERSHOT	
Do	11/1/17		Battalion in Brigade Reserve at AGNY. (M 8 d 51 B SW FRANCE) Working parties found.	
Do	12/1/17		do Working parties found.	

Army Form C. 2118.

WAR DIARY
or
INTELLIGENCE SUMMARY.
(Erase heading not required.)

Instructions regarding War Diaries and Intelligence Summaries are contained in F. S. Regs., Part II. and the Staff Manual respectively. Title pages will be prepared in manuscript.

Place	Date	Hour	Summary of Events and Information	Remarks and references to Appendices
AGNY (M.8.d) 51.B.S.W.	13/1/17		Battalion relieved in Rentan Brigade Reserve (M.8.d) by 5th Ox. & Buck. L.I. and afterwards proceeded to relieve 9th K.R.R. Corps in trenches in left sector. (G.17 to G.nt)	
left sector AGNY (51.B.S.W)	14/1/17		Battalion in trenches in left sector. AGNY. Disposition as follows:- A Coy in Reserve (M.9.H.O to M.9.C.11) B Coy in trenches G.16.6.20 (M.15.b.9.9 to M.15.a.9.H) 51.B.S.W. C " " trenches G.17 to G.nt (M.10.C.56 to M.15.6.9.8) D Coy in trenches G.17.6. G.16 (M.15.a.8.4 to M.15.C.1.8)	
Do	15/1/17		do. Enemy aircraft active during the night	
Do	16/1/17		do Considerable Aeroplane Activity. Situation quiet.	
Do	17/1/17		do.	
Do DAINVILLE (L.29.C) S/C FRANCE	18/1/17		do The Battalion was relieved by the 9th K.R.R. Corps and afterwards proceed to billets at DAINVILLE (L.29.C) S/C FRANCE	

WAR DIARY
or
INTELLIGENCE SUMMARY.

Army Form C. 2118.

Place	Date	Hour	Summary of Events and Information	Remarks and references to Appendices
DAINVILLE L.29.c (SIC. FRANCE)	19/1/17 to 20/1/17		Battalion in billets at DAINVILLE. (L.29.c) SIC FRANCE). Snow.	
Do	21/1/17		2/Lieuts 19.J. RADCLIFFE and 2/Lieut D.H. LLOYD joined the Battalion today	
Do	22/1/17		Weather, frosty	
Do	23/1/17		The Battalion relieves the 9th KRRC in trenches L.17 to L.7 rt. in L.9 Left Sector. AGNY (51 BSW). Disposition of Coy as follows:- A Coy in trenches L.17 to L.16 (M.15.c.1.8 to M.15.c.1.8). B Coy in Reserve (M.9.b.9.0 to M.9.c.1.1). C Coy in trenches L.21.L rt. (M.10.c.5.6 to M.15.b.9.8) 51 BSW. D Coy in trenches L.16 to L.20 (M.15.b.9.8 to M.15.a.8.4) 51.BSW.	
AGNY (L. Left Sector)	24/1/17		Battalion in trenches in L Left Sector (AGNY) 51 B.S.W. 2/Lieut A.C. BERNARD joined today. Between 10.15 A.M. and 11.00 A.M. today, our artillery fired several H.E. on enemy front line opposite A Coys front, Lewis guns fired at short intervals along enemy's front line & wire. No patrols were sent out owing to the snow.	
Do	25/1/17		Battn in trenches L Left Sector (AGNY) 51 B.S.W. Enemy searchlight active during the night.	

Army Form C. 2118.

WAR DIARY
or
INTELLIGENCE SUMMARY.
(Erase heading not required.)

Instructions regarding War Diaries and Intelligence Summaries are contained in F. S. Regs., Part II. and the Staff Manual respectively. Title pages will be prepared in manuscript.

Place	Date	Hour	Summary of Events and Information	Remarks and references to Appendices
9. Left Section (AGNY)	26/1/17		Battalion in trenches in 9 Left Sector AGNY. (51 B.S.W). Between 2 and 4 pm today, the enemy's Trench mortars very active, over 90 heavy ones falling between these lines. 18 pdr. & Stokes mortar on enemy front line. Our Artillery replied with H.S.	
Do	27/1/17		Do	
Do	28/1/17		A Draft of 137 O.R. joined today. The Battalion was relieved by the 9th K.R.R. Corps & afterwards moved into Brigade Reserve at AGNY. (M.8.d. 51.B.S.W). 2 Lieut. C.M.I. HAMER joined the Battalion	
AGNY (51.B.S.W) (M.8.d.)	29/1/17		Battalion in Brigade Reserve in AGNY. (M.8.d. 51.B.S.W). Working parties found for R.E. 11th Kings Regt. & both Battns in the line	
Do.	30.1.17		Do.	

Army Form C. 2118.

WAR DIARY
or
INTELLIGENCE SUMMARY.

(Erase heading not required.)

Place	Date	Hour	Summary of Events and Information	Remarks and references to Appendices
AGNY (51 BSN) M&d	31/1/17		Battalion in Brigade Reserve at AGNY (M&d. 51 BSN) Bronillie 1.0th Wounded. Several working parties found for R.E, 11 Kings Regt, and both Battalions in the linen. 2/Lieut. W.J.G. YEOMANS joined the Battalion today.	

G. Turner Capt
Commanding 5th King Shropshire L.I.

WAR DIARY

CONFIDENTIAL

UNIT 5th Shops. L.I.

DATE From 1-2-17 to 28-2-17

VOL NO 15

WAR DIARY
or
INTELLIGENCE SUMMARY.
(Erase heading not required.)

Army Form C. 2118.

Place	Date	Hour	Summary of Events and Information	Remarks and references to Appendices
AGNY (M.8.d) 51BSN	1/2/17		Battalion in Brigade Reserve AGNY (M.8.d) 51.B.S.W. FRANCE. WEATHER - FROSTY.	
Do	2/2/17		Battalion relieved in Brigade Reserve by 5th Oxford Bucks LI and afterwards proceeded to relieve 9th K.R.R. Corps in left sector AGNY. (51BSW) Disposition of Coys as follows:- D Coy on right, in trenches G.17 to M.1, (M.15.a.8.H. 51BSW) A Coy on the left, in trenches G.21 to M.7, (M.10 c.5.b to M.15. t.9.8), B Coy in the centre, G.16 to 10, (M.15.t.9.8 to M.15.a.8.H) Reserve. (M.G. & H.O. to M.G.C.11). B Coy in the centre were also in the afternoon. Weather still frosty. Our Artillery (18 pdrs) were active firing on enemy front and support lines.	M1.15.C.18 51BSW
GLENT. AGNY (M.8.d)	3/2/17		Disposition of Battalion same as yesterday. Several lance Bombs fell in neighbourhood of G.S. line and GROUSE ST about 9.45 am doing no damage, in retaliation to this, our Stokes Mortar fired from 11 to 12 noon.	
Do (51BSW)	4/2/17		Disposition of Battalion same as 3rd inst. Our H.S. and 6" guns registered at 11 A.M. and also at 3-30 p.m., on enemy's front and support lines. Enemy Artillery was active this morning between 7 & 8 A.M., firing light shells, chiefly on front of D & B Coy.	
Do (51.BSW)	5/2/17		Disposition of Battalion same as 3rd inst. Our Artillery fired during the afternoon on enemy front and support lines.	

A 5834 Wt. W 4973 M 687 750,000 8/16 D.D. & L. Ltd. Forms/C.2118/13.

WAR DIARY
or
INTELLIGENCE SUMMARY.
(Erase heading not required.)

Army Form C. 2118.

Place	Date	Hour	Summary of Events and Information	Remarks and references to Appendices
G.S.F. SECTOR (51 BSW) ACHICOURT & ARRAS (51 B)	6/9/17		Battalion in trenches. N/Lt. Col. AGNY (51 BSW) in the afternoon, the Battalion was relieved by 2nd Yorks Regt, and afterwards proceeded to ACHICOURT (G.33.C. 51 B FRANCE), after which there by 19 Manchesters, the Battalion marched to billets in ARRAS, (H.Q. situate G.27.d.5.6. 51 BSW)	No Casualties occurred during recent tour.
ARRAS (G.27.d.5.6) 51B	7/9/17.		Battalion in billets in ARRAS. (G.27.d.5.6. 51 B FRANCE) Hostile aeroplanes flew over ARRAS during the morning and were heavily fired on by our Anti-A. Batteries.	
Do (G.27.d.5.6) 51B	8/9/17		Battn in billets in ARRAS (G.27.d.5.6) 9 found working parties to take up during the number of 500 OR. Lieut R. Lee R.A.M.C. joined the Battn today. Co Capt JO Snell MC who left today. Working parties supervised by the	
Do (G.27.d.5.6) 51B	9/9/17 10/9/17 11/9/17		Battn in billets in ARRAS (G.27.d.5.6) Battn the same as 8/inst	
Do (G.27.d.5.6) 51B	12/9/17		Battn in billets in ARRAS (G.27.d.5.6) MAJOR M.C. RICHARDS, 2 LIEUTS A.W. GROVES, & W.S. GARTON joined the Battalion today	
Do (G.27.d.5.6)	13/9/17		Battalion in billets in ARRAS (G.27.d.5.6) 2 LIEUT J.H. IKIN joined today	

WAR DIARY
or
INTELLIGENCE SUMMARY.

Army Form C. 2118.

Place	Date	Hour	Summary of Events and Information	Remarks and references to Appendices
ARRAS (G.27, a 5 b)	14/7/17		Battalion in Billets in ARRAS (G.27.d.5.b.) Weather - frosty & cold. Working parties found the same as 13th inst.	
Do	15/7/17		Battalion in Billets in ARRAS (G.27.a.5.b.) Working parties found same as 14th inst. Lieut. S.G. BUDGETT and 2/Lieut G.P. BULNER proceeded to join the R.F.C. to-day	
Do RONVILLE	16/7/17		Battalion was relieved in ARRAS by 9th K.R.R. Corps, and afterwards proceeded to relieve 5th Ox & Bucks L.I. in trenches in H left sector RONVILLE B, C, and D Coys in front line. A Coy in reserve. (M.4.d.3.7 to G.35. d. 8.0) 51B. TRANCH	
H LEFT SECTOR (RONVILLE)	17/7/17		Battalion in trenches in H left sector RONVILLE. Patrols went out from B & D Coys during the night. Observation was difficult owing to extreme darkness & mist. Found in "No Mans Land" 2 new enemy O.Ps. badly cut up. Trenches in a deplorable state, owing to thaw having set in.	
Do (RONVILLE)	18/7/17		Battalion in trenches in H left sector RONVILLE. Own artillery shelled enemy trench line from 10-30 A.M. to 2-30 p.m. also to night 9 2.36 from 2 to 3 p.m. Enemy sent artillery fire & rifle light shells about H 35.3H TMS line at 9 p.m. Also one heavy shell in direction of RONVILLE Officers patrol went out from B Coy and 2 men across front at H.34 & H.35, but nothing encountered.	

WAR DIARY
or
INTELLIGENCE SUMMARY.

Army Form C. 2118.

Place	Date	Hour	Summary of Events and Information	Remarks and references to Appendices
A Sek tector	19/7/17		Battalion in trenches H/left sector. At 3.5 pm. today our heavy artillery fired on enemy's new long obstacle 31.3H.-35, also 18 pdr. fired on this front line & appeared to knock which good effect, a patrol was sent out from 3t 33 (B.C.) at 9.30 pm - nothing unusual to report and no enemy patrols encountered - Patrol returned at 10.45 pm	
Do	20/7/17		Battalion in trenches. H/left sector. Enemy fired 3 heavy shells (from a position in rear of 3t 3Ht) in the direction of ARRAS.	
Do	21/7/17		Battalion was relieved by 9th R. Iole, and afterwards moved into Bde Reserve in RONVILLE. At 10-35 PM today, 3 of the enemy were observed getting out of their reserve trench, they opened hand & rifle fire by our post of 4 men in 3t 3H; one was seen to throw up his arms & fall to the ground; remainder of the party jumped back into the trench.	
RONVILLE	22/7/17		Battalion in Brigade Reserve, RONVILLE. Working parties found to the number of 500 OR's for work to line, also storage trench, and bringing cable between Munich and Halifax streets.	
Do	23/7/17		Battalion in Brigade Reserve RONVILLE. Working parties found same as yesterday. 2/Lieut H.S. GRIFFIN joined the Battalion today.	

Army Form C. 2118.

WAR DIARY
or
INTELLIGENCE SUMMARY.
(Erase heading not required.)

Place	Date	Hour	Summary of Events and Information	Remarks and references to Appendices
RONVILLE (G.34.a) 51 B.	24/5/17 to 26/5/17		Battalion in Brigade Reserve. RONVILLE. (G.34.a 51B FRANCE). Working parties found for working on C/line, & Hooge trench, burying cable between Italian & Hindu streets, and carrying parties to 2 M.T.M. Battery. 2/Lieut. P.M. LEE joined the Battalion today.	
Do (G.34.a) 51B & (K.29.c) 51C. FRANCE	27/5/17		Battalion relieved in Brigade Reserve. RONVILLE. by 9 K.R.R. Corps. and afterwards proceeded to Billets at DAINVILLE. One of our aeroplanes was attacked by several enemy machines, and observer was seen to descend in flames in or near to ARRAS.	
Do (K.29.c) FRANCE	28/5/17		Battalion in billets in DAINVILLE (K.29.c) 51C FRANCE.	

G.A. Helms Murray Lieut-Col
Commanding 5th King's Shropshire L.I.

No 17

17.S.
7 sheet

WAR DIARY.

CONFIDENTIAL.

UNIT, 5th Shrops. L. I.

PERIOD. From 1-3-1917 To 31-3-1917.

VOLUME NO. 16

Army Form C. 2118.

WAR DIARY
or
INTELLIGENCE SUMMARY.

(Erase heading not required.)

Instructions regarding War Diaries and Intelligence Summaries are contained in F.S. Regs., Part II. and the Staff Manual respectively. Title pages will be prepared in manuscript.

Place	Date	Hour	Summary of Events and Information	Remarks and references to Appendices
DAINVILLE (L.29.c) FRANCE 51.C	1/3/17		Battalion in Billets at DAINVILLE (L.29.c FRANCE) (51C) Major L.B. Wingfold proceeded to MONDICOURT, to take over Command of 7th Corps Infry School	
Do	2/3/17		Do During the afternoon the enemy fired about 12 shells into DAINVILLE. Casualties 3 O.R. wounded	
Do	3/3/17 to 6/3/17		Battalion in billets. DAINVILLE (L.29.c) FRANCE, and found working parties daily to the number of about 450 O.R. for work under 7th Corps Signals in the neighbourhood of ACHICOURT.	
Do	7/3/17 to 10/3/17		Battalion in DAINVILLE. (L.29.c.) FRANCE, daily for 7th Corps Signals. Provided working parties	
Do	11/3/17		The Battalion proceeded to RONVILLE at 5-15 pm and relieves the 5th Ox & Bucks I.I. in Brigade Reserve there.	
RONVILLE (G.34.a.51.B. FRANCE)				
RONVILLE (G.34.a.51.B.) FRANCE	12/3/17		Battalion in Brigade Reserve at RONVILLE. (G.34.a) (51R FRANCE) found working parties	
Do (G.34.a.51.B.) FRANCE	13/3/17		Battalion in Brigade Reserve at RONVILLE. (G.34.a) (51.B FRANCE) Usual working parties found.	

WAR DIARY
or
INTELLIGENCE SUMMARY.
(Erase heading not required.)

Army Form C. 2118.

Place	Date	Hour	Summary of Events and Information	Remarks and references to Appendices
RONVILLE (G.34.a) 51B FRANCE	14/3/17		Battalion in Brigade Reserve. RONVILLE.(G.34.a.51B France) A and C. Coys moved into DUNEDIN CAVE. RONVILLE. Usual working parties found.	
Do	15/3/17		HqtoCoys in DUNEDIN CAVE RONVILLE (G.34.a.51BFrance)B&D.Coys in billets in RONVILLE. During greater part of morning and afternoon, the enemy fired H.T.s; which fell on and in the vicinity of, RONVILLE BRIDGE. to also sent over several heavy shells in the afternoon. Casualties 1 O.R. wounded. Usual working parties found.	
Do	16/3/17		Battalion in Bde Reserve at RONVILLE. (G.34.a.) 51B FRANCE) Enemy Aeroplanes displayed unusual activity today.	
Do	17/3/17		The Battalion relieved the 9th Rifle Brigade in tr Sector RONVILLE, in trenches H39 to H47. A Coy on the Right, C Coy on the Left, B Coy in (G.35.c.3.4 to G.35.d.9.8. BRITISH MAP) Reserve, D Coy in the HUILERIE RONVILLE. (G.34.a.51BFRANCE) Capt C. Lunch, 2/Lieut AW Parsons and H O.R. rejoined from 3rd Army School. 2/Lieut H.W. R Evans joined the Battalion today.	

WAR DIARY or INTELLIGENCE SUMMARY

Army Form C. 2118.

Place	Date	Hour	Summary of Events and Information	Remarks and references to Appendices
H. SECTOR (LEFT) RONVILLE (G.35.c.3.1) to (G.35.d.9.8) ARRAS TRENCH MAP.	16/3/17		Battn in trenches H 38 to H 47 (G.35.c.3.1 to G.35.d.8.8 ARRAS TRENCH MAP) at 2.59 A.M the enemy put up a heavy barrage of fire on our front & patrol lines, and which continued for some time. The fixed several signals during this bombardment, but nothing in the nature of offensive action took place. At 3.14 A.M. O.C. A Coy got into touch with C H 6 Battery, who immediately put up a very heavy barrage on enemy front line opposite H 38, 39, who situation was normal by H.5. A.M. Casualties 2 O.R. wounded. Several fires were observed during the night of 17/18 inst. in rear of enemy lines. 6 explosions were heard in rear of enemy support & front lines. During the afternoon patrols were sent out by this Battn. and met with no resistance, finding the German 1st, 2nd & 3rd line of trenches un-occupied, but in a very bad state. Patrols report that most of the enemy dug-outs had been demolished by him before leaving.	

WAR DIARY
or
INTELLIGENCE SUMMARY.

Army Form C. 2118.

Place	Date	Hour	Summary of Events and Information	Remarks and references to Appendices
14. LEFT SECTOR RONVILLE	19/3/17		A & C Coys moved up into German 1st, 2nd & 3rd June System. B & C Coys relieving them in our original front line. Batn HQ moved from FACTORY at (G34.b.95.90) to Headqr situate in HUNTER ST. (Late B Coy Hdqrs) Patrols were sent out by A & C Coys, and at night the German 4th line was reoccupied, from M.5.b.95.05 to G.36.c.6.v. Our new sector was heavily shelled during the day, by 8", 5", 9" & H.V's and considerable casualties were sustained. The digging of a communication trench from our old front line to late enemy 3rd line was commenced during the day, but was 9 interrupted greatly by enemy shelling. The trenches were in a deplorable condition, chiefly owing to the rain	
Do	20/3/17		Batn in RONVILLE SECTOR. Enemy shelled new front line, support line & HUNTER ST during the night of 19th inst, from the direction of TILLOY WOOD. Work of consolidating new front lines & digging new communication trench progressed during the day.	

WAR DIARY
or
INTELLIGENCE SUMMARY.
(Erase heading not required.)

Army Form C. 2118.

Place	Date	Hour	Summary of Events and Information	Remarks and references to Appendices
RONVILLE SECTOR	21/3/17		Desultory shelling of our new front line during the day; heavy shelling at night. The Battalion was relieved by the 9th Rifle Brigade, A&C Coys proceeding to DUNEDIN CAVE, B&D to RONVILLE, Ruton Street at factory G.34.b.95.70 (51 B + FRANCE) RONVILLE was shelled during the night. Total casualties during recent tour in trenches. 11 O.R. Killed. 48 O.R. wounded.	
Do	22/3/17		B & D Coys moved into DUNEDIN CAVE in the morning. RONVILLE was again shelled today. Casualties 1 O.R. killed 1 O.R. wounded.	
Do	23/3/17		Disposition of Battn same as 22nd. Considerable aeroplane activity in the afternoon.	
Do & DAINVILLE	24/3/17		The Battalion was relieved by the 7th Rifle Bde, and afterwards proceeded to Billets in DAINVILLE (A.29.d)	
Do	25/3/17 to 27/3/17		Battalion in billets at DAINVILLE (A.29.d). On 27th inst, an unloading party of 50 O.R. was found by the Battalion for unloading trains at DAINVILLE STATION	

Army Form C. 2118.

WAR DIARY
or
INTELLIGENCE SUMMARY.
(Erase heading not required.)

Place	Date	Hour	Summary of Events and Information	Remarks and references to Appendices
DAINVILLE to FOSSEUX (SHEET 51C FRANCE)	28/3/17		The Battalion moved to FOSSEUX (SHEET 51 C. FRANCE) into huts. Vacated yesterday by 9th K.R.R.Corps. Transport moved to from BARNVILLE to Camp at SIMENCOURT (SHEET 51.C. FRANCE)	
FOSSEUX	29/3/17 to 31/3/17		Battalion in huts at FOSSEUX (SHEET 51C. FRANCE). Time was spent chiefly in training, in accordance with S.S. 143 & S.S.144 "Organization of Platoons etc" and "Normal Formation for the Attack"	

G.H. Helme-Murray. Lieut-Col.
Commdg 5th Kings Shropshire L.I.

CONFIDENTIAL

WAR DIARY

UNIT   5th King's Shropshire L.I.

PERIOD   Apl: 1st to 30th 1917

VOLUME   No 18

WAR DIARY
or
INTELLIGENCE SUMMARY.

(Erase heading not required.)

Army Form C. 2118.

Place	Date	Hour	Summary of Events and Information	Remarks and references to Appendices
FOSSEUX (P.10.d) SIC.	1/4/17 2/4/17		Battalion in huts at FOSSEUX (P.10.d) SIC. FRANCE. The Training, as shewn in Diary of last month, was much interfered with by the inclement weather.	
do	3/4/17		At 2-45 pm today, the Battalion, (less details to the number of 7 Officers & 80 O.R., who remained at Fosseux) marched to huts situate at SIMENCOURT. (Q.10.b) SHEET 51.C. FRANCE	
SIMENCOURT (Q.10.b) SHEET 51.C. FRANCE				
SIMENCOURT (51.C. FRANCE) (Q.10.b)	4/4/17		Battalion in huts at SIMENCOURT (Q.10.b SHEET 51.C. FRANCE) Transport camp was also here.	
Do DAINVILLE	5/4/17		Battn in huts at SIMENCOURT (Q.10.b). Weather still cold & wet. At 5-45 pm the Battn marched to Billets at DAINVILLE (L.29.c). Transport remains at SIMENCOURT	
DAINVILLE (L.29.c) SHEET 51.C.	6/4/17		Battn in billets at DAINVILLE (L.29.c). Weather improving	
Do & H. SECTOR RONVILLE (51.C MAP)	7/4/17		At 6-145 pm today the Battalion moved off from DAINVILLE & proceeded to relieve the 9th K.R.R. Corps in H. SECTOR (RONVILLE). After relief, the distribution of Battn was as follows:- A, B & C Coys in 51.B MAP RESERVE LINE, D Coy in the Support Line, Battn H.Q. at HOP ALLEY. Details moved to BREVILLERS. (T.1.b) SI.C. FRANCE	

Army Form C. 2118.

WAR DIARY
or
INTELLIGENCE SUMMARY.

(Erase heading not required.)

Instructions regarding War Diaries and Intelligence Summaries are contained in F.S. Regs., Part II. and the Staff Manual respectively. Title pages will be prepared in manuscript.

5/5/1

Place	Date	Hour	Summary of Events and Information	Remarks and references to Appendices
H. SECTOR RONVILLE (SIC TRENCH) SHEET	8/4/17		Distribution of Batt[alio]n, same as 7 inst. A copy of circular letter recd from 14 Divn is attached at back of diary. This letter refer to the good & hard work accomplished in pushing our line forward to within assaulting distance of the enemy. Weather fine, but cold.	I (Divl letter)
Do SHEET 51 B5W (M.6.c.9) N.7.c.	9/4/17		The Battalion takes part in the Battle of ARRAS. A detailed report, as rendered to Army Infantry is given herewith:— "I was in command of B Coy, 5th K.S.L.I. operating on the right flank of the Batt[alio]n and detailed to capture the COJEUL SWITCH from EYE LANE to DOG LANE inclusive. On attaining objective I was to take charge of Battalion front on BLUE LINE. The Battalion was formed up in assembly trenches by 2.10 A.M. and the zero were made to lie down to avoid observation by the enemy. The assembly trenches were not shelled. At 7.30 A.M. our barrage commenced, and the Batt[alio]n advanced. At this time there were two tanks just in front of assembly trenches and I put behind, the condition of the ground seemed to make their progress very slow and in my line of advance I saw nothing more of them any they played no part in the operations. Our enemy barrage, which appeared to be fairly heavy, was drawn across the crest of TELEGRAPH HILL immediately WEST of TELEGRAPH WORK. At this point the attacking line also came under heavy M.G. fire from the direction of NEVILLE TRENCH and TILLOY. Slight resistance was encountered in TELEGRAPH HILL TRENCH & HEAD LANE, but this was immediately overcome and my company captured between 50 & 75 prisoners here. No resistance was offered in POLE TRENCH, but enemy had a M.G. from NOUVION LANE. On a patrol being sent forward the enemy abandoned NOUVION LANE and ran to the rear, but were shot down by gun fire. The enemy M.G. was captured. The D.T.L. of 43rd Bde had converged slightly into my area (continued)	

1577 Wt.W10791/1773 500,000 1/15 D.D.&L. A.D.S.S./Forms/C. 2118.

WAR DIARY or INTELLIGENCE SUMMARY

Army Form C. 2118

Place	Date	Hour	Summary of Events and Information	Remarks and references to Appendices
RONVILLE H SECTOR (N.7.d) 51 BSM	9/4/17		that I occupied POLE TRENCH from N.7.d. 85.70 to N.7.7.70.75 that I establish communication with the D.L.I. on my right by 8.45 A.M. Germans in dug outs were cleared out by 9.10 A.M. and work was forthwith started on consolidating the line. I captured & consolidated this line with the remnants of A B & C Coy. D Coy had meantime stand their objective in SILENT WORK and by 10 A.M. communication had been established with the SUFFOLKS on their left and with the O.B.L. in the STRING and NEGRINE TRENCH. At 1.15 p.m. the R.B's pressed through my line to establish an outpost line in advance. They appeared to encounter no resistance whatever. OUR BARRAGE was very effective, but in my opinion the enemy moved much too slowly. Three units heard mixed, it would be almost impossible to prevent this line advancing right into our own barrage, and I am convinced that a large proportion of casualties especially in the two leading Battns of the Brigade may be attributed to this. ENEMY BARRAGE With the exception of that put down on TELEGRAPH HILL, enemy artillery fire was almost negligible. CASUALTIES The greater proportion of our casualties resulted from M.G. fire from the left flank. TOTAL CASUALTIES in the Battn as far as can be ascertained at present amount to 12 Officers and 189 other ranks. TROPHIES Only one enemy M.G. was captured, but the trench system is so smashed up by our Artillery fire that it is very possible several others are buried in the debris. Also I noticed every man in my final objective & could not send men back to search TELEGRAPH HILL TRENCH — the enemy front line. We have seized several hundred rifles, and a large quantity of ammunition, bombs, and equipment. PRISONERS I would estimate that the prisoners taken by this Battalion numbered over 300." Signed O.S. Bentinck Lieut Col 5 K.R.R.	

Army Form C. 2118.

WAR DIARY
or
INTELLIGENCE SUMMARY.
(Erase heading not required.)

Instructions regarding War Diaries and Intelligence Summaries are contained in F.S. Regs., Part II. and the Staff Manual respectively. Title pages will be prepared in manuscript.

Place	Date	Hour	Summary of Events and Information	Remarks and references to Appendices
TELEGRAPH HILL (N.7.b.51BSW)	10/4/17		Battalion in captured German position on TELEGRAPH HILL (N.7.b.51BSW) a copy of which received from 4th Infbde congratulating the Bde on the success of yesterday, is attached at back of diary	(2)
Do (N.7.b) 51.B.S.W. M&R.	10/4/17		Do. Lieut Col. H.W. SMITH D.S.O assumes command of 5th King Shropshire L.I. Complimentary order rec'd from 4th Inf Bde on his order who to recent success is attached at back of Diary.	(3) Ref/5th
Do	11/4/17		The Battalion moved off from TELEGRAPH HILL in the evening and after short stay in to billets at WANQUÉTIN (K.32.A) during the march a proceeded to DAINVILLE RAILWAY halt was made at RONVILLE CAVES BRIDGE, where hot tea was served to the Battn.	
WANQUÉTIN (K.32.A) 51C.M&R				
WANQUÉTIN (K.32.A) 51C.M&R	12/4/17		At 6pm the Battalion moved off from WANQUÉTIN (K.32.a) and marched to huts at NOYELETTE. (J.18.b 51C.TRANCE)	
NOYELETTE (J.18.b)				
NOYELETTE (J.B.b) 51 C. TRANCE	13/4/17		At a Battalion Parade held this morning, the commanding officer addressed the Battn with reference to the recent operations, and also read out the various congratulatory messages received. In the afternoon, the G.O.C. 14th Inf Bde addressed the Battn, and expressed his pleasure at the success gained by the Battn during operations of 9th inst.	

WAR DIARY
or
INTELLIGENCE SUMMARY.

(Erase heading not required.)

Army Form C. 2118.

Place	Date	Hour	Summary of Events and Information	Remarks and references to Appendices
NOYELLETTE (T.15.a)	14/4/17		The Battn moved off from NOYELLETTE at 9 AM. today, and marched to billets at LIENCOURT. (I.32.c SIC MAP) A Copy of a circular letter received from 1st Divn is attached at back of diary	Congratulatory letter from Divn (H)
LIENCOURT (I.32.c SIC MAP)	15/4/17		Battalion in billets at LIENCOURT. (I.32.c SIC MAP). Lieut R. LEE R.A.M.C. proceeded to 6th Bn & joined the Battn today. Lieuts R.C. MORGAN and E.G. TAITHORN & drafts of 8 O.R. joined the Battn today. Capt. JOHNSON R.A.M.C. from today. Details from the Battn from BREVILLERS (T.15) SIC.	
Do (I.32.c SIC MAP)	16/4/17		Battn in billets at LIENCOURT. (I.32.c SIC MAP) Letter from O.C. Brigade ref to C-in-C went to him & congratulation is attached herewith.	(5)
Do (I.32.c SIC MAP)	17/4/17		do. Sgt WHITNEY was Infantry Gas N.C.O inspected the Rest Respirators of the Battn today	
Do (I.32.c SIC FRANCE)	18/4/17		Battn at LIENCOURT. (I.32.c)	
Do (I.32.c SIC FRANCE)	19/4/17		Do. A draft of 175 O.R., composed of 1st & 16th Gloucesters, Herefords & Shropshires, joined the Battalion today	
Do (I.32.c SIC FRANCE)	20/4/17		Battn in Billets at LIENCOURT. (I.32.c SIC FRANCE)	

WAR DIARY or INTELLIGENCE SUMMARY

Army Form C. 2118

Place	Date	Hour	Summary of Events and Information	Remarks and references to Appendices
LIENCOURT (I.32.c.) S.I.C. FRANCE	21/4/17		Battn in billets at LIENCOURT (I.32.C.) Lieut ATKINSON, Divl. GAS OFFICER lectured the recent drafts on Gas Defence measures. Capt G.P. CAREY 5th R. Pes joins the Battn today on appointment as temporary 2nd in Command. Major G.A. Delme-Murray proceeds to join 1st K.S.L.I. today.	
Do (I.32.C.) 51C MAP FRANCE	22/4/17		Battn in billets at LIENCOURT (I.32.C.) During the time in which the Battn was billeted in LIENCOURT training in offensive action was carried out. Re-fitting of Coys was also done so far as possible.	
Do (I.32.C.) HAUTEVILLE (J.35.a)	23/4/17		The Battalion marched from LIENCOURT this morning, to billets at HAUTEVILLE. (J.35.C.) 5I.C.	
HAUTEVILLE (J.35.a) SICMAP G ROSSVILLE (R.25.a) & 51C HARP (N.7.b.) 51.13.SW	24/4/17		At 6.30 a.m. today, the Battalion moved off from HAUTEVILLE, and marched to billets at GROSSVILLE (R25a) Moved from latter place at 5.50 pm to relieve 4th Battn East Yorks Regt. in the HARP. (Battn. H.Q. N.7.C.4.9. SHEET 51.B.S.W.) Details to the number of 7 offrs & 90 o.R., together with transport moved to RONVILLE.	

Army Form C. 2118.

WAR DIARY
or
INTELLIGENCE SUMMARY.
(Erase heading not required.)

Instructions regarding War Diaries and Intelligence Summaries are contained in F.S. Regs., Part II and the Staff Manual respectively. Title pages will be prepared in manuscript.

Place	Date	Hour	Summary of Events and Information	Remarks and references to Appendices
THE HARP & VANCOURT (N.14.c.0.5) SIBSY. MAP.	25/4/17		Battalion in the HARP TRENCHES at 6pm today. The Battn moved from here to SUPPORT TRENCHES in neighbourhood of VANCOURT (N.14.c.0.5) relieving a Battn (9th Durhams D.) of the 151st Brigade. A Coy, B Coy, & 2 platoons of D Coy in trenches, 2 Coy & remaining 2 platoons of D Coy in SUNKEN ROAD. HEADQRS of D Coy (N.14.c.0.5) A Coy came under the orders of O/c 5th Cpt Brooks) tonight also in SUNKEN ROAD. (SIBSY)	
VANCOURT (N.14.c.0.5) SIBSY. MAP	26/4/17		Battn in support near VANCOURT (N.14.C.0.5) (SIBSY MAP). Distribution of Battn same as 25th. T.H. is Chiefly Enemy shelled SUNKEN ROAD frequently today, with 5.9s & trenches were, however, lightly shelled. The Battn provided a working party of HQ BR. under Major D.W.D. Evans, for work under the R.E., who were engaged in wiring support line.	
VANCOURT (N.14.c.0.5) SIBSY. MAP.	27/4/17		Battn in support near VANCOURT (N.14.C.0.5) SIBSM. Disposition same as 26th. Enemy shelled trenches heavily up to 3.45pm. After that time most of his attention was directed on 15 Division on our left. Our aeroplanes took advantage of the prevailing fine weather, constantly flying over enemy lines.	Nil Casualties during the term O.R. 5 killed O.R. 32 Wounded
Do (N.14.c.0.5) (N.16.C.0.5) SIBSM.	28/4/17		O/c A Coy came under order of O/c 7 KRR. At night the Battn (with the exception of C Coy, who took over trench lately occupied by A Coy) was relieved by the 7 Rifle Brigade (41st Bde), and afterwards proceeded to relieve of 7 K.R.R. in NIGER TRENCH (N.16.C.0.5) SIBSY. Hostile aircraft was only seen at infrequent times.	

Army Form C. 2118.

WAR DIARY
or
INTELLIGENCE SUMMARY.

(Erase heading not required.)

Instructions regarding War Diaries and Intelligence Summaries are contained in F. S. Regs., Part II. and the Staff Manual respectively. Title pages will be prepared in manuscript.

Place	Date	Hour	Summary of Events and Information	Remarks and references to Appendices
NANCOURT (N16.c.0.5) 5IBSW.	29/4/17		Battn in trench (NIGER) near NANCOURT (N16.C.O.S. SIRSWT.RANCE) Enemy bur heavies fired most of the morning, and again at night. Enemy shells village of NANCOURT, he afterwards dropped shells all over the Area, Battn provided working parties at night as if searching for batteries	
Do (N.16.c.0.5) 5IBSW.	30/4/17		Battn in NIGER TRENCH near NANCOURT.(N16.C.05) SI36W and the vicinity. Enemy again shelled NANCOURT TRENCH this afternoon, and a lot of light shells fell in rear of NIGER TRENCH this afternoon, and in front and about the Batteries of Heavy guns which had been firing all morning. The Battn provided working parties at night, for digging assembly trenches.	

H m Smith
Lieut. Col.
Commdg 5" Kings shropshire L.I.

APPENDIX
1

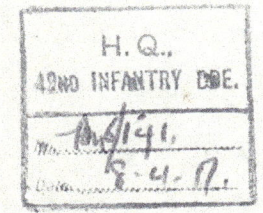

14th Division
G.S. 2678.

41st Infantry Brigade
42nd Infantry Brigade
43rd Infantry Brigade
C.R.E.
11th King's Liverpool Regt.

    The G.O.C. wishes to convey to all ranks his great appreciation of the amount of hard and difficult work which has been accomplished by the R.E., Infantry and Pioneers of the Division in pushing our line forward to within assaulting distance of the enemy.

    The determination and good spirit thus shown is a good augury to the operations now about to be carried out.

    As everyone is doing his best then it is certain that the Division will accomplish the task which has been set to it and maintain the name and reputation gained during the Battle of the Somme.

Lieut Colonel
General Staff
14th (Light) Division

April 7th, 1917.

APPENDIX 3

COMPLIMENTARY ORDER.

The Commander-in-Chief has personally requested me to convey to all ranks of the 14th (Light) Division his high opinion of the excellent fighting qualities shown by the Division.

The commencement of the great offensive of 1917 has been marked by an initial success in which more than 11,000 prisoners and 100 guns have been taken on the first day alone.

The Division has taken a prominent part in achieving this success and maintained the reputation gained last year on the SOMME and added to the laurels of the gallant regiments of which it is composed.

V. Couper.
Major-General
Comdg. 14th (Light) Division

10th April, 1917.

APPENDIX 4

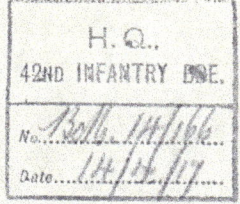
H.Q.
42ND INFANTRY BDE.
No. B.M. 14/166
Date 14/4/17

14th Division
G.S.2711

All Units, 14th Division.

The following is a copy of a letter which has been received from VII Corps.

"As the 14th (Light) Division is leaving the Corps "for a well earned rest, the Corps Commander takes the "opportunity of congratulating you and all in your "command on the manner in which they have conducted "themselves during the victorious advance. The Division, "not only by its spirited advance, but by the hard work "put in previously, has added to its long list of honours. "The Corps Commander wishes the Division the best of luck "and hopes he will be fortunate enough to soon again "include such a hard fighting Division in his command."

C.R. Meade-Waldo
Major
for
Lieut.Colonel
General Staff
14th (Light) Division

14/4/1917

APPENDIX 5

5th Oxf & Bucks L.I.
5th Shrops L.I.
9th K.R.Rif.C.
9th Rif Brig.
42nd Machine Gun Company.
42nd Trench Mortar Battery.

42nd Inf Bde.

B.M. 14/167.

The Commander-in-Chief came to Brigade H.Q. to-day, and personally congratulated the Brigadier on the fine work done by the Brigade on April 9th.

He requested that his thanks might be conveyed to all Commanding Officers, Officers, N.C.Os. and Men of the Brigade for what they have done, which had exceeded his expectations, and was proof of the high fighting qualities, possessed by all ranks.

16th April 1917.

Capt,
Bde Major,
42nd Inf Bde.

APPENDICES

1
2 } Congratulatory
3 } Messages
4 } are attached
5 } at back of
       diary

APPENDIX 2

"A" Form.
MESSAGES AND SIGNALS.
Army Form C.2121 (in pads of 100).

Prefix **SY** Code **M4** m.
Words **25**
ZAB

TO **SCARLET**

Sender's Number: **BM/513**
Day of Month: **9th**
AAA

GOC brigade sends hearty congratulations to all ranks on the fine performance of PINK CRIMSON & SCARLET to day

From
Place **RED**
Time **12·25 pm**

CONFIDENTIAL

WAR DIARY

5th SHROPSL. L.I.

1st – 31st MAY 1917

VOL 18

WAR DIARY
or
INTELLIGENCE SUMMARY
(Erase heading not required.)

Army Form C. 2118

Place	Date	Hour	Summary of Events and Information	Remarks and references to Appendices
Hévincourt (N.16.c)	1/5/17		Battalion in NIGER TRENCH NEAR WANCOURT. (N.16.c & 51.8.s.w.) Working parties at night.	
Do (51.8.s.w.)	2/5/17		Battalion in NIGER TRENCH AT WANCOURT (N.16.c, 51.8.s.w.) Battalion moved into Assembly Trenches as follows:- At 10 p.m. A, B & D Coys in PANTHER TRENCH (O.19.a) C Coy in TIGER TRENCH (N.24.d & O.19.a).	
Do	3/5/17		Battalion takes part in action of 3/5/17. A copy of report on the action is given herewith:— (forwarded 6th & 9th 5/46) (1) "Dispositions prior to ZERO. — 3 Coys in PANTHER, 1 Coy in TIGER. (2) Orders issued verbally and in writing, for the advance were as follows:- Two Coys viz B & D Coys under CAPT TURNER were to advance from PANTHER to HON at ZERO. They were to advance very gradually and in such formation as seemed most suitable at the time to avoid shelling and yet not lack cohesion. They were told to ascertain before each step to step advance from trench to trench, that there was room for them in the trench whither they were bound before leaving the trench in which they then were. A Coy (the 3rd Coy in PANTHER) was to follow on the 1st trench to the 1st leading Coys, always keeping one trench in rear. C Coy (the Coy as a support to B & D Coys similarly ordered to follow behind A Coy the two leading Coys were told not to go beyond APE without a written order from me. It was previously impressed on all officers that the role of the Battn was to further, and at any moment be ready to assist actively in the forward movement of the Brigade, & secondly that it should be ready to assist in the holding of any ground gained either by repelling a counter attack or by delivering any small attack to restore victory to cover retreat. (3) The above instructions were obeyed to my entire satisfaction as I received reports from my Coy Commanders during their forward movement. At 5.30 a.m. I had reports that my Companies had reached their final positions viz. B & D Coys were	

/1875 Wt. W593/826 1,000,000 4/15 J.B.C. & A. A.D.S.S./Forms/C. 2118.

WAR DIARY or INTELLIGENCE SUMMARY

Army Form C. 2118

Place	Date	Hour	Summary of Events and Information	Remarks and references to Appendices
VANCOURT (N.14.d.9) O.19.a (51B SW) FRANCE	3/5/17		"CAPT TURNER in APE, A Coy in BOAR, C Coy in LION. I ascertained by personal inspection that they were in the positions described above and returned to Bn HQ in STAG at 10.40 a.m. I was informed by the Brigadier General that a heavy counter attack by the enemy was in progress. He ordered me to go forward, make sure of holding the APE, and as I thought best on the spot, and to keep him informed of the progress of events if possible by personal report. A pigeon message was received by me about this time from CAPT TURNER in APE confirming report of German counter attack. On my way to APE I met small parties of R.B. & OxfBucks L.I. mostly wounded. On arrival at APE about 11-15 a.m. I proceeded from end to end of APE and found the disposition of troops as follows:- APE TRENCH. D Coy 5 KRRifs on rt of JUNGLE ALLEY, B Coy on left of JUNGLE ALLEY. 3 Machine guns on extreme rt flank, 2 M.G.'s on extreme left flank. A number of NCOs and men of Ox & Bucks L.I. and R.B. were mixed up with my men and also an Officer and about 10 men from the Brigade on our left. Col PICKERING, 9th R.B. had taken command of the whole of APE. I directed him to continue in command. Capt CRAWFORD Ox & Bucks L.I. was also in the trench. I ordered the officers of all Corps to distribute themselves along the front and take over command of the men of their sectors of whatever corps. I hastened on the cutting of fire steps, collected ammunition from wounded or any men going to the rear and sent down for my Stokes Gun carrying party to bring up more ammunition. I then reported to Bde H.Q. by runner. BUCK TRENCH was garrisoned by R.B. and Ox & Bucks L.I. under Lieut WOOD. I directed him to remain there. BOAR TRENCH was garrisoned by my A Coy. I hastened on the preparation of fire-step here. I had removed a platoon of my B Coy from APE to BOAR to relieve the congestion caused by the influx of troops from the front. All this time more parties of wounded and stragglers men were returning from the front. The wounded were sent straight down, the unwounded were collected by Col WOOD in BUCK TRENCH. I saw no sign of the enemy but I had not time for very careful observation. There was little or no shelling of the front trench. Left wounded that APE was secure. M.G.'s Lewis guns of 2nd Companies and men of all corps were distributed and full of fighting spirit."	

WAR DIARY
or
INTELLIGENCE SUMMARY
(Erase heading not required.)

Army Form C. 2118

Instructions regarding War Diaries and Intelligence Summaries are contained in F.S. Regs., Part II. and the Staff Manual respectively. Title Pages will be prepared in manuscript.

Place	Date	Hour	Summary of Events and Information	Remarks and references to Appendices
M.A.M.C. O.D.R.T. (N. 7d. d 8) O. 19. a 51/3 S 1.17	3/5/17	2	Left the command in the hands of Col PICKERING & reported the situation personally to Bde H.Q. Neither Col PICKERING or Col WOOD could give me any definite information as to what number or position of any of their men in front of APE. I now made my Battn JTQ at junction of BOAR & JUNGLE ALLEY. About 1pm a soldier of the Ox & Bucks reported to me that a party of his Regt under an officer had been surrounded and taken prisoners, but guns opened a barrage about this time which cut off the capture of this party. The man in question (whose name at my direction was taken by Capt CRAWFORD) said to the men of this party "Lets run for it" they apparently ran & all got in except the officer who was wounded. Only my direct order prevented this man from going back to take his wounded officer in. I permitted to do this at night time. A Corporal of the R.B. at about 4pm came in from the front and reported to me that our barrage was falling on a party of his Battn consisting of two officers & two platoons. The matter seemed urgent to me & I sent my Adjt at top speed to Bde HQ to try & stop our barrage on his way he had to pass through a heavy relieve German barrage and was slightly wounded but barrage was stopped. I ordered the party of R.B. to return to the APE about 6 am 4 May I again moved my Bn HQ by direction of the Brigadier to STAG. There was now very little firing of any sort. At 7.40 pm an R.B. runner brought me a note from Lt. ROUND. R. Bde. timed 6.45. He stated he was situated about 500 or 600 yards in front of APE & a party of Germans such a main about 50 yds in front of him. He asked for more ammunition &c. I ordered him to use his judgment & retire at nightfall. He had several wounded men and only 12 able bodied men with him. I reported personally to the Brigadier thinking he might possibly wish me to consolidate further forward as by Lt. ROUND's report it became apparent that the Germans were not nearer to us in that part of the line than 600 yards. Lt. ROUND and party reported to me about 9-45 pm. Lt. ROUND sent his men back from the forward position at once on receipt of my order but he himself absolutely refused to leave until stretchers had arrived for the evacuation of his wounded men. I cannot speak too highly of the conduct of the regimental stretcher bearers who both by daylight and after dark were indefatigable in collecting the wounded on 3rd May and on the 4th & night of 4th May. (Sgd) Wm. Smith Lt Col Comdg 5th Lond R	

1875 Wt. W593/826 1,000,000 4/15 J.B.C. & A. A.D.S.S./Forms/C. 2118.

Army Form C. 2118.

WAR DIARY
or
INTELLIGENCE SUMMARY.
(Erase heading not required.)

Instructions regarding War Diaries and Intelligence Summaries are contained in F. S. Regs., Part II. and the Staff Manual respectively. Title pages will be prepared in manuscript.

Place	Date	Hour	Summary of Events and Information	Remarks and references to Appendices
WANCOURT (from) 51 BSM	4/5/17		The Battalion was placed at night by the 6th Comp. F.J. and afterwards proceeded to trenches East in N.13.a. (Old German trench system)	
Trenches in N.13.a	5/5/17 to 8/5/17		Battalion in Old German trenches in N.13.a. (S.F.Bsn) During this period the Battalion came under the tactical command of 43rd Inf Bde & found working parties daily as ordered by that Bde.	
Do	9/5/17		The Battn relieved the 6th Of. & Bucks L.J. in POL TRENCH. (N.1.a)	
N.1.a (51 BSM)	10/5/17 to 13/5/17		Battalion in trenches (POL etc) in N.1.a. Found parties daily for salvage work, collecting wire, pickets etc. Enemy shelled occasionally, three principally falling in direction of Wadi Tanks a front 1000 yds	Enemy very frequent 3.5
Do	13/5/17		The Battalion moved into NEPAL TRENCH at N.77.a.9.5.10 N.M. to T.O. & came under tactical command of 41st Inf Bde & found working parties daily as ordered by them.	
Do	14/5/17		do Enemy fired several heavy shells, which fell near & about Bn HQ.	

1577 Wt.W10791/1773 300,000 1/15 D.D. & L. A.D.S.S./Forms/C. 2118.

Army Form C. 2118.

WAR DIARY
or
INTELLIGENCE SUMMARY.
(Erase heading not required.)

Instructions regarding War Diaries and Intelligence Summaries are contained in F. S. Regs., Part II. and the Staff Manual respectively. Title pages will be prepared in manuscript.

Place	Date	Hour	Summary of Events and Information	Remarks and references to Appendices
NEPAL TRENCH HINDENBURG LINE (N.15.d.3.d)	15/5/17		Battalion in NEPAL TRENCH HINDENBURG LINE (N.15.d.3.d) & found working parties daily under 41st Inf Bde	
Do	16/5/17		do	
Do	17/5/17		do	
Do	18/5/17		do. Major Sir R. WINGFIELD rejoined the Battn from 1st Corps S of Wales.	
Do	19/5/17		Commencing from Officers reconnoitred from line trenches	
D	19/5/17		The Battalion, at night proceeded to relieve 9th R.W.R. in COTEUL SWITCH, from PANTHER LANE to PORE exclusive, N.20.b - N.Y.C. - N.20.d.	

1577 Wt.W10791/1773 500,000 1/15 D.D.&L. A.D.S.S./Forms/C. 2118.

WAR DIARY
or
INTELLIGENCE SUMMARY

(Erase heading not required.)

Army Form C. 2118

Place	Date	Hour	Summary of Events and Information	Remarks and references to Appendices
PANTHERS & PORE TRENCHES N20B-N21C - N20D (51BiW)	20/5/17		Battalion in PANTHER & PORE TRENCHES N20B-N20C-N20D & 51B.W. (51B.W.) Found working party of 50 o.R. for road making under 11 Kings (Liverpool R.)	
do	21/5/17		do	
do	21/5/17		Working party of 150 OR provided at night	
do	22/5/17		do	
do	23/5/17		do	
do (O.26.a & D.25.d.)	24/5/17		The Battalion relieved the 8th K.R.R.Corps in the Right Sectn. Dispositions as follows:— A Coy on the Right, in FONTAINE & BULLFINCH, B Coy on Left in JACKDAW, C Coy in Centre in MALLARD. (O.26 a & O.K.d.) D Coy in support in BULLFINCH. 51B.S.W.	
do	25/5/17		At 3 am today the 18th Durm on my right put over gas which, owing to the unfavourable wind, drifted back to our trenches, causing us casualties as follows:— Died from asphyxiating M.G. Gas etc, suffering from Gas poisoning 17 OR	

WAR DIARY
or
INTELLIGENCE SUMMARY

(Erase heading not required.)

Army Form C. 2118

Place	Date	Hour	Summary of Events and Information	Remarks and references to Appendices
RIGHT SECTOR O.10.a.9 O.15.d (N.31.B.5.4)	25/5/17		Battalion in Right Section (O.X.a & O.15.d). Early this morning the 26th R.I.R., wearing his gas mask, walked into our trenches & gave himself up. It appeared that he was one of a party of 5 who had been caught by our fire & was the only survivor of the party. Hostile aeroplane flew very low over our front line at 4.30 am & appears to be making our dispg m.g. positions. At 8.30 p.m. a large party of Germans were observed to be making their way to an advanced post, they were fired on by Lewis guns & Rifle and suffered heavy casualties. The enemy heavily bombarded our line on night of 26th inst.	
Do	26/5/17		Heavy shelling of our line tonight. Hostile aeroplane again flew low over our line in the early hours of the morning.	
Do	27/5/17		An Enemy party of about 50 attempted to raid on B Coy front, but were repulsed by rifle & M.G. fire :- A message read from Mid Infantry runs as follows:- "5th K.S.L.I. B.M. 77 of 28 inst." "The G.O.C. Brigade directs me to say that he is very pleased with the manner in which your Battn. repulsed a hostile raiding party last night by means of rapid rifle fire 777". Please convey his appreciation of their good work to those concerned. (Sgd) G.T. Pritchard D. A.J.A. & Brig.	
Do N.30.b. etc.	28/5/17 29/5/17 30/5/17 31/5/17		The Battalion was relieved on night of 29 inst. & afterwards moved to trenches vacated by 2nd Batt. as follows:- Headqrs. & A Coy in THE NEST (N.30.a) B Coy in DUCK EGRET C Coy in NEPAL VALLEY in EGRET (N.30.B) The night of 31st the enemy fired a number of gas shells.	

Hm Smith Lt. Col
Commdg. 5th Inns. Rifles L.S.

CONFIDENTIAL.

WAR DIARY

Unit.   5th Kings Shropshire. L.I.

Period   1st to 30th June 1917.

Volume.   No 19

Army Form C. 2118.

WAR DIARY
or
INTELLIGENCE SUMMARY.
(Erase heading not required.)

Instructions regarding War Diaries and Intelligence Summaries are contained in F. S. Regs., Part II. and the Staff Manual respectively. Title pages will be prepared in manuscript.

Place	Date	Hour	Summary of Events and Information	Remarks and references to Appendices
PUCHEVILLIERS (N.27.a.57)	19/6/17		Battn in Billets at PUCHEVILLIERS (N.27.c.57D)	
Do	20/6/17		Do	
			Capt. G.B.BUCKLEY MC R.A.M.C. and 2/Lieut. R.B.D. MALDEN joined the Battn today. Capt. T.E. JOHNSON R.A.M.C. proceeded to join 1/1st Field Ambulance.	
Do	21/6/17 22/6/17 23/6/17 24/6/17 25/6/17		Battn in Billets at PUCHEVILLIERS (N.27.c.57D MAP). Training was carried out daily in accordance with APPENDIX 2. During this period, Rifle, football & other competitions were held.	APPENDICES 1, 2 & 3 attached for Diary
Do	26/6/17		Battn in Billets at PUCHEVILLIERS (N.27.c.57D MAP) 1st Divl Horse Show was held today at MARIEUX (H.31.b.57D MAP)	
Do	27/6/17		Battn in Billets at PUCHEVILLIERS (N.27.c.57D MAP) 2/Lieut. C.M. STRONG joined the Battn today	
Do	28/6/17 29/6/17		Battn in billets at PUCHEVILLIERS (N.27.c.57D MAP) Training in accordance with attached appendices.	
Do	30/6/17		The O/C Brigade inspected the Battalion today at the AERODROME, VERT GALAND FARM (M.9.C) in the execution of a Drill Attack in accordance with S.S.144.	

C.F.Pitman Major
Commdg 5" King's Shropshire L.I.

WAR DIARY or INTELLIGENCE SUMMARY

Army Form C. 2118.

Place	Date	Hour	Summary of Events and Information	Remarks and references to Appendices
WANCOURT. SUPPORT TRENCHES (N 30.6. S1 BSW)	1/6/17		Battalion in support trenches near WANCOURT. (S1 BSW MAP). Disposition as follows:- Headqrs & A Coy in THE NEST. (N30 a.7.3) B Coy in DUCK'S EGRET trenches (N30.b.) C Coy in NEAR TRENCH. (N 21 c+d) D Coy in EGRET (N30.b) SHEET.S1BSW. During the night enemy fired a large quantity of gas shells, which fell chiefly in rear of Battn HQ., no casualties were sustained. The Battn provided carrying party for S. Stafford's (,) & also working parties under 11 King's Liverpool Regt. for work in trenches. Reinforcements of 23 OR. joined the Battn today. The Commanding Officer congratulates the following recipients of the MILITARY MEDAL. No 9440 C.S.M. WILLIAMS. F. D Coy. No 10788 PTE. BARRETT H.H. BCoy. No 19807 PTE. OHMAN S. BCoy. No 8/10170 PTE RAYNER. C.W. CCoy. 11135 PTE TREVOR.O.W. CCoy. 10856 ME. ASHWORTH F.M. ACoy.	
Do	2/6/17		Battalion in support trenches near WANCOURT. Disposition same as 1st inst. Working & carrying parties found at night.	
Do	3/6/17		Battalion in support trenches near WANCOURT. (S1 BSW) At midnight the Battalion was relieved by the 6th K.O.Y.L.I. & afterward	
NEUVILLE VITASSE (N 20 a 15.50 S1BSW)			proceeded into Divisional Support Area at NEUVILLE VITASSE. (Bn HQ situate at N. 20 a. 15.50 S1BSW Map)	

Army Form C. 2118.

WAR DIARY
or
INTELLIGENCE SUMMARY.
(Erase heading not required.)

Instructions regarding War Diaries and Intelligence Summaries are contained in F. S. Regs., Part II. and the Staff Manual respectively. Title pages will be prepared in manuscript.

Place	Date	Hour	Summary of Events and Information	Remarks and references to Appendices
NEVILLE VITASSE (N 10 a. 15.50)	4/6/17		Battn in bivouac at NEVILLE VITASSE (N 10 a. 15.50) During the afternoon the Battalion was relieved by 7th RIFLE BRIGADE & afterwards moved into Divl Reserve at M.10.d. (Nr BEURAINS) 51 B.S.W	
BEURAINS (M.10.d.)	5/6/17		Battn in RESERVE CAMP at M.10.d. (Nr BEURAINS) 51.B.S.W.) Hostile aeroplanes were heard passing overhead, in the direction of ARRAS	
BEURAINS (M.10.d.) (51-B.S.W.)	6/6/17		Battn in RESERVE CAMP at M.10.d. (Nr BEURAINS) 51.B.S.W.) Y.O.C. Hants Inf Bde inspected the Camp today	
Do	7/6/17		Battn in RESERVE CAMP at M.10.d. (Nr BEURAINS) 51.B.S.W). The following extract from Part II.	
	8/6/17		Orders appears in Batt'n orders of 8 inst No10843 R.Q.M.S. F.H. GRIMLEY, appointed Hon./Lieut Qr. Mr. and posted 6.5KSL.1 Authy H.Q 4th DIV. A 9/384	
Do	9/6/17		At 6.10 am today, the Battalion moved off from M.10.d. & marched to billets at MONCHIET. (Q.21.0.9.6) 51 C map) which place was reached about 9 A.M	
MONCHIET (Q.21.C.9.6)	10/6/17		At 6.10 am the Batt'n marched off from MONCHIET (Q.21.C.9.6) & marched to billets at SAULTY & GOMBREMETZ. (Y.v.C.) these places being reaches about 9 am	
SAULTY & GOMBREMETZ (Y.V.C)	11/6/17		The Battalion moved off from SAULTY & GOMBREMETZ at 5.30 am & marched to billets at PUCHEVILLERS (N.27.b. SHEET 57D MAP) length of march 13 Lieut. Col. J.M. SMITH D.S.O proceeded to H.Q. 42nd Inf Bde, & assumed command of 42nd Infantry	
SAULTY & GOMBREMETZ (Y.V.D)510				
PUCHEVILLERS (N.27.b. 57.D.MAP)				

T2131. Wt. W708—776. 500'000. 4/15. Sir J.C. & S.

WAR DIARY
or
INTELLIGENCE SUMMARY.
(Erase heading not required.)

Army Form C. 2118.

Place	Date	Hour	Summary of Events and Information	Remarks and references to Appendices
PUCHEVILLIERS (N.27.c) (Sh.57 D.T.FRANCE)	12/6/17		Battalion in billets at N.27.c. (Map 57 D.T. France) The following extract from 1st Div: Routine Orders of 11/6/17, was republished in Battn. orders of today, together with the Commanding Officer's congratulations:- "Extract. The General Officer Commanding has great pleasure in announcing that under authority of H.M. THE KING, the Field Marshall Commanding-in-Chief, has made the following awards for acts of gallantry in the field during recent operations:- 5th K.S.L.I. THE MILITARY CROSS.- LIEUT & ADJT W.J. MILTON. D.C.M. 20008 CPL. J.W. CATTLIN.	
Do	13/6/17		Battalion in billets at PUCHEVILLIERS. (N.27.c. Sh.57D. Map) Training was carried out in accordance with "Programme of Work" (attached to back of this diary). MAJOR C.E. ATCHISON. D.S.O. joined the Battalion today.	APPENDIX 1.
Do	14/6/17		Battn. in billets at PUCHEVILLIERS (N.27.c.57D) MAJOR. C.E. ATCHISON D.S.O. assumed command of the Battn. Training in accordance with APPENDIX 1 was carried out today.	
Do	15/6/17 16/6/17 17/6/17 18/6/17		Battn. in billets at PUCHEVILLIERS (N.27.c.57D). Training in accordance with APPENDICES 1 & 2 was carried out today	

PROGRAMME OF WORK
Week ending June 16. 1917.

Date	Time	Unit Nature of training	Locality	Remarks
13th inst	6-30/7-30	Physical exercises Bayonet fighting	Sheet 57d 1/40,000	Specialists will drill & train under their Specialist Officers.
	9/10 am	Platoon & Company drill	N.27.c.	
	10/11 am	Rifle Exercises & Musketry	"	Lectures will be given in the evenings.
	11/12 noon	Extensions, Signals, and Extended Order drill		Gas Respirator drill periodically.
14th inst	6-30/7-30	Physical Exercises Bayonet fighting	"	
	9/10 am	Platoon and Company Drill		General cleaning and all inspections were carried out on the 12th inst.
	10/11 am	Rifle Exercises & Musketry	"	
	11/12 noon	Extensions, Signals, Extended Order Drill		
15th inst	Route March		PUCHEVILLERS LE VAL DE MAISON HERISSART TOUTENCOURT PUCHEVILLERS	
16th inst	6-30/7-30	Physical Exercises	Sheet 57d. 1/40,000	
	9/10 am	Platoon & Company drill	N.27.c.	
	10/11 am	Rifle Exercises & Musketry.		
	11/12 noon	Extensions, Signals, Extended Order Drill		

(sd) C.R.B. Wingfield,
Major.
5th K.S.L.I.

APPENDIX 1

PROGRAMME OF WORK FOR

W/E June 23rd 1917.

Date	UNIT	Time	Coy	Nature of training	Locality	Remarks
18th		6-30/8 am	A	Range practice 5 rds delib 10 rapid 1 min	Sheet 57D 1/40,000 N.27.c. Left of PUCHE- VILLERS - VAL-DE- MAISON RD	Breakfast under Coy arrangements
		10/12-30 pm		Coy drill and attack practice (in waves)		
		8/9-30 am	B	Range practice 5 rds delib 10 rds rapid 1 min	Ditto	Coy drill include Platoon drill
		10/12-30 pm		Coy drill and attack practice (in waves)		
		9-30/11 am	C	Range practice 5 rds delib 10 " rapid 1 min	Ditto	
		11-15/12-45 pm		Coy drill and attack practice (in waves)		
		9/10-45 am	D	Coy drill and attack practice (in waves)		
		11/12-30 pm		Range practice 5 rds delib 10 rds rapid 1 min		
19th		9/4 am	All Coys	Route march to Aerodrome. Attack practice according to Pamphlet 40/W.O./3995	VERT GALAND FARM	Breakfasts at 8 am. Cookers will be taken. Dinners at Aerodrome
20th		9/10-45 am	A	Company drill & attack practice (in waves)	N.27.c.	Breakfasts under Coy arrangements
		11/12-30 pm		Range practice 5 rds delib 10 " rapid 1 min		
		6-30/8 am	B	Range practice 5 rds delib 10 " rapid 1 min	N.27.c.	
		10/12,30 pm		Coy drill & attack practice (in waves)		

APPENDIX. 2

Date	Coy	Time	Unit Nature of training	Locality	Remarks
	C	8/9-30 am	Range practice 5 rds delib 10 rds rapid 1 min		
		10/12-30 pm	drill Coy attack and attack practice (in waves)		
21st	All Coys	6-30/7-30 am	Physical training		
		9/9-30 am	Bayonet fighting	N.27.c.	
		9-30/10am	Attack practice		
		10-15/10-45 am	Rapid loading		
		10-45/11-15 am	Gas Drill		
		11-15/12 noon	Coy Drill		
22nd	A	8/9-30	Range practice 5 rds delib 10 rds rapid 1 min		
		10/12-30 pm	Coy drill & attack practice (in waves)		
	B	9/10-45am	Coy drill & attack practice (in waves)		
		11/12-30 pm	Range practice 5 rds delib 10 rds rapid 1 min		
	C	6-30/8 am	Range practice 5 rds delib 10 rds rapid 1 min.		
		10/12-30 pm	Coy drill and attack practice (in waves)		
	D	8/9-30 am	Range practice 5 rds delib 10 rds rapid 1 min		
		10/12-30 pm	Coy drill and attack practice (in waves)		

Date	Time	Unit	Nature of training	Locality	Coy	Remarks
23rd	8/9-30 am		Range practice 5 rds delib 10 rds rapid 1 min		A	
	10/12-30pm		Coy drill and attack practice (in waves)			
	9-30/11 am		Range practice 5 rds delib 10 rds rapid 1 min		B	
	11-15/12-45 pm		Coy drill and attack practice (in waves)			
	9/10-45 am		Coy drill and attack practice (in waves)		C	
	11/12-30 pm		Range practice 5 rds delib 10 rds rapid 1 min			
	6-30/8 am		Range practice 5 rds delib 10 rds rapid 1 min		D	
	10/12-30 pm		Coy drill and attack practice (in waves)			

On Mondays, Wednesdays and Fridays, tactical exercises and lectures, at 2 pm to 3-30 pm.

Specialists will drill and train under their own Specialist Officers.

Lectures will be given in the evenings.

Officers under the Commanding Officer.

N.C.O's under the Adjutant and R.S.M.

                    (sd)   J. Milton.

                           Lieut & Adjutant,
                           5th K.S.L.I.

PROGRAMME OF WORK FOR
WEEK ENDING JUNE 30th

Date	Time	Unit	Nature of work	Locality	Coy	Remarks.
M.25th	6-30/8am		Range practice Grouping & rapid. (10 rounds p.min)	N.27.c.	A	Breakfast under Coy arrangements.
	10/12-30pm		Company Drill Bayonet fighting Gas Drill			
	8/9-30 am		Range practice Grouping & rapid. (10 rds p.min)		B	
	10/12-30pm	5th. Battalion King Shropshire Light Infantry	Company drill Bayonet fighting Gas drill			
	9-30/11 am		Range practice Grouping & rapid (10 rds p.min)		C	
	11-15/12-45 pm		Company drill Bayonet fighting Gas drill			
	9am/10-45am		Company drill Bayonet fighting Gas drill		D	
	11am/12-30 pm		Range practice Grouping & rapid (10 rds p.min)			
T.26th	9am/4pm		Route March to Aerdrome. Artillery formations with Battn. Dinners out. March back in the afternoon.	VERT GALAND FARM	All Coys	Specialists under their own Officers & N.C.O's. Cookers taken.
W.27th	9/10-45am		Bayonet fighting Artillery formation	N.27.c.	A	
	11am/12-30pm		Range practice Grouping & rapid. (10 rds p.min)			

APPENDIX 2

2.

Date	Time	Unit	Nature of work	Locality	Coy	Remarks
	6-30/8pm		Range practice Grouping & rapid (10 rds p.min)		B	
	10am/12-30pm		Bayonet fighting Artillery formation			
	9/9-30am		Range practice Grouping & rapid (10 rds p.min)			
	10am/am-30pm	King's Shropshire Light Infantry	Bayonet fighting Artillery formation			
	9-30am/11am		Range practice Grouping & rapid (10 rds p.min)			
	11-15/12-45pm		Bayonet fighting Artillery formation			
Th.28	6-30/7-30am		Physical training		All Coys	
	9am/12 noon		Company drill Artillery formation Extended order drill			
29th	9-30/11am	5th Battalion	Range practice Grouping & rapid (10 rds p.min)	A.T.O	A	Lecture will be given in the evening
	11-10am/12-40pm		Bayonet fighting Extended order drill			
	9am/10-45am		Bayonet fighting Extended order drill			
	11am/12-30pm		Range practice Grouping & rapid (10 rds p.min)			
	6-30/8am		Range practice Grouping & rapid (10 rds p.min)			
	10am/12-30pm		Bayonet fighting Extended order drill			

Date	Time	Unit	Nature of work	Locality	Coy	Remarks
	6/7-30am		Range practice grouping & rapid (10 rds p.min)		D	Lecture will be given in the evening
	10am/12-30pm		Bayonet fighting Extended Order drill			
5.30th	6-30/7-30	5th Batt. Kings Shropshire L. Inf.	Physical training		All Coys	
	9-12 noon		Company drill Extended order drill			
	5pm/6-30pm		Mondays, Wednesdays and Fridays, Tactical exercises and Lectures. Officers under C.O. N.C.O's under Adjutant and R.S.M. On Musketry days, Rifle Grenadiers will have practice firing rifle grenades,both fused and unfused, under Company arrangements.			

The Lewis Gun and Miniature Range will be used concurrently with the 100 - 300 yards range.

J. Milton
Lieut & Adjutant,
5th K.SL.I.

CONFIDENTIAL

WAR DIARY.

Unit: 5th King's Shropshire. L.I.

Period: 1st to 31st July 1917.

Volume No: No 20

Army Form C. 2118.

WAR DIARY
or
INTELLIGENCE SUMMARY.
(Erase heading not required.)

Instructions regarding War Diaries and Intelligence Summaries are contained in F. S. Regs., Part II. and the Staff Manual respectively. Title pages will be prepared in manuscript.

Place	Date	Hour	Summary of Events and Information	Remarks and references to Appendices
PUCHEVILLERS (N.27.c) SHEET 57 D	1/7/17		Battalion in billets at PUCHEVILLERS (N.27.c. 57D SHEET). at 7.45 a.m the Battalion paraded & proceeded on a route march, returning about 1.45 p.m	
do	2/7/17 3/7/17 4/7/17		Battalion in billets at PUCHEVILLERS (N.27.c. 57D SHEET) training on the same lines as shewn in APPENDIX III of JUNE WAR DIARY, was carried out during this period.	
do	5/7/17		do Major C.R.BYNG FIELD proceeded to ENGLAND today	
do	6/7/17		do 10 Junior Officers course at ALDERSHOT Battn in billets at PUCHEVILLERS (N.27.c. 57D SHEET) The Battalion executed a Practice Brits Attack at VERT GALAND FARM	
do	7/7/17		Battn in billets at PUCHEVILLERS (N.27.c. 57D SHEET). Practice Drill Attack at VERT GALAND FARM by the Battalion today.	
do	8/7/17		Battn in billets at PUCHEVILLERS. (N.27.c. 57D SHEET) Lieut H.D. CORBET and 38 O.R. joined for duty today	
do	9/7/17		Battn in billets at PUCHEVILLERS.(N.27.c. 57D SHEET)	
do	10/7/17		do Lieut. Col. H.M.SMITH. D.S.O. returned from H's'rs Int Bde and resumed command of the Battn	

WAR DIARY
or
INTELLIGENCE SUMMARY.
(Erase heading not required.)

Army Form C. 2118.

Place	Date	Hour	Summary of Events and Information	Remarks and references to Appendices
PUCHEVILLERS (N.7.d.57D)	11/7/17		Battalion in billets at PUCHEVILLERS. (N.27.c.57.D.FRANCE) 2/Lieut L.G. MACKLIN proceed to join R.F.C.	
do	12/7/17		The Battalion moved off at 1-45 a.m. & proceeded to CANDAS, entrained at that place at 6-50 A.M., and after a long railway journey, detrained at BAILLEUL (S.26.a.b.3) at 1-50 p.m., & marched to camp situate at (S.1.d.8.6) arriving at this place about 2-30 p.m. 2/Lieut. C.P. COOKE joined the Battn today.	
BAILLEUL (S.1.d.8.6) SHEET 28	13/7/17		Battalion in camp at S.1.d.8.6, near BAILLEUL. (SHEET 28) in Camp. Rapid-loading exercises, Rifle inspections were carried out & during the day, as no parade ground was available for Drill movement.	
Do	14/7/17		Battn in camp at S.1.d.8.6 near BAILLEUR. (SHEET 28) The commanding officer presented cards recording Honours gained by N.C.O.s men of the Battn during present campaign. The recipients names are shown on the Battn order of 13th July 17, attached to back of this diary.	
Do	15/7/17		Battalion in camp at S.1.d.8.6 near BAILLEUL. (SHEET 28) Enemy aeroplanes dropped several bombs in neighborhood of BAILLEUL, in the early hours of the morning. 2/Lieuts Yr R. WESTON & L. BURLAND joined the Battalion today from R.F.C. 2 " C.C. ABRAHAM proceeded to join R.F.C.	

WAR DIARY
or
INTELLIGENCE SUMMARY.

Army Form C. 2118.

Place	Date	Hour	Summary of Events and Information	Remarks and references to Appendices
BAILLEUL (S.1.d.8.6)	16/9/17		Battalion in camp near BAILLEUL (S.1.d.8.6) SHEET 28. Parades today were as follows: Physical training 6.30 to 7.30 a.m, parades under Coy arrangements from 9 a.m to 12.30 p.m, special attention being paid to training of all specialists i.e. Lewis Gunners, Bombers, Rifle Grenadiers etc.	
do	17/9/17 18/9/17		Battalion in camp near BAILLEUL (S.1.d.8.6) SHEET 28. Parades under Coy arrangements were held to-day on similar lines as 16th inst.	
do	19/9/17		Battalion in camp near BAILLEUL (S.1.d.8.6) SHEET 28. Proceeded to 6th K.O.Y.L.I. at M.20.a.0.6. (SHEET 28). A lecture was delivered at Regt. Hqrs. 5th O.B.L.I. by an officer of 53rd Squadron R.F.C., by on "Contact Patrols", Commanding Officer, Signalling Officer & one Officer & one N.C.O. per Coy attended.	
do	20/9/17		Battalion in camp near BAILLEUL (S.1.d.8.6) do	
do	21/9/17		At 7.30 a.m today, the Battalion moved off & proceeded to Training Ground, S.E. of BAILLEUL & carried out an attack practice in conjunction with contact aeroplane, operation order reference this practice are attached to end of this Diary.	

T.2134. Wt. W708—776. 500000. 4/15. Sir J. C. & S.

WAR DIARY
or
INTELLIGENCE SUMMARY.
(Erase heading not required.)

Army Form C. 2118.

Place	Date	Hour	Summary of Events and Information	Remarks and references to Appendices
NEAR BAILLEUL (S.1.d.9.b)	22/7/17		Battn in camp near BAILLEUL (S.1.d.8.b) SHEET 28	
Do	23/7/17		do. Parades today were as follows:- 6.30 to 7.30 A.M. Physical Drill 9 am to 12.30 am Attack Practice in short rushes (particular attention being paid given to covering fire, his orders and the responsibility of the Section Leader as a fire control Commander) Medical Officer inspected all Coys at various times during the day	
Do	24/7/17		do. Training in musketry etc was carried out during the day. Practice in wearing Box Respirators continuously for one hour during night-time was done by C & D Coys.	
Do	25/7/17		Battn in camp near BAILLEUL (S.1.d.8.b) Parades today:- openings of Kit Inspections, Bomb throwing etc.) Physical Drill	
Do	26/7/17		Battn in camp near BAILLEUL (S.1.d.8.b) SHEET 28 Inspection of H/d Int Bde by General Sir H PLUMER G.C.M.G. K.C.B. A.D.C. Commdg the Second Army to whom operation orders of this Battn respecting the inspection are attached to one of the Diary.	

Army Form C. 2118.

WAR DIARY
or
INTELLIGENCE SUMMARY.
(Erase heading not required.)

Instructions regarding War Diaries and Intelligence Summaries are contained in F. S. Regs., Part II. and the Staff Manual respectively. Title pages will be prepared in manuscript.

Place	Date	Hour	Summary of Events and Information	Remarks and references to Appendices
NR BAILLEUL (S.I.d.8.6) SHEET 29	27/7/17		Battalion in camp near BAILLEUL (S.I.d.8.6) at 5-30 am today. The Battalion proceeded on a route march	
do	28/7/17		Battalion in camp near BAILLEUL (S.I.d.8.6). The Battalion paraded at 6.30 am at 28.S.I.d.2.7. for Battalion Drill.	
do	29/7/17		Battalion in camp near BAILLEUL (S.I.d.8.6). Lieut J.C.THOMPSON proceeded to join R.F.C. 30/7/17 SHEET 78	
do	30/7/17 31/7/17		Battalion in camp near BAILLEUL (S.I.d.8.6). Heavy artillery fire commenced soon early this morning & continued for the greater portion of the day.	
			APPENDICES	
			APPENDIX.I. CORPS COMMDRS LETTER.	
			" 2. Bde. Commdrs "	
			" 3 BATT'N ORDERS of 12/7/17	
			" 4 " Operation order 20/7/17	
			" 5 " " 25/7/17	

Wm Smith
Lieut. Col.
Commdg. 5th Kings Shropshire L.I.

Type 4 copies
1 each to Ifc. bye.

H.Q.,
42ND INFANTRY BDE.
No. Belle 14/228
Date. 10/7/17

VII Corps
G.C.R. 889/3.

14th Division.

    The Corps Commander is unable to let the 14th (Light) Division leave the Corps without recording his appreciation of the way the 14th Division fought and endured, not only when the main fighting was in progress but also during the very long time the Division was in the line; during the heavy fighting in April and May the Division gallantly carried on the traditions of the Light Division of Peninsula fame.

    He wishes the Division the best of luck and is certain that wherever it goes it will add to its previous grand record.

                              sd/ T. BURNETT STUART,
                                    Brigadier-General,
                         General Staff, VII Corps.

8th July, 1917.

14th Division
G.S. 3207.

All units, 14th (Light) Division.

              Forwarded.

                                    Lieut Colonel
                                    General Staff
                             14th (Light) Division

8th July, 1917.

Appendix 1

42nd Inf. Bde.
S.C.317/6.

The Brigade Commander wishes to place on record his appreciation of the excellent behaviour of the troops during the past month.

No complaints have been received from the civilian inhabitants but on the other hand only words of thanks and praise, which in themselves pay a great tribute to the discipline of the Brigade.

He feels sure that this record will accompany the Brigade wherever it may go, and wishes all ranks to be informed of the contents of this letter.

(sd) K. GLADSTONE,
Captain,
Staff Captain
42nd Inf. Bde.

10/7/17.

BATTALION ORDERS
BY
LIEUT-COL. H.M. SMITH D.S.O.
COMMANDING
5TH KING'S SHROPSHIRE LIGHT INFANTRY

July 15th 1917.

Part 1.

1. **DUTIES.**
   Orderly Officer for tomorrow, 2/Lt W.J.C. Wood.
   Next for duty, 2/Lt C.P. Cooke.
   Battalion O. Sergeant. Sgt Cook "A".

2. **HONOURS & AWARDS:**
   The undermentioned, W.O's, N.C.O's and men will parade at Orderly Room tomorrow, at 9-45 am, for presentation by the Commanding Officer, of cards recording the awards gained by each of the undermentioned.

   A COMPANY
   C.S.M. Price.   No 20060 Cpl J. Blacklock
   a/R.Q.M.S. J. Manning   20008 " J.W. Cattlin
   No 10667 Sgt J. Rogers   17003 L/" C. Herring
                                            10856 Pte F.M. Ashworth.

   B. COMPANY
   No 8373 C.Q.M.S. Thomas   14962 a/L.Cpl W.P. Manford
      9444 Sgt D. Jones   11409   "   L.W. Watkins
     11915 L/Cpl A. Fidler   10788 Pte H.H. Barrett
     17488   "   J. Hopwood   10721   " H.W. Gough
     18075   "   R. Morris

   C. COMPANY
   11064 Sgt C. James   11135 "   C.W. Trevor
   26120 Pte C.W. Rayner   25390 "   A. Watts

   D. COMPANY
   No 9440 C.S.M. E. Williams   11607 L/Cpl A. Davies
      17229 Sgt H. Bufton   17722 a/" C. Holmes,
      18076 " S. Roberts   16350 Pte J. Challinor.

3. **PARADES.**
   Parades will be carried out tomorrow from 6-30 to 7-30 am, and from 9 am to 12-30 pm, in Camp Grounds.

4. **PASSES.**
   N.C.O's and men may proceed to St. Jans Capel without a pass.
   N.C.O's and men granted a pass to BAILLEUL will parade at 4-45 pm each day, properly dressed, for inspection by the Orderly Officer, who will issue the passes.

Part 2.

5. **REVERTION.**
   No 235883 Pte (a/Cpl) H.A. King, reverts to permanent grade - i.e. Private, on joining the Battalion 28/6/17.

6. **APPOINTMENTS.**
   The undermentioned are appointed paid L/Cpls from 15/6/17:
   No 11036   Pte H. Davies   "C"
      18288   " G. Davies   "C"
      14887   " D. Long   "C"

(sd) J.W. JACKSON,
Lieut. & a/Adjutant,
5th K.S.L.I.

OPERATION ORDERS
BY
CAPT. C.S.BERROW-ROWE M.C.
COMMANDING
5TH KING'S SHROPSHIRE LIGHT INFANTRY
IN "CONTACT CONTROL" DEMONSTRATION
July 20th 1917.

Tomorrow, 21st July, the Battalion will carry out an attack practice in conjunction with contact aeroplanes, on the new Training Ground S.E. of BAILLEUL.

MARCH.   Companies will be ready to move off at 7-25 am.
STARTING POINT.   Entrance to Camp.
TIME.   7-30 am.
ORDER OF MARCH.   B.C.D.A.
DRESS.   Fighting Order.
NARRATIVE.   The Battalion is ordered to capture two objectives. The first objective will be attacked by 2 coys in two waves, and the 2nd objective by "leap-frogging" one coy, in one wave, through the two coys detailed for the capture of the 1st objective. One coy will be in Battalion Reserve.

ORDERS FOR ATTACK.
A & D Coys are detailed to attack the 1st objective.
A Coy on the left, D Coy on the right.
B Coy is detailed to capture the 2nd objective.
C Coy will be in Battalion Reserve.

At 9-30 am watches will be synchronised with that of the C.O.
At 9-40 am the Battalion will be disposed as follows:-
A & D Coys. 2 platoons of each coy constituting the 1st wave, in line, in the Assembly trenches.

APPENDIX 4

Operation Orders 2.

2 platoons of each coy constituting the 2nd wave, in line, 10 yards in rear of the 1st wave.

B Coy.   In line 10 yards in rear of the 2nd wave.

C Coy.   To the right rear of Battalion Headquarters.

Bayonets will be fixed, and all arrangements made for the attack by this time.

At 9-55 the Creeping Barrage, represented by men with flags will come down 50 yards short of the 1st objective.

ZERO at 10 am.

At Zero A & D Coys will advance at a steady walk in sections in file (at the high port). 70 yards short of the 1st objective they will extend into line.   15 yards between lines, 50 yards between waves. 40 yards short of objective they will kneel down. At Zero plus 4 minutes advance at steady walk for 15 yards then charge. The 2nd line of the 1st wave and the 2nd wave will conform exactly to all movements of the 1st line, except that the 2nd wave will not charge but advance at steady double.

B Company. At Zero plus 4 minutes B Coy will advance at steady walk in sections in file (at the high port). They will pass through the 1st objective, and, 70 yards short of the 2nd objective will extend into 2 lines, 15 yards apart. At 40 yards short of 2nd objective they will kneel down. At Zero plus 13 minutes they will advance at steady walk for 15 yards, then charge.

At Zero plus 29 minutes six patrols of 4 men each under an Officer or N.C.O. will be pushed forward under the barrage for about 350 yards in front of 2nd objective and will establish posts.
Patrols will move in extended order.

Operation Orders 3.

On obtaining objectives men will lie down and immediately commence consolidation.

The contact aeroplane will call for flares at ZERO plus 20 minutes and again at ZERO plus 50 minutes.
At the first call flares will be lit by troops in the 2nd objective, and at the 2nd call by troops holding posts pushed in advance of the 2nd objective.

On 2 bugle blasts being sounded Coys will close, and march back to assembly trenches forming mass on A Coy (Right Coy).

Jackson
Lieut & a/Adjutant,
5th K.S.L.I.

OPERATION ORDERS
BY
LIEUT-COL. R.M. SMITH D.S.O.
COMMANDING
5TH KING'S SHROPSHIRE LIGHT INFANTRY

July 25th 1917.

1. General Sir HUBERT PLUMER, G.C.M.G., K.C.B., A.D.C., commanding the Second Army, will inspect the 42nd Inf.Bde. at 10-30 am on the 26th inst on the 9th K.R.R.C. Parade Ground (SH.8.c.o.8.9).

2. The Brigade will be drawn up facing SOUTH in line of Battalions in close column of companies with the M.G.C. and T.M. Battery on the LEFT, the T.M. Battery in rear of the M.G.C.
   There will be 10 paces interval between units, and 15 paces distance between the M.G.C. and T.M. Battery.
   Battalions will be in the following order from RIGHT to LEFT:-

   5th Oxs & Bucks L.I.   5th K.S.L.I.   9th K.R.R.C.
                   9th R.B.

3. The whole Battalion will parade for this Inspection with the following exceptions:-

Orderly Room	8	Sanitary Men	8
Police	4	(2 per coy)	
H.Q. Mess	5	Corporal Jarvis	1
Cooks (Coy & offs)	19	L/Cpl Taylor	1
Transport & Grooms	50	L/Cpl Laden	1
Watercart	4	Coy Storemen	
Canteen	2	(1 per coy)	4
Q.M. Stores	10	Signalling S'man	1
Officers' Servants		Lewis Gun	
(1 per coy)	4	Storeman	1

   TOTAL 119 and Sick.

4. The Battalion will parade in the road outside the Camp, ready to move off at 9-30 am, facing EAST, in the following order:-

   A. B. C. D.

5. Signallers, Cyclists, Stretcher Bearers etc, and Regimental Employ will be in the ranks.

6. The Dress will be Drill Order with steel helmets and P.H. Helmets, which latter will be worn slung from the left shoulder down the left side. Small Box Respirators will not be carried.
   All ranks will wear Cap Badges in the covers of their steel helmets.
   Officers will carry sticks.
   Commanding Officers only, will be mounted.

APPENDIX 5.

Operation Orders 2.

7. Companies will size by platoons.

8. The Buglers of the 9th K.R.R.C. will play the General Salute.
The Band of the 5th Oxs & Bucks L.I. will play Selections during the Inspection, and will also play for the March Past if there is one.

9. A plan of the disposition of Officers, Warrant Officers and N.C.O's on parade may be seen at the Orderly Room.

                                                          Captain & Adjutant,
                                                          5th K.S.L.I.

CONFIDENTIAL 42/14 225. 17 sheets

Vol 22) WAR DIARY

Unit   5th King's Shropshire. L.I.

Period   1st to 31st August 1917

Volume No   21

CONFIDENTIAL

WAR DIARY or INTELLIGENCE SUMMARY.

Army Form C. 2118.

Place	Date	Hour	Summary of Events and Information	Remarks and references to Appendices
BAILLEUL 28 S.I.d.9.6	1/8/17		Battalion in camp near BAILLEUL. (28 S.I.d.9.6)	
do	2/8/17		Held today, (teams 6 a side) was won by A Coy. Inter-Coy Jumping Competition. Reinforcement of 120 O.R. joined.	
do	3/8/17		Battalion in camp near BAILLEUL. (28 S.I.d.8.6) 'Parade' held today. Coy arrangements. 2/LIEUT. H.G. HUGHES and 14 O.R. joined today.	
do	4/8/17		Battalion in camp near BAILLEUL. (28 S.I.d.9.6). Battalion route march today as follows. TIME - 9.30 AM. ROUTE - CROIX-DE-POPERINGE - MONTNOIR - BERTHEN - ST JANS CAPPEL, - back to billets.	
do	5/8/17		Battalion in camp near BAILLEUL. (28 S.I.d.8.6) Draft of 14 O.R. joined today.	
do CAESTRE AREA	6/8/17		At 9.10 am the Battalion moved off & proceeded to billets camp in the CAESTRE AREA. (H.Q. and transport at Y.5.a.5.1, A Coy at Y.13.a.11.2, B Coy at Y.13.c.3.9, C Coy at Y.11.d.6.4, D Coy at Y.11.c.6.6.	
CAESTRE AREA, SHEET 27. (Y.5.c.5.1)	7/8/17		Battalion in camp billets nr CAESTRE Y.5.c.5.1 A Draft of 31 O.R. joined the Battn today.	
Do	8/8/17		Do	

Army Form C. 2118.

WAR DIARY
or
INTELLIGENCE SUMMARY.

(Erase heading not required.)

Instructions regarding War Diaries and Intelligence Summaries are contained in F.S. Regs., Part II. and the Staff Manual respectively. Title pages will be prepared in manuscript.

Place	Date	Hour	Summary of Events and Information	Remarks and references to Appendices
CAESTRE AREA. V.5.C.S.1	9/8/17		Battalion in tents & billets in the CAESTRE AREA. (V.5.C.S.1) MAJOR BETTS, A.G.S. instructed one platoon of each Coy. in Bayonet fighting. Enemy shelled HAZEBROUCK during the day.	
Do	10/8/17 11/8/17 12/8/17 13/8/17 14/8/17		Battalion in tents & billets in CAESTRE AREA (V.5.C.S.1) Parades were held under Coy arrangement during this period. Lieut DYMOND, T.R. joined the Battn on 10 inst. 2 " W. STANLEY & 8 O.R, R.E. SHELDON joined on 11 inst. 2 " W. BULLOCK & 88 O.R. joined the Battn on 12 " 2 " A.H. DAY & 6 O.R. joined the Battn on 13 inst.	
Do OUDERDOM	15/8/17		The Battalion moved off at 7am, and marched to 27.N.19.a.0.2, where it entrained at 8.15 am, and proceeded to 2nd Corps area, de-training at 28.Q.14.d.0.0. & afterwards marching to camp situate at Q.29.C. (SHEET 28 N.W) NEAR OUDERDOM	
OUDERDOM G.29.C.	16/8/17		Battn in tents at camp near OUDERDOM. (G.29.C. SHEET 28 N.W.)	
Do DICKEBUSCH & HALFWAY HOUSE	17/8/17		Battn moved off early this morning and marched to camp near DICKEBUSCH and after a stay of several hours, proceeded to the dugouts at HALFWAY HOUSE at I.17.C.4.8. (ZILLEBEKE MAP)	
HALFWAY HOUSE I.17.C.4.8 (ZILLEBEKE)	18/8/17		Battalion in dugouts near HALFWAY HOUSE (I.17.c.4.8). Enemy shelled the vicinity of the dugouts & trenches with gas shells during the evening. Casualties:- 2 LIEUTS. R.F. SHELDON & BURLAND D.M.O.R. wounded. 1 O.R. killed.	

WAR DIARY
or
INTELLIGENCE SUMMARY.
(Erase heading not required.)

Army Form C. 2118.

Place	Date	Hour	Summary of Events and Information	Remarks and references to Appendices
HALFWAY HOUSE I.17.c.4.6. (ZILLEBEKE)	19/8/17		Battalion in dugouts at HALFWAY HOUSE (I.17.C.4.6. ZILLEBEKE). Enemy shelling intermittent during the day. Casualties – 2/Lieut. P.MORTON and 5 O.R. wounded.	
Do	20/8/17		Battalion in dugout at HALFWAY HOUSE (I.17.C.4.8. ZILLEBEKE) at 9 p.m. tonight, the Battalion proceeded to relieve the 5th Ox.& Bucks L.I. in the line. Dispositions of Coys. & details of the relief, are shewn in the Operation orders attached to end of this diary.	APPENDIX 1
Trenches (E of YPRES)			On the operation orders attached to end of this diary. Fairly heavy shelling was experienced by A Coy & H.Q. Coy on the way up to the trenches, especially on the MENIN ROAD, (near the HOOGE CRATER at J.18.b.1.5.)	
IN THE LINE (E of YPRES)	21/8/17		Battalion in the line, East of Ypres. Casualties. 5 O.R. killed Hostile Artillery active throughout the day. & 19 O.R. wounded.	
Do	22/8/17		The Battalion executed an attack on the Dyzulye (J.14 & J.20.10 to J.& C.60.25) allotted to it. Operation orders concerning this are attached to end of this diary. The following is a copy of a report on the operation, as rendered to Brig. Infde. "Report on the action of Aug 22.1917. Carried out by the 5th Battn. Kings Shropshires L.I., to the East of YPRES. The objective to be attacked and held extended from the RIGHT of the trenches held by the KINGS ROYAL RIFLES on our LEFT, who were to remain stationary, to a point which such the "L" farm on our RIGHT where we were to connect with the	

WAR DIARY
or
INTELLIGENCE SUMMARY

Army Form C. 2118.

Place	Date	Hour	Summary of Events and Information	Remarks and references to Appendices
			LEFT Battn. of the 43rd Infde., who were also advancing (600 yards) Prior to the attack I disposed of my Battn. as follows:- "B" Company (Vanguard the RIGHT) "K1" on the LEFT), under CAPT. O.S. BENBOW-ROWE M.C. were situated in JARGON TRENCH, with strong outposts to their front in GLENCORSE WOOD. One Coy. (D Coy) under CAPT. E.G.R. HOYD was situated as a support in JARGON SWITCH, one Coy (C Coy) under 2/LIEUT. H.W.D. EVANS was situated as Battn. Reserve in IGNORANCE TRENCH. ZERO hour was given as 7 AM (SEVEN A.M.) and the advance was to take place then simultaneously with the 43rd Bde on our RIGHT. Prior to ZERO I issued the following orders. A & B Coys were to withdraw all outposts into JARGON TRENCH from GLENCOURSE WOOD before daybreak, there was to be no movement in any of the Companies before ZERO HOUR. At ZERO, A & B Coys were to advance in two lines maintaining connection as they advanced with the 43rd Bde. B Coy were to advance from JARGON SWITCH to JARGON TRENCH, but were on no account to advance beyond that line. C Coy were to advance from IGNORANCE to the trenches in the vicinity of Battn. H.Q. holding the high ground at the bend in the MENIN ROAD. This scheme carried out the principle of	

Army Form C. 2118.

WAR DIARY
or
INTELLIGENCE SUMMARY.
(Erase heading not required.)

Instructions regarding War Diaries and Intelligence Summaries are contained in F. S. Regs., Part II. and the Staff Manual respectively. Title pages will be prepared in manuscript.

Place	Date	Hour	Summary of Events and Information	Remarks and references to Appendices
			of Defence in Depth and provides for 3 successive lines over which the enemy would have to cope. In addition the whole of Battn. H.Q. were told off into sections for Defence should they be called on. Action at ZERO and afterwards. Immediately on ZERO going, A and B Coys advanced in small section Columns through the WOOD and quickly obtained their objective throughout the line with the exception of the RIGHT flank which was "refused" in order to obtain connection with the 43rd Bde whose progress was held up by Machine Gun Fire from "W" FARM. Within 5 minutes of the advance, all the officers of the RIGHT Coy became casualties and only one Junior Officer remained with the LEFT Coy. Considerable opposition was encountered during the advance, especially by Machine Gun fire. D & C Coys carried out their instructions for action on ZERO, and on my being informed of the other casualties in A and B Coys, I ordered CAPT. LLOYD forward from D Coy to take charge of the two advanced Coys. (This occurred at 8.75 A.M). CAPT. LLOYD found on arrival that B Coy had withdrawn from its advanced position, and owing to lack of leaders, the fire and again advanced B Coy, effectually establishing communication	

with F Coy, though touch with the 43rd Bde which had been lost, was not regained about this time; the enemy was observed in the SUNKEN ROAD occupying dugouts and we attacked him by means of Rifle Grenades, the result of this procedure could not be ascertained. At 10.20 am I personally directed 2/LIEUT. H.D EVANS, Connely. C Coy to send 2/LIEUT. COOKE to the assistance of CAPT. HOYD in view of the officer casualties in A Coy, and later, moved my O.C details for all officers at the Camp to be sent up to me immediately. At 11.10 pm I wrote to the O/C C Coy. 4th Bucks. (?) asking him to hold the Coy of his, that was at my disposal, in the trenches on the NORTH side of the MENIN ROAD, and to report to me at my Headquarters. I did this because I realised that at least a fourth of my Battalion had by this time become casualties, and wished to be prepared adequately for any counter-attack which might follow. At 12.48 pm I received information from Capt HOYD that connection had been established with the 43rd Brigade and this was maintained until the relief of my Battalion. In the morning of the 23rd and at about 4.30 am, a heavy counter attack was launched against the 43rd Bde. And it was only on my extreme RIGHT that we been Germans were able to penetrate in repelling it, and considerable execution was done by them in the field the enemy ranks, firing half right. We continued to hold the ground gained on the Rotten trench

WAR DIARY
or
INTELLIGENCE SUMMARY

Army Form C. 2118

(Erase heading not required.)

Place	Date	Hour	Summary of Events and Information	Remarks and references to Appendices
			until relieved by the 5th Battn. O. & Buch L.I. on the night of 23/4/17 incl. (Signed) Wm. Smith) Lieut. Col. "Commanding 5th K.R.L." Casualties. KILLED 2.LIEUT. C.P. COOKE and 19 OR. WOUNDED CAPT. O.S. BENBOW-ROYLE. M.C. LIEUT. H. ATKINSON. 2. Lt. M. CUTLER. 2. Lt. M.S. PORTER and 107 O.R. MISSING 12 O.R.	Supplementary Orders respecting this operation are attached to end of this Diary. APPENDIX 1 APPENDIX 2
	23/4/17		The Battalion was relieved tonight by the 5th Battn. O & Bucks L.I. and afterwards proceeded to dugouts at HALFWAY HOUSE. LIEUT. F.R. DYMOND 712 O.R. wounded	
HALFWAY HOUSE (11.r.c.1.r.8.) SHEET 1/40 NW	24/4/17		Battn. in dug out at HALFWAY HOUSE. Enemy shelled the vicinity during this morning. Casualties — 9 OR. wounded (slightly)	
do	25/4/17		At 6 p.m. today, the Battn. moved off and marched to camp near CAFE BELGE (28 H.29.c.), stayed here for the night, and	
K.141 a.5.b. (SHEET 27)	26/4/17		tomorrow next morning and proceeded to billets and camp at M.K.M.a.5.J.	

WAR DIARY or INTELLIGENCE SUMMARY

Army Form C. 2118

Place	Date	Hour	Summary of Events and Information	Remarks and references to Appendices
K.M.a.5.H. (SHEET 27) Q.29.d.9.3	27.8.17 28.8.17 29.8.17		Batn in billets & camp at 27 K.24.a.5.H. 2/Lieuts R.L. PRICE, A.W.R. TRANTER, H.A. TURNER, C.R.T. SHEPHERD 7/60R. joined on 28th inst. The Battalion moved off at 9.30 am today & marched to billets & camp in the THIENSHOUK AREA.	
THIENSHOUK AREA (SHEET 27) Q.29.d.8.3	29.8.17 to 31.8.17		Batn in billets & camp in the THIENSHOUK AREA (Q.29.d.8.3) SHEET 27. Inspection of Bn Respirators of the Battn were carried out by the Bde Gas N.C.O on 31st inst. 2/Lieuts. H.C. TRUMPLER, T.E. FLYNN, C.W. JEFFERIES, and 29 O.R. joined on 31st inst. LIEUT. D.E.G. PREECE rejoined on 31st inst., together with a draft of 65 O.R. Attached to end of diary Appendix. 1 Operation order of 20 inst. " 2 Complementary orders " " " " " " " act to action of 22nd inst.	

Wm Smith
Lieut Col
Commandg 5th Hampshire R.S

APPENDIX I

Operation Orders by Lieut. Col
H.M. Smith D.S.O. Commdg. LoBE.
Aug. 31st 1917

Ref 10,000 Trench Map. HOOGE and
Sheet. 28 N.W. 1/20,000.

1. The Battalion will execute an attack tomorrow (ZERO hour will be notified later) in conjunction with the 43rd Inf Bde. on our RIGHT.

2. The Objective allotted to the Battalion is the GREEN Line J.14.b.20.40 to J.8.c.60.25. Immediately after the capture of this line, and still under cover of the Creeping Barrage, patrols with Lewis Guns, and Rifle Grenadiers and Bombers will be pushed forward to the line J.14.b.20.40 to J.14.b.15.90 and will occupy this line if no serious opposition is met with, and will form a defensive flank from J.14.b.15.90 to

J.8.z.66.25.

3. Distribution of the Battalion :-
(1) A and B Coys under Capt O.S. Benbow-Rowe, will form the first wave of the assault and will be distributed in depth in 2 lines at 40 yards distance.

At 4.15 a.m. these 2 Companies will be in their assembly trench (JARGON TRENCH) J.8.c.25.25 to J.14.a.40.60 to J.14.a.30.30.

These 2 Companies will advance to their objectives in small columns, making every use of the ground.

(2) D Coy. under Capt. E.E.R. Lloyd, will, by 4.15 a.m. be distributed in line in JARGON SWITCH, forming the 2nd Wave, immediately in rear of the 1st Wave.

Immediately on ZERO he will advance his Company, and will occupy JARGON TRENCH, vacated by the assaulting wave. He will, on no account, advance beyond this Line.

(3) C Coy, under Lieut. H.W.D. Evans, will, by 4.15 a.m. move up, with his Coy. to Batt the Trenches in the vicinity of Battalion HQtrs NORTH of the MENIN ROAD. He will himself be at Battn. HQrs. and will be at the disposal of the O.C. Battalion.

4. Distribution of Machine Guns:—
The 3 Guns, under Lieut. Lascelles, will remain in the Tunnel under the MENIN ROAD, at his Head Quarters, and will await orders.

5. It is of the utmost importance that no movement is visible to the enemy after daybreak till ZERO hour. The importance of this order will be impressed on all ranks.

6. 2 Barrage Maps have been issued to each Coy. By 4.15 a.m. tomorrow, all troops will be withdrawn to positions not less

than 200 yards WEST of the opening Barrage Line

7. The assembly area is liable to be gas-shelled. Box Respirators will therefore be worn unbuttoned.

8. (1) The leading troops of the Battn. will burn RED flares at — (1) ZERO plus 1 hour (2) at all other times when called for by the Contact Plane, sounding a succession of A.s. on a KLAXON HORN, or dropping a WHITE Light

(2) The Contact Aeroplane will be marked by 2 Oblong Black Panels, fixed at Right Angles to the Lower Plane (Rear edge).

(3) Infantry will not burn flares if called for by an aeroplane which does not carry the above markings.

9. A small S.A.A., Lewis Gun Ammunition and Bomb Dump has been placed in JARGON TRENCH.

10. Water Bottles will be filled.

11. ZERO hour will be communicated. It will be announced at 10 pm tonight and watches will be synchronised at the same hour.

12. Every endeavour will be made to keep up communication with Battn. H.Q. throughout. ~~the Commanding Off~~
Half-hourly situation reports, whether positive or negative, will be sent commencing at ZERO.
Important messages should be sent by more than 1 route.

13. No Maps, Papers or Letters, likely to be of use to the enemy are to be taken into action.

14. Medical Arrangements.
The First Aid Post will be at Battn. H.Qrs. which will not move.

J. Milton
Capt & Adjt
HOBN

APPENDIX 2

14th Division Order No 141.

1. The G.O.C. wishes the following brought to the notice of all ranks.
2. On the night of the 17th/18th August the Division took over the most important part of the line on the present Flanders Battle Front.
3. On the 22nd August after hard and stubborn fighting still further portions of valuable commanding ground were wrested from the enemy.
4. Between the 22nd and 28th August the Germans, alarmed at the inroads made into the key of their defensive position, made repeated and violent counter attacks to regain some of the lost ground. These counter attacks were supported by a very heavy artillery fire and some by attacks with Flammenwerfer. Only one of the numerous counter attacks had any success and that was very limited.
5. The counter attack of the 24th August was undoubtedly made with the object of driving us from the STIRLING CASTLE GLENCORSE RIDGE. Despite a hostile artillery fire of an intensity never before experienced by the Division and repeated attacks by fresh enemy troops brought up specially for the purpose the Infantry and Machine Guns, ably assisted by the artillery, succeeded in maintaining the greater part of the advanced line gained on the 22nd August and in addition inflicted very serious losses on the enemy.
6. The result of the fighting from which the Division has just returned is that a small but very valuable advance has been made to the EAST of the important STIRLING CASTLE-GLENCORSE RIDGE, and that a determined effort to retake this ridge has been thrust back with severe loss to the enemy.
7. One noticeable and gratifying feature in the operations under review has been the increased use of the rifle and Lewis Machine Gun for beating off counter attacks and causing loss whenever targets offered. The G.O.C. thanks all the Instructors who have been so successful in reveiving the musketry spirit in the Division and he urges all ranks to pay increased attention to this important branch of training.
8. The recent operations have again added to the high reputation already held by the Division. The G.O.C. thanks all ranks who by their gallantry, devotion to duty and hard work have helped to achieve this result. He particularly desires to record his appreciation of the work done by the Runners, Signallers, and Carrying parties who carried out their duties regardless of losses and in face of unusual danger and difficulties caused by very heavy shell fire and bad weather.

           (sd) G.D. BRUCE,
               Lieut. Colonel,
               Gen. Staff,
August 31st 1917.   14th (Light) Division.

APPENDIX 2

14th Division.
G.S.177.

The following has been received from Fifth Army:-

The Army Commander wishes to thank all ranks 14th (Light) Division for gallant work they have done while with Fifth Army.

Despite difficulties of ground, bad weather and determined resistance of enemy, they made valuable progress along ridge on 22nd August and maintained positions in face of heavy shell fire and repeated counter attacks, inflicting heavy losses.

Division has maintained high reputation in some of heaviest fighting on this front.

(sd) GD. BRUCE.
Lieut. Colonel,
Gen. Staff.
14th (Light) Division.

August 30th 1917.

Confidential

Vol 23

War Diary

23.S.
9 sheets

Unit   5th King's Shropshire L.I.

Period   1st to 30th September 1917

Volume No.   22

Army Form C. 2118.

WAR DIARY
or
INTELLIGENCE SUMMARY.
(Erase heading not required.)

Instructions regarding War Diaries and Intelligence
Summaries are contained in F.S. Regs., Part II.
and the Staff Manual respectively. Title pages
will be prepared in manuscript.

Place	Date	Hour	Summary of Events and Information	Remarks and references to Appendices
THIEVSHOEK AREA (27.Q.M.d.5.3) & NEUVE EGLISE (36.S.17.C.8.8)	1/9/17		The Battalion moved off from THIEVSHOEK AREA at 1-5 pm & marched to camp in the NEUVE EGLISE AREA at 36.S.17.C.8.8.	
NEUVE EGLISE (36.S.17.C.8.8) & MESSINES (SHEET 28 SW.T.5.E)	2/9/17		The Battalion moved off from S.17.C.8.8. at 6.30pm & proceeded to relieve the 18th Battn MANCHESTER REGT in SUPPORT, immediately NORTH of MESSINES. (SHEET 28 SW.T.5.E). Battn HQ at O.32.d.6.2 (SHEET 28 SW.T.5.E). CAPT. F R BURKTON Joined the Battn today	
MESSINES (O.32.d.6.2)	3/9/17		Battalion in dugouts and trenches in SUPPORT LINES, NORTH of MESSINES (O.32.d.6.2) Enemy shelled the area in rear of Battn HQ in the evening.	SHEET 28 S.W.T.5.E. Casualties: Pte T.R.A. MORGAN WOUNDED CAPT DUTY 1 OR KILLED. 3 OR WOUNDED
Do	4/9/17		Battalion in support NORTH of MESSINES. (O.32.d.6.2) SHEET 28 S.W.T.5.E. In the evening the enemy fired a considerable number of Gas Shells which fell in the neighbourhood of Battn HQ. The Battn found working parties for R.E. & carrying parties for the Battn in the line. (9th K.R.R. Corps)	Casualties - 1 OR KILLED. 10 OR WOUNDED
Do	5/9/17		Battalion in support NORTH of MESSINES (O.32.d.6.2) Considerable aeroplane activity on both sides. Working & carrying parties provided at night.	Casualties. 3 OR Wounded
Do	6/9/17		The Battalion proceeded at night to relieve the 9th K.R.R. Corps in the front line trenches. A Coy on the CENTRE. (O.35.t.05.10 to O.35.d.80.20) B Coy in SUPPORT. (H.Q. O.34.d.55.95) C Coy on the LEFT (O.35.a.6.5 to O.35.t.1.1.1) D Coy on the RIGHT (U.5.5.9 to O.35.d.8.3) Battn HQ at O.34.c.9.3	Casualties 10R KILLED 1 OR WOUNDED

T./134. Wt. W708-776. 50C090. 4/15. Sir J. C. & S.

Army Form C. 2118.

WAR DIARY
or
INTELLIGENCE SUMMARY.
(Erase heading not required.)

Place	Date	Hour	Summary of Events and Information	Remarks and references to Appendices
MESSINES	7.9.17		Battalion in trenches at MESSINES, disposition same as 6 inst. Situation quiet during the day, enemy sniper were active at night.	
Do	8.9.17		Do Enemy Trench mortars were active in the early hours of the morning, one appearing to fire from the neighbourhood of O.35.d.80.50. Our Artillery shelled enemy front and support lines at 1 am today.	
Do	9.9.17		Battn in trenches at MESSINES (H.Q at O.34.b.9.3) at dawn today, one of the enemy was observed to hung over and drop in shell hole 60 yards in front of our wire at O.35.d.80.50 (A Coy front), he was unarmed & carried a small white flag. Two hostile Trench Mortars firing from neighbourhood of KIWI FARM were very active during the night. Enemy M. Guns occasionally swept track between B Coys HQ and Regtl Aid Post.	Casualties 1 O.R. Killed & 1 O.R. Wounded
Do	10.9.17		Battn in trenches at MESSINES HQ (O.34.b.9.3) The Battalion was relieved at night by the 8th Rifle Bde (41st Inf Bde) and afterwards proceeded to billets at NEUVE EGLISE. During the relief, hostile artillery was very active, chiefly in the direction of HUNS WALK, a large number of shells falling near the Battn Ration Dump Musco.	1 O.R. Killed. 6 O.R. Wounded

Army Form C. 2118.

WAR DIARY
or
INTELLIGENCE SUMMARY.
(Erase heading not required.)

Place	Date	Hour	Summary of Events and Information	Remarks and references to Appendices
NEUVE EGLISE (Sh.T.1S. a. 0. 4)	11/9/17		Battn in billets at NEUVE EGLISE (78.T.15.a.O.4). The following announcements of Honours and Awards appeared in Batt Orders of 7th inst. re-published in Battn orders together with the Commanding Officers congratulations. "The General Officer Commanding has great pleasure in announcing that, under authority of His Majesty the King, the Field Marshal Commanding-in-Chief has made the following awards for acts of gallantry in the Field during ward operations - 5th Army Shropshires. THE DISTINGUISHED SERVICE ORDER - A/CAPT. E.G.R. LLOYD. THE MILITARY MEDAL - No 10847. SGT RILEY O. ACoy - 1101? PTE. WOODEND L. BCoy - 16679. PTE. HOPKINS J.M. CCoy - 19471k PTE MWILLIAMS D. DCoy - 16075 H.CPL. MORRIS. R. BCoy - 17716 PTE. BROOKS. S. ACoy - 11453 PTE. WRIGHT H DCoy - 204130. H.CPL. WALKER.T. ACoy - 16994 PTE. BROOME T. ACoy - 10917 PTE. MABBUTT. F.V. BCoy - 6495 PTE. W. EDWARDS ACoy - 10984 H.CPL. KYNASTON. F. DCoy.	
Do	12/9/17		Battn in billets at NEUVE EGLISE (78 T.15. a. 0 4) Battn provided working parties for work on trench tramways at WULVERGHEM. (T.S. 6.) (Sheet 28)	
Do	13/9/17		Battn in billets at NEUVE EGLISE (78.T.15. a. 0 4) Working parties found same as 12/not	

WAR DIARY or INTELLIGENCE SUMMARY

Army Form C. 2118.

Place	Date	Hour	Summary of Events and Information	Remarks and references to Appendices
NEUVE EGLISE	14/9/17		Battn in billets at NEUVE EGLISE. Battn found working parties for work on French Tramways etc at WULVERGHEM.	(T.S.6) WULVERGHEM
Do	15/9/17		The Battn moved off at 8.35 am today & proceeded by route march to billets in the BERQUIN AREA between BERQUIN and DOULIEU (36A.L.11.a.10.10) where 49th Inf Bde replaced the 143rd Inf Bde in the reserve to the 57th Division who were holding the line FLEURBAIX – BOIS-GRENIER – ARMENTIERES AREA.	DOULIEU (36A.L.11.a.10.10)
DOULIEU AREA (36A.L.11.a.10.10)	16/9/17		Battn in billets in the DOULIEU AREA at 36ª L.11.a.10.10. 2/Lieut A.Y. MACKENZIE and 2/Lieut W.H. POWELL joined the Battalion today. The following announcement of Honours Awards appeared in R.Routine Order of today:– "The GOC has great pleasure in announcing that under authority delegated by the Field Marshal Commanding in Chief, the Corps Commander has made the following awards for acts of gallantry during recent operations :– 5125 L/Cpl S. 11695 Sgt URION G (DCap) 16888 PTE. GARNER W.H – 16407. SGT. HINCHLEY. V.C.¬ 9778 SGT HEATH J.YV. (BCap)." This announcement was republished in Battn Orders together with the congratulations of the Commanding Officer.	

WAR DIARY
or
INTELLIGENCE SUMMARY.
(Erase heading not required.)

Army Form C. 2118.

Place	Date	Hour	Summary of Events and Information	Remarks and references to Appendices
DOULIEU AREA 36A.M.11.a.10.10	17/9/17		Battalion in billets at 36A. L. 11.a. 10.10 in the DOULIEU AREA.	
Do	18/9/17		The Battn. moved off today at 2.15 p.m. & marched to Hutments at CANTEEN CORNER. 28. T.76.c.5.1.	
CANTEEN CORNER. 28 T.76.c.5.1	19/9/17		Battalion in camp at CANTEEN CORNER (T.76.c.5.1) 2/Lieut. L.A.T. SPEER joined the Battn. today.	
Do	20/9/17		Battn in camp at CANTEEN CORNER (T.76.c.5.1) The following is an extract from 1st Routine Orders of today :- "The G.O.C has great pleasure in announcing that under the authority of H.M. THE KING the Field Marshal Commanding-in-Chief has made the following awards for acts of gallantry in the Field during recent operations:- "5th K.S.L.I. THE MILITARY CROSS – 2/LIEUT. C.M.I. NAMIER – 2/LIEUT. W.R. WESTON – 9324. C.S.M. T. GINES. THE DISTINGUISHED CONDUCT MEDAL. – 17779. SGT. BUTTON. H. b394. SGT. JONES. J. – 10963 – SGT. LEWIS. W. –11327. CPL. FULLER. W.	
Do	21/9/17		Battn in camp at CANTEEN CORNER. (T.76.c.5.1). The following programme of work was carried out by Coys today :- Patrol Work and Outpost Schemes. During which Men exercise Box Respirators were worn for ½ an hour.	

Army Form C. 2118.

WAR DIARY
or
INTELLIGENCE SUMMARY.
(Erase heading not required.)

Instructions regarding War Diaries and Intelligence Summaries are contained in F. S. Regs., Part II. and the Staff Manual respectively. Title pages will be prepared in manuscript.

Place	Date	Hour	Summary of Events and Information	Remarks and references to Appendices
CANTEEN CORNER (28.T.26.c.5.1) CAMP	22/9/17		Batta in camp at CANTEEN CORNER. (28.T.26.c.5.1) The Battalion proceeded on Route March today at 7AM, as per following details:- ORDER of MARCH - Signallers - H.Q.Coy - Buglers - B Coy - C Coy - D Coy - A Coy. DRESS. MARCHING ORDER. ROUTE - ROAD JUNCTION - B1. central - CROSS ROADS B.27.a.9.1 - CROSS ROADS B.21.d.1.4 - THORNTON ROAD - CROSS ROADS S.23.a.9.7 - ROAD JUNCTION S.17.d.5.8 - ROAD JUNCTION S.17.d.7.9 - WATERLOO ROAD - Back to Billets. A Draft of 68 OR. joined the Battn today	
Do	23/9/17		Batta in camp at CANTEEN CORNER (28.T.26.c.5.1). An aeroplane shell, (fired by one of our Anti-Aircraft Batteries at hostile aeroplane flying overhead) what failed to explode in the air, fell in one of the huts occupied by our H.Q. Signals causing casualties to the number of 2 O.R. killed and 12 O.R. wounded. (1 at duty) 2/Lieut J.C. JACKSON-TAYLOR and 2/Lieut T.A. ALLEN joined the Battalion today.	
Do	24/9/17		Batta in camp at CANTEEN CORNER (28.T.26.c.5.1) and found working parties to the number of 330 O.R. for work chiefly on Trench Tramways WULVERGHEM. FANNYS AVENUE , NEW CROSS AVENUE , CHURCH ARMY HUT, BAILLEUL, 2nd Australian CCS and LA CRECHE AMMUNITION DUMP. 2/Lieut J. WILDE joined the Battalion today	

Army Form C. 2118.

WAR DIARY
or
INTELLIGENCE SUMMARY.
(Erase heading not required.)

Instructions regarding War Diaries and Intelligence Summaries are contained in F. S. Regs., Part II. and the Staff Manual respectively. Title pages will be prepared in manuscript.

Place	Date	Hour	Summary of Events and Information	Remarks and references to Appendices
CANTEEN CORNER (28 T.26 c.5.1)	26/9/17		Batt in camp at CANTEEN CORNER (28 T.26 C.S.1). Coys carried out training as follows:- Physical Training, Bayonet fighting 6.30/7.30 am. Rifle Exercises 9 to 10 am. Wiring 10 to 11 am. Coy Route March 11 to 12 noon. During the day 10 minutes Box Respirator Drill was carried out. Lewis Gunners, Lignalers, Stretcher Bearers and Snipers were, from 10 am at the disposal of their Instructors.	
Do	26/9/17		Batt in camp at CANTEEN CORNER. (28 T.26 C.S.1) Parades were under Coy arrangements	
Do	27.9.17		Batt in camp at CANTEEN CORNER. (28 T.26 C.S.1) 2/LIEUT. W.T.C.WOOD reports from Hospital	
Do	28.9.17		Batt in Camp at CANTEEN CORNER (28 T.26 C.S.1) Proceeded to Support Position in 28.O.32 at 5.30 pm.	
Do	29.9.17		Batt. in Support Position in 28.O.32. No Casualties. 2/LIEUT. T.A. ALLEN Evacuated Sick	
Do	30.9.17		Batt. in Support Position in 28.O.32	

W.Jackson Lt. and Adjt.
for Major
O/C. 5th Kings (Shropo L.I.)

Confidential

WAR. DIARY

5th King's (Shropshire. Light Infantry)

1st to 31st October 1917

Volume No. 23

Army Form C. 2118.

WAR DIARY
or
INTELLIGENCE SUMMARY.

(Erase heading not required.)

Instructions regarding War Diaries and Intelligence Summaries are contained in F.S. Regs., Part II. and the Staff Manual respectively. Title pages will be prepared in manuscript.

Place	Date	Hour	Summary of Events and Information	Remarks and references to Appendices
MESSINES.	1-10-17		Battalion in support NORTH of MESSINES. (O.32.d.6.2.) Sheet 28. S.E. & S.W. The Battalion found working & carrying parties for R.E. & for the Battn: in the line (9th K.R.R.Corps).	
Do.	2-10-17		Battalion in support NORTH of MESSINES. (O.32.d.6.2.) Sheet 28. S.E. & S.W. Considerable airoplane activity on both sides. Working & carrying parties provided at night. Casualties. 1. O.R. Wounded.	
Do.	3-10-17		The Battalion proceeded at night to relieve the 9th K.R.R. Corps in the front line trenches. A. Coy. in the Centre (O.35.b.05.10 to O.35.d.80.20.) "B" Coy in Support (H.Q. O.34.d.55.95.) "C" Coy on the left (O.35.a.6.5 to O.35.b.1.1.) "D" Coy on the right (U.5.b.8.7 to O.35.d.8.3.) Battn: Hd: Qrs: at O.34.b.9.3.	
Do.	4-10-17		Battalion in trenches at MESSINES disposition same as 6th inst: Situation quiet during the day, at night hostile artillery was active, number of shells falling near Battn: Hd: Qrs: "B" Coy: Hd: Qrs: and Regt: Aid Post but no damage done. 18. Other Ranks reinforcements joined the Battn: to-day	

Army Form C. 2118.

WAR DIARY
or
INTELLIGENCE SUMMARY.
(Erase heading not required.)

Instructions regarding War Diaries and Intelligence Summaries are contained in F. S. Regs., Part II. and the Staff Manual respectively. Title pages will be prepared in manuscript.

Place	Date	Hour	Summary of Events and Information	Remarks and references to Appendices
MESSINES	5-10-17		Battalion in trenches at MESSINES disposition same as 3rd & 4th inst. During the day the enemy fired a few shells which fell in the vicinity of Battn: Hd. Qrs: no damage was done. 2nd Lieut: H. T. Clarke admitted to Hospital to-day. (Wounded) discharged to duty	
MESSINES.	6-10-17		Battalion in trenches at MESSINES, disposition same as 3rd 4th & 5th inst. Situation quiet during the day, enemy snipers were active at night. 2nd Lieut: H. T. Clarke admitted to Hospital. Wounded	
do.	7-10-17		Battalion in trenches at MESSINES disposition same as 6th inst. Situation quiet.	
do	8-10-17		Battalion in trenches at MESSINES, disposition same as 6th inst. Situation quiet. 19. Other Ranks joined the Battn: to-day. At night the Battn: was relieved by the 5th Battn: Scottish Rifles, and proceeded to huts at KORTEPYP. A. Camp T 26. C 50. 60. Ref: sheet 28.	

Army Form C. 2118.

WAR DIARY
or
INTELLIGENCE SUMMARY.
(Erase heading not required.)

Instructions regarding War Diaries and Intelligence Summaries are contained in F. S. Regs., Part II. and the Staff Manual respectively. Title pages will be prepared in manuscript.

Place	Date	Hour	Summary of Events and Information	Remarks and references to Appendices
KORTEPYP. (T.26.c.50.60. Ref: sheet 28)	9-10-17		Battalion in huts at KORTEPYP A Camp T.26.c.50.60. Ref: sheet 28.	
do	10-10-17		The Battn: moved off from KORTEPYP A.Camp at 10.0 am and marched to the BERTHEN Area Q.30.d.3.4. Ref: sheet 27 1/40.000. Lieut. D.E.J. Pierce admitted to hospital	
BERTHEN Area Q.30.d.3.4. Ref: sheet 27 1/40.000	11-10-17		The Battn: moved off from BERTHEN Area Q.30.d.3.4. at 10.0 am and marched to RIDGE WOOD. (N.5.a.8.4. Ref: sheet 28.)	
RIDGE WOOD N.5.a.8.4. Ref: sheet 28	12-10-17		Battalion in huts at RIDGE WOOD. N.5.a.8.4. Ref: sheet 28.	
do	13-10-17		— do —	
do	14-10-17		— do — 57 Other Ranks joined the Battn: to-day	
do	15-10-17		— do — 48 Other Ranks joined the Battn: to-day	

WAR DIARY
or
INTELLIGENCE SUMMARY.

(Erase heading not required.)

Army Form C. 2118.

Place	Date	Hour	Summary of Events and Information	Remarks and references to Appendices
RIDGE WOOD N.5.9.8.4. Ref sheet 28	1/10/17		The Battalion moved off from RIDGE WOOD at 1.0pm and proceeded to relieve the 8" Batt: K.R.R.Corps in the Support Trenches, NORTH of the MENIN ROAD, (Battn Hd.Qrs. at J.14.d.90.20. Ref: GHELUVELT 28 N.E. Enemy Artillery very active during relief. Casualties. 2nd Lt: G.W. Jeffreys T.1. O.R. Missing 11. O.Rs. Killed. 29. O.Rs. Wounded. 2nd Lieut G.W. Jeffreys Shepherd admitted to hospital	
J.14.d.90.20.17-10-17 GHELUVELT 28.N.E.			Battn: in the Support Trenches, NORTH of the MENIN ROAD. (J.14.d.90.20). Party provided to carry rations from CLAPHAM JCT: (J.13.d.90.50) to the Battn: in the front line (9th K.R.R. Corps). Enemy Artillery very active, in the evening several Gasshells fell in the vicinity of Battn: Hd: Qrs. Casualties:- 14 O.Rs. Wounded. In the morning a hostile Aeroplane was brought down by our Anti-Aircraft Gun Fire at (J.14.c.30.40.) The Observer and Pilot (names unknown) were killed and were buried at (J.14.c.30.40.)	
do:	18/10/17		Battn: in the Support Trenches, NORTH of the MENIN ROAD. (J.14.d.90.20). Considerable Aeroplane activity by both sides. Party provided to carry rations up to the Battn: in the line 9th K.R.R. Corps. Enemy Artillery put up occasional barrages from (J.21.a.60.10 to J.15.d.30.40.) and J.15.c. to J.14.c. central. Casualties.1 O.R. Killed 5.O.Rs Wounded.	

WAR DIARY or INTELLIGENCE SUMMARY.

Army Form C. 2118.

Place	Date	Hour	Summary of Events and Information	Remarks and references to Appendices
J.14.d.90.20 GHELUVELT 28.N.E	19-10-17		The Battalion in the Support Trenches NORTH of the MENIN ROAD (J.14.d.90.20). Artillery activity by both sides. Casualties. 6. Other Ranks killed. 11. O.Rs Wounded. 2"Lieut: T.W.B.Francis proceeded to BOULOGNE to report to 16 Inf. Bn. Labour Corps for duty. 5. Other Ranks Reinforcements joined the Battn. to-day.	
do	20-10-17		The Battalion in the Support Trenches NORTH of the MENIN ROAD (J.14.d.90.20). Found party for ration carrying to the Battn. in the front line (9th O.& B.L.I. Corps) Enemy Artillery very active, at night several Gas Shells fell in the vicinity of Battn. Hd.Qrs. and To. Coy. Hd. Qrs. Capt: F.W.Groves and Lieut: H.C.Trumpler admitted to Hospital. 2"Lieut: A.K.Mackenzie. M.C. assumed command of "C" Coy. Casualties. 3. Other Ranks Wounded. At night a working party of 1. Off + 10.O.Rs was found for burying cable.	
do	21-10-17		The Battalion in the Support Trenches NORTH of the MENIN ROAD (J.14.d.90.20). Found party for ration carrying to the Battn. in the front line (9th O.& B.L.I.Corps) Considerable Artillery and Aeroplane activity by both sides. At 5.45 pm the Battn. proceeded to relieve the 5 "Battn. Oxf: Bucks: L.I. in	

WAR DIARY
or
INTELLIGENCE SUMMARY.
(Erase heading not required.)

Army Form C. 2118.

Place	Date	Hour	Summary of Events and Information	Remarks and references to Appendices
J.14.d.90.20. GHELUVELT. 28.N.E.	21-10-17 Cont'd		The front line trenches in the Right Sector. "C" Coy. right Coy. from J.21.C.70.10. to J.22.a.10.30. "D" Coy. left Coy. from J.22.a.10.30. to J.22.a.40.60. "A" Coy. right support J.21.C.20.20. "B" Coy. left support J.21.C.60.50. Battn: Head Qrs: J.21.a.90.40. Enemy Artillery quiet during relief. Casualties 3. O.Rs. Killed. 2. O.Rs. Wounded.	
J.21.a.90.40 GHELUVELT. 28.N.E	22-10-17		The Battalion in the front line trenches in the Right Sector disposition same as 21st inst. At 5.30 a.m. our Artillery bombarded the Enemy's front line trenches and wire, at 6.0 a.m. the Enemy dropped a heavy barrage in front and in Rear of our trenches and continued for an hour. During the day our Artillery bombarded POLDERHOEK CHATEAU several direct hits were observed. At dusk "A" Coy. carried rations to "C" Coy. and "B" Coy. carried to "D" Coy. Enemy Artillery very active at night, a considerable number of shells falling in the vicinity of Battn: Hd: Qrs: Casualties. 7. O.Rs Killed. 2nd Lt: 6.W. Storey and 23. O.Rs Wounded 7. Other Ranks Reinforcements joined the Battn: to-day.	

Army Form C. 2118.

WAR DIARY
or
INTELLIGENCE SUMMARY.
(Erase heading not required.)

Instructions regarding War Diaries and Intelligence Summaries are contained in F.S. Regs., Part II. and the Staff Manual respectively. Title pages will be prepared in manuscript.

Place	Date	Hour	Summary of Events and Information	Remarks and references to Appendices
J.21.a.90.4.0 GHELUVELT 28 N.E	23-10-17		The Battalion in the front line Trenches in the Right Sector disposition same as 22nd inst. Throughout the day our Artillery bombarded Enemy's Pill Boxes at about J.21.d.75.85. for this bombardment the Right Support Coy. withdrew to the concrete buildings in the vicinity of Battn. Hd. Qrs. and the Right Front Coy. withdrew and dug themselves in on line N.E. from point 28 I 22.a.20.30. Left Front and Left Support Coys. remained in their present positions. At 5.0pm our bombardment ceased and the Right Front & Right Support Coys. reoccupied the positions evacuated by them in the morning. Enemy Artillery active during the day, Aeroplane activity by both sides. At night hostile Artillery shelled Battn. Hd. Qrs. and the area in rear. Casualties. 1. O.R. Killed. 5. O.Rs. Wounded.	
do.	24-10-17		Battn: in the front line Trenches in the Right Sector disposition same as 23rd inst. The Enemy showed increased activity in Sniping and Machine Gun Fire, a relief was suspected to have taken place on the night previous. Both Artillery & Aeroplane activity by both sides during the day. At night the Battn: was relieved by 2 Coys: of the 9th Devons and by 2 Coys: of the 2nd Royal West Kents. The Left Front & Left Support Coys: relieved by 2 Coys: of the 2nd Royal West Kents. The Right Front & Right Support Coys: relieved by 2 Coys of the 9th Devons. Battn. Hd. Qrs: relieved by the 9th Devons. During relief hostile Artillery was very quiet. Casualties 1. O.R. Missing 1. O.R. Killed 11. O.Rs. Wounded.	

WAR DIARY
or
INTELLIGENCE SUMMARY.
(Erase heading not required.)

Army Form C. 2118.

Place	Date	Hour	Summary of Events and Information	Remarks and references to Appendices
J.21.a.90.40. GHELUVELT. 28 N.E (cont'd)	24-10-17		After relief the Battn. proceeded to TROIS ROIS (J.20.c.5.9) where hot drinks were supplied. At this point the Battn. embussed, and debussed at the CROSS ROADS.(Q.30.c ref:sheet 27) and marched to Billets in the BERTHEN area. Battn: Hd: Qrs. X.1.c.2.2.(Ref:sheet 27).	
BERTHEN AREA X.1.c.2.2. Sheet 27	25-10-17		The Battn: in billets in the BERTHEN area. Battn: Hd: Qrs. X.1.c.2.2. "A" & "B" Coys. X.1.c.2.2. "C" Coy. X.1.a.central. "D" Coy. X.1.a.6.5. Transport X.1.c.central	
do	26-10-17		The Battn: in billets in the BERTHEN area, disposition same as 25th inst. Lieut:Col: H.B. Smith D.S.O. assumed tem: command of 42nd Infy.Bgde. Major G. Turner M.C. assumed command of the Battn. Capt: C.I.Smith 2i/c Command. 2nd Lieut: H.W.D. Evans assumed command of 2 Coy. 2nd Lieut: R.C. Morgan assumed command of D Coy. Parades under Coy: arrangements.	
do	27-10-17		Battn: in billets in the BERTHEN area, disposition same as 26th inst. Parades under Coy: arrangements.	

Army Form C. 2118.

WAR DIARY
or
INTELLIGENCE SUMMARY.
(Erase heading not required.)

Instructions regarding War Diaries and Intelligence Summaries are contained in F. S. Regs., Part II. and the Staff Manual respectively. Title pages will be prepared in manuscript.

Place	Date	Hour	Summary of Events and Information	Remarks and references to Appendices
BERTHEN AREA X.I. G.2.2. Ref. Sheet 27	28-10-17		Battn: in billets in the BERTHEN area, disposition same as 27th inst. Wet weather interfered with training.	
do	29-10-17		Battn: in billets in the BERTHEN area, disposition same as 28th inst. The following programme of work was carried out by Coys: today:- Physical Training, Bayonet Fighting, Musketry, Platoon & Coy: Drill, Visual Training on 2 mile route march by Coys: The following is an extract from 14 Div: Routine orders of to-day:- "The J.O.C. has great pleasure in announcing that under authority of H.M. the King the Field Marshal Commanding-in-Chief has made the following awards for acts of gallantry in the Field during recent operations:- x "C. J. E. J. THE MILITARY MEDAL No: 17975 PTE G. WARD.	
do	30-10-17		Battn: in billets in the BERTHEN area. The following programme of work was carried out by Coys: to-day:- Physical Drill, Bayonet Fighting, Extended Order Drill, Rapid Wiring Drill, Route march by Coys: (Gas Helmet & Aeroplane drill en route).	

T2134. Wt. W708-776. 50000. 4/15. Sir J. C. & S.

Place	Date	Hour	Summary of Events and Information	Remarks and references to Appendices
BERTHE AREA X.1. C.2.2 Alipsheet 27	31-10-17		Battn. in billets in the BERTHEN area, disposition same as 30th inst. The following programme of work was carried out by Coys:-today:- Bathing, Extended Order Drill and Musketry 4 OR Reinforcements joined the Battn. to-day.	
	1-XI-17			

E. Turner
Major
Comdg 5th K.S.L.I.

Confidential

War Diary

5th Kings Shrops L.I.

1st to 30th November 1917

Volume No 24.

WAR DIARY
or
INTELLIGENCE SUMMARY.
(Erase heading not required.)

Army Form C. 2118.

Place	Date	Hour	Summary of Events and Information	Remarks and references to Appendices
BERTHEN AREA X.1. C.2.2. Ref: sheet 27.	1-11-17		The Battn: in billets in the BERTHEN AREA. Battn: Hd: Qrs: X.1. C.2.2. A. & B. Coys: X.1. C.2.2. C Coy: & Transport X.1. a central. D Coy: X.1. a. 6.5. The Battn: paraded for Route March at 8.30 a.m. and returned at 12.0 noon	
"	2-11-17		Battn: in billets in the BERTHEN AREA. Training carried out was as follows:- Physical Training. Bayonet Fighting. Kit Inspection. Wiring and Night Outpost. 4 N.C.Os attended Brigade Hd: Qrs: for instructions in P.T. & B.F.	
"	3-11-17		Battn: in billets in the BERTHEN AREA. Training carried out was as follows:- Physical Training. Bayonet Fighting. Box Respirator Inspection. & Overhauling of Equipment.	
"	4-11-17		Battn: in billets in the BERTHEN AREA. To-day being Sunday the Battn paraded in the morning for Divine Service.	
"	5-11-17		Battn; in billets in the BERTHEN AREA. Training carried out as under:- Physical Training, Bayonet Fighting, Platoon & Coy: Drill, Visual Training. Rapid Loading & Gas Drill. Lieut: Col: H.M. Smith. D.S.O. returned from 42 Inf: Bgde: and resumed command of the Battn: Major J. Turner M.C. resumed 2 in command of the Battn: & Capt: C.J. Smith resumed command of "C" Coy:	

Army Form C. 2118.

WAR DIARY
or
INTELLIGENCE SUMMARY.
(Erase heading not required.)

Instructions regarding War Diaries and Intelligence Summaries are contained in F. S. Regs., Part II. and the Staff Manual respectively. Title pages will be prepared in manuscript.

Place	Date	Hour	Summary of Events and Information	Remarks and references to Appendices
BERTHEN AREA X.1.c.2.2. Ref: sheet 27 and 13.G.7.4. Ref sheet 28	6.11.17		The Battn: moved to-day to the Canadian Corps forward Area for work under the 1st Canadian Division, entrained at 11.45 am on the FLETRE-THIEUSHOEK ROAD and detrained at H.12.d.6.4. and then proceeded by march route to Camp at I.3.G.7.4. ref: sheet 28. arriving at 5.15 p.m. The following is an extract from 14th Divl. Routine Orders of to-day. The G.O.C. has great pleasure in announcing that, under authority of H.M. the King the Field Marshall Commanding-in-Chief has made the following awards for acts of gallantry in the Field during recent operations:— 5th R.I.L.I. Bar to Military Medal No.17003 L/Cpl. C. Heenan. Military Medal. No: 14667. L/Cpl. N. Dixon. 5926. Pte. W. Lincox. 10969. " E. Hughes. 6327. " W. Kirkham.	
1.3.G.7.4. Ref. sheet 28	7.11.17		Battn: in Camp at 13.G.7.4. sheet 28. During the day the following working parties for Road Cleaning, Repairing and Drainage were found. 2. Off: 7.100. O.R.s under the 19th Labour Coy: at HELLFIRE CORNER. I.10.d.1.2. 2. " " 100. " " " 314 Rd: Const. Coy: at GODLEY RD. 5 " " 250. " " R.E. at MILLCOT at I.4.G.9.7.	

Army Form C. 2118.

WAR DIARY
or
INTELLIGENCE SUMMARY.
(Erase heading not required.)

Instructions regarding War Diaries and Intelligence Summaries are contained in F. S. Regs., Part II. and the Staff Manual respectively. Title pages will be prepared in manuscript.

Place	Date	Hour	Summary of Events and Information	Remarks and references to Appendices
I.3.c.7.4. Ref. sheet 28	8-11-17		Battn: in Camp at I.3.c.7.4. Working parties found as on the 7th inst.	
do	9-11-17		do. Lieut: C.M.J. Hamer admitted to Hospital to-day	
do	10-11-17		Battn: in Camp at I.3.c.7.4. Working parties found as on the 7th inst.	
do	11-11-17		do	
do	12-11-17		1. O.R. Wounded. Capt: C.J.R. Lloyd. D.S.O. assumed command of "D" Coy. Battn: in Camp at I.3.c.7.4. Working parties found as on the 7th inst.	
do	13-11-17		do	
do	14-11-17		During the morning Enemy Aeroplanes were very active and dropped several bombs in the vicinity of the Camp. Casualties 1. O.R. Wounded. Battn: in Camp at I.3.c.7.4. Working parties same as on the 7th inst. 2nd Lieut: H.T. Turner assumed command of "B" Coy. to-day. Aeroplane activity by both sides during the day.	
do	15-11-17		Battn: in Camp at I.3.c.7.4. Working parties same as on the 7th inst. 1. O.R. Wounded. The Commanding Officer presented Cards, granted by the G.O.C. 14th Division for gallant conduct in the Field on Oct: 22/17	

Cont'd:

WAR DIARY
or
INTELLIGENCE SUMMARY.

(Erase heading not required.)

Army Form C. 2118.

Place	Date	Hour	Summary of Events and Information	Remarks and references to Appendices
I.3.C.7.4. Ref: sheet 28.	15-11-17 Continued		To the following N.C.Os and men of the Battalion:- No:10893 T/Cpl. F.E. James. 11036 T/Cpl. T. Davies. 11751 Pte T. Vaughan. 11315 Pte. H. Kendal. 10576. Pte. H. Wakefield and 17029. Pte R. Birtwhistle.	
do	16-11-17		Battn: in Camp at I.3.C.7.4. Working parties found same as on the 7th inst: Considerable Aeroplane activity by both sides during the day.	
do	17-11-17		Battn: in Camp at I.3.C.7.4. No working parties found to-day. The Battn: spent the day in bathing at I.1.d.9.8.	
do	18-11-17		Battn: in Camp at I.3 C.7.4. Working parties found as on the 7th inst: Casualties. 2. O.Rs Killed. 4. O.Rs. Wounded. Capt: H. Atkinson joined the Battn; to-day and assumed command of "A" Coy:	
do	19-11-17		Battn: in Camp at I.3.C.7.4. Working parties found as on the 7th inst: Transport section moved to-day to Camp at: H.9.C.4.6. ref: sheet 28.	
do	20-11-17		Battn: in Camp at I.3.C.7.4. The same working parties as on the 7th inst: Considerable Aeroplane activity by both sides during the day.	

WAR DIARY or INTELLIGENCE SUMMARY

Army Form C. 2118.

Place	Date	Hour	Summary of Events and Information	Remarks and references to Appendices
I.3.c.7.4. Ref: sheet 28	21-11-17		Battn: in Camp at I.3.c.7.4. Ref: sheet 28. The following Working Parties were found during the day. 3. Offrs and 125. O.Rs. under the 62nd Field Coy: R.E., working on the SINGLE PLANK TRACK. D.14.c.0.7. 3. Offrs and 125. O.Rs under the 61st Field Coy: R.E. doing similar work. 2. Offrs and 80. O.Rs under the 218th Field Coy: R.E. 25. O.Rs. under 11th King's Liverpool Regt: unloading lorries and carrying material from KANSAS CROSS to ROAD in D.15.a. sheet 28. Casualties. 1. O.R. Wounded.	
do	22-11-17 to 28-11-17		Battn: in Camp at I.3.c.7.4. Working Parties were supplied as on the 21st inst. Casualties. 1. O.R. Wounded. 22nd inst: 2. O.Rs. Wounded 27th inst. 37. O.Rs. Reinforcements joined the Battn: 27th. Casualties. 2. O.Rs. Wounded 28th inst.	
I.3.c.7.4. Ref: sheet 28 & Q.22.d.6.2. sheet 27	29-11-17		Battn: relieved by the 1/1st Battn: Herts: Regt. At 10.a.m the Battn: moved off and proceeded to YPRES RLY: STATION entraining there at 11.a.m. detrained at GODEWAERSVELDE at 12.40.pm and marched to billets in the EECKE area, arriving at 1.30.pm. Battn: Hd: Qrs: at Q.22.d.6.2. Ref: sheet 27. Transport section moved by road.	

Army Form C. 2118.

WAR DIARY
or
INTELLIGENCE SUMMARY.

(Erase heading not required.)

Instructions regarding War Diaries and Intelligence Summaries are contained in F. S. Regs., Part II. and the Staff Manual respectively. Title pages will be prepared in manuscript.

Place	Date	Hour	Summary of Events and Information	Remarks and references to Appendices
Q.22.d.6.2 Ref: Sheet 27	30-4-17		Battn: in Billets in the EECKE area.	
			The following Inspections were carried out during the day. Rifle, S.A.A, Box Respirator and Medical Inspection.	

Wm Smith
Lieut: Col:
Comdg: 5 King's Shropshire L.I.

War Diary

5th Shrops L.I.

December 1917.

Volumn 25

From:- O.C. 5th Battn. K.S.L.I.

To:- Headquarters, 42nd Infy Bde.

Herewith "War Diary" duly completed for the month of December 1917.

E. Turner
Major,
Commanding, 5th Bn K.S.L.I.

D.69/19
2-1-18.

Army Form C. 2118.

WAR DIARY
or
INTELLIGENCE SUMMARY.
(Erase heading not required.)

Instructions regarding War Diaries and Intelligence Summaries are contained in F. S. Regs., Part II. and the Staff Manual respectively. Title pages will be prepared in manuscript.

Place	Date	Hour	Summary of Events and Information	Remarks and references to Appendices
Q.22.d.6.2. Ref: sheet 27	1-12-17		Battalion in Billets in the EECKE area. Battn. Hdr: Qrs at Q.22.d.6.2. Ref: sheet 27. 2nd Lieut: J.T.A. Flynn assumed command of "E" Coy.	
"	2-12-17		Battalion in Billets in the EECKE area	
" G.6.d.4.4. Ref: sheet 28.	3-12-17		At 10.50 am to-day the Battalion moved off by route march to "B" CAMP BRANDHOEK at G.6.d.4.4. Ref: sheet 28. ROUTE:- GODESWAERSVELDE, R.B.JCT: ABEELE, POPERINGHE arriving in Camp at 3-0 pm. Transport Section moved to Camp at J.3.c.6.5. ref: sheet 28.	
G.6.d.4.4. Ref: sheet 28.	4-12-17		Battalion in Huts at "B" CAMP BRANDHOEK. (G.6.d.4.4. sheet 28). Capt. H.T. Colburn reassumed command of "B" Coy. During the morning Kit Inspections and parades were carried out under Coy: arrangements.	
"	5-12-17		Battalion in Huts at "B" CAMP. Parades carried out under Coy: arrangements.	
"	6-12-17		Battalion in Huts at "B" CAMP. During the day the following working parties were supplied:- 6. Offr: 170. O. Ranks under the 306th, J.6. Coy, repairing roads in the forward area 3 " 95 " " " 314 " " " " 2 " 50 " " " 306 " " " carrying material	

Army Form C. 2118.

WAR DIARY
or
INTELLIGENCE SUMMARY.
(Erase heading not required.)

Instructions regarding War Diaries and Intelligence Summaries are contained in F. S. Regs., Part II. and the Staff Manual respectively. Title pages will be prepared in manuscript.

Place	Date	Hour	Summary of Events and Information	Remarks and references to Appendices
G.6.d.4.4. Ref: sheet 28	7-12-17		Battalion in Huts at "B" Camp. 2nd Lieut: E.J. Faithorn assumed command of "E" Coy. Working parties were supplied on the 6+7 inst:	
"	8-12-17		Battalion in Huts at "B" Camp. Parades carried out under Coy: arrangements during the morning	
G.6.d.4.4 + G.37.d.1.11 Ref: sheet 28	9-12-17		At 5.30 pm the Battn. moved off from B Camp to relieve the 6th Somerset L.I. in Divisional Support at G.37.d.1.11. Ref: sheet 28. arriving at 7.30 pm. Enemy Artillery very quiet during relief.	
G.37.d.1.11 Ref: sheet 28	10-12-17		Battalion in Divisional Support at G.37.d.1.11. Ref: sheet 28. Early morning working parties were supplied as follows:- 4 Offs + 120. Other Ranks under the 62nd Field Coy: R.E.s repairing roads in the forward area 3 Offs 75. O.Rs. under the 89th Field Coy: R.E.s working on Pack Transport lines at Divisional Hd. Qrs: 1. Off. 25. O.Rs under the 22nd Durham L.I. Pioneer Regt. working on Transport lines. Considerable hostile Aeroplane activity during the day.	

Army Form C. 2118.

WAR DIARY
or
INTELLIGENCE SUMMARY.

(Erase heading not required.)

Instructions regarding War Diaries and Intelligence Summaries are contained in F.S. Regs., Part II. and the Staff Manual respectively. Title pages will be prepared in manuscript.

Place	Date	Hour	Summary of Events and Information	Remarks and references to Appendices
C.18.d.5.6. Sheet 28.	16-12-17		"B" & "Hd.Qrs." Coys in dugouts at CAPRICORN CAMP. "C" & "D" Coys in dugouts at CALIFORNIA CAMP. The day was spent in cleaning equipment etc. Considerable Aeroplane activity by both sides during the day.	
"	17-12-17		Battn: in dugouts at CAPRICORN, and CALIFORNIA CAMPS. " on working parties under the R.D.L.R. repairing roads in the forward area. 2nd Lieuts: W.J. Herbert, A.N. Donaldson & J.J. Goodchild joined the Battn: to-day.	
"	18-12-17		Battn: in dugouts at CAPRICORN and CALIFORNIA CAMPS. Considerable Aeroplane activity by both sides during the morning. One of our Observing Planes was brought down near CAPRICORN CAMP. The Pilot, and Observer were both killed. Capt: E.S. Smith reassumed command of "C" Coy.	

Army Form C. 2118.

WAR DIARY
or
INTELLIGENCE SUMMARY.
(Erase heading not required.)

Instructions regarding War Diaries and Intelligence Summaries are contained in F. S. Regs., Part II. and the Staff Manual respectively. Title pages will be prepared in manuscript.

Place	Date	Hour	Summary of Events and Information	Remarks and references to Appendices
C.37.d.1.11. Ref: sheet 28.	11-12-17		Battalion in Divisional Support at C.37.d.1.11. ref. sheet 28. Working parties supplied to work under the A.D.L.R. on roads in the forward area.	
"	12-12-17		At 6.30 p.m the Battn: moved off to relieve the 10"Battn: Durham L.J in front line trenches NORTH of PASSCHENDAELE. Disposition of Coys:- D"Left Coy: V.29.a.50.70 to V.29.c.70.60. C"Centre Coy: V.29.c.70.60 to V.29.c.40.60. A" Right Coy: V.29.c.6.6 to V.30.a.05.75. B"Coy: Support 1 platoon V.29.c.9.5. 1 platoon V.29.c.7.5. 1 platoon V.29.c.6.5. Enemy Artillery very quiet during relief.	
V.29.C.6.6 Ref: sheet 27.	13-12-17 to 14-12-17		Battalion in the front line trenches NORTH of PASSCHENDAELE. Disposition of Coys: the same as on the 12"inst: Enemy Artillery very quiet. Casualties 1 O'Rank killed in Action 14" inst.	
" to C.18.d.5.6 Ref: sheet 28.	15-12-17		At night the Battn: was relieved by the 10"Durham L.J. "A", "B" & Bn: Hd. Qr: Coys: proceeded to CAPRICORN CAMP at C.18.d.5.6. ref: sheet 28. C & D Coys proceeded to CALIFORNIA CAMP. Owing to the wet state of the ground, relief was rather difficult and was not complete until about 12.0 m.m. Enemy Artillery fairly Active during relief. Casualties 1. O.R Killed in Action 5 O'Rs Wounded.	

*D. D. & L., London, E.C.
(A804) W. W1711/M32 31 730,000 5/17 Sch. 93 Forms/C2118/11

Army Form C. 2118.

WAR DIARY
or
INTELLIGENCE SUMMARY.
(Erase heading not required.)

Instructions regarding War Diaries and Intelligence Summaries are contained in F.S. Regs., Part II. and the Staff Manual respectively. Title pages will be prepared in manuscript.

Place	Date	Hour	Summary of Events and Information	Remarks and references to Appendices
C.18.d.5.6. Ref: Sheet 28. + D.4.d.5.4 Ref: Sheet 28	19-12-17		Battn: in dugouts at CAPRICORN, and CALIFORNIA CAMPS. Lieut: Col: H.M. Smith D.S.O. Commdg: Officer proceded on short leave to England to-day. Major. G. Turner M.C. assumed command of the Battn: Capt: C.J. Smith assumed 2nd in Command and 2 Lieut: H.M.D. Evans assumed command of "C" Coy. At 6.30 p.m. the Battn: moved off to relieve the 6th K.O.Y.L.I. (43rd Brigade) in the Support Trenches. H.Q. D & Bd: Qrs: at BELLEVUE. D.4.d.5.4. Ref: sheet 28. "B" Coy: at VINE COTTAGES. Relief was completed at about 8.30 p.m. Enemy Artillery fairly active during relief. Casualties 2.O.Rs Wounded	
D.4.d.5.4 Ref: sheet 28	20-12-17 + 21-12-17		Battn: in the Support Trenches. H.Q. D & Bd: Qrs: at BELLEVUE. D.4.d.5.4 Ref: sheet 28. "B" Coy: at VINE COTTAGES. At 6.0 p.m. parties were found to carry water to the 9th Batt. K.R.R.C. in the front line trenches. Enemy Artillery fairly quiet both by day and night. Casualties. 2nd Lieut: C.J. Turner K.R.R.C. wounded 20-12-17.	

Army Form C. 2118.

WAR DIARY
or
INTELLIGENCE SUMMARY.
(Erase heading not required.)

Instructions regarding War Diaries and Intelligence Summaries are contained in F.S. Regs., Part II. and the Staff Manual respectively. Title pages will be prepared in manuscript.

Place	Date	Hour	Summary of Events and Information	Remarks and references to Appendices
B.4.d.5.4. Ref. sheet 28	22-12-17		Battn: in the Lakpoort Trenches. F.C.D. & Hd.Qrs. at BELLEVUE D.4.d.5.4. sheet 28. B.Coy. at VINE COTTAGES.	
C.27.C.8.8. Ref. sheet 28		At 9.0 pm.	the Battn. was relieved by the 9th Battn. K.R.R. Corps and proceeded to huts at JUNCTION CAMP (C.27.c.8.8 sheet 28) arriving at 1.30 am. Enemy Artillery very active during relief, chiefly with 5.9s and gas shells, no casualties were caused.	
C.27.C.8.8. Ref. sheet 28	23-12-17		Battalion in huts at JUNCTION CAMP. (C.27.c.8.8 sheet 28). At night Hostile Aeroplanes were very active, dropping several bombs in the vicinity of the Railroad near JUNCTION CAMP. no damage was done.	
"	24-12-17		Battalion in huts at JUNCTION CAMP. Early morning working parties were found as follows:-	
		3.50 am.	2. Offs. + 60. O.Rs. under the 89th Field Coy. R.E.s carrying material.	
		3.50 am.	2. Offs. + 60. O.Rs. " " " " wiring BELLEVUE.	
		5.30 am.	1. Off. + 30. O.Rs. " " " " " ABRAHAM SWITCH.	
			Capt. F.W. Groves rejoined from wounds to-day. At 2.15 pm the Corps Commander presented Medal Ribbons to the following recipients of immediate rewards, at GRAND PLACE YPRES. No: 9324. C.S.M. Grimes. J. M.C.+M.M. 20430. Cpl: J.W. Walker. M.M. 16075. Cpl. R. Morris.M.M. 17483. L/Cpl. L. Colwood. M.M. 11409. L/Cpl: E.W. Watkins. M.M. 5926. L/Cpl. W. Linnox. M.M. 16994. Pte. T. Broome. M.M. 6392. L/C. J. Jones. D.C.M. 11327. Cpl. W. Fuller. D.C.M.	

WAR DIARY or INTELLIGENCE SUMMARY.

Army Form C. 2118.

Place	Date	Hour	Summary of Events and Information	Remarks and references to Appendices
6.27.C.8.8. Ref. sheet 28 + HAZEBROUCK S.A	25-12-17		Battalion in Huts at JUNCTION CAMP. At 5.30.a.m a working party consisting of 2 Offrs. and 40 O.Rs was supplied to work under the 59 Field Coy R.E. for wiring at BELLEVUE. About 2.0.pm Enemy Artillery dropped several shells near ST JEAN STATION and on the road leading through JUNCTION CAMP. Casualties 1. O.R. Wounded. At 3.15 p.m the Battn; marched to ST JEAN STATION where they entrained for WIZERNES, detrained there at 8.30 p.m, and hot cocoa and biscuits were issued to the troops. At 9.0 p.m the Battn marched to billets at LONGUENESSE a distance of 3 kilometres, arriving there at 10.0 p.m	
LONGUENESSE Mr ST OMER ref. HAZEBROUCK S.A	26-12-17		Battalion in billets at LONGUENESSE. 24. O.Rs joined the Battalion to-day.	
"	27-12-17		Battalion in billets at LONGUENESSE.	
"	28-12-17		Battalion in billets at LONGUENESSE. The following Parades were carried out during the morning 6.45 am to 7.45 am Physical Training and Bayonet Fighting 9 to 10 am Section + Platoon Drill. 10/11.45 am Musketry. 11.45/12. noon Ceremonial Drill.	

Army Form C. 2118.

WAR DIARY
or
INTELLIGENCE SUMMARY.

(Erase heading not required.)

Instructions regarding War Diaries and Intelligence Summaries are contained in F. S. Regs., Part II. and the Staff Manual respectively. Title pages will be prepared in manuscript.

Place	Date	Hour	Summary of Events and Information	Remarks and references to Appendices
LONGUENESSE Nr ST OMER (nr.) HAZEBROUCK S.A.	29-12-17		Battalion in billets at LONGUENESSE. Parades carried out as follows:- 6.45/7.45 am Physical Training and Bayonet Fighting. 9/10 am Musketry. 10/11 am Section & Platoon drill. 11/12 noon Short march (and Gas Drill en route). 6 Other Rank reinforcements joined the Batt. to-day.	
"	30-12-17 Sunday		Battalion in billets at LONGUENESSE. 8 Other Ranks reinforcements joined the Battn. to-day.	
"	31-12-17		Battalion in billets at LONGUENESSE	Appendix 1. Complimentary orders re good work when in the X.I. Corps.

Comdg. 5 King's Shropshire L.I.
Major

War Diary

5th King's Shropshire L.I.

January 1915

Volumn 26

Army Form C. 2118.

WAR DIARY
or
INTELLIGENCE SUMMARY.

(Erase heading not required.)

Instructions regarding War Diaries and Intelligence Summaries are contained in F. S. Regs., Part II. and the Staff Manual respectively. Title pages will be prepared in manuscript.

Place	Date	Hour	Summary of Events and Information	Remarks and references to Appendices
LONGUENESSE	1-1-18		At 5.20pm. the Battn. marched off to ST. OMER. Station, where they entrained at 7.20pm. for EDGEHILL, detraining at 9.20am. 2-1-18. Cocoa & Biscuits were served to the troops	
Heptonrick 32 cd. 12 1/100,000 Ref Amiens 17, 1/100,000			at 10.30am. The Battn. then marched to Huts at SUZANNE, about 15 kilometres distant arriving in Billets at 3.0pm. No men fell out on the march.	
SUZANNE.	2-1-18.		Battn. in Billets at SUZANNE. One man. No. 237698. Pte. Carlin. J.V. absent.	
SUZANNE.	3-1-18.		Battn. in Huts at SUZANNE. Parades under Coy. arrangements. Capt. A.W. Groves. proceeded on leave. Parade:- 6.45am to 7.45am. Bayonet Fighting & Physical Training. 10.0am to 11.0am. Musketry. 11.0am to 11.45am Platoon & Coy. Drill. 11.45am to 12 noon. Ceremonial Drill.	
SUZANNE.	4-1-18.		Battn. in Huts at SUZANNE. Parades:- 6.45 to 7.45am. R.J. & B.J. 9/11am. Outpost & Attack Practice. 11/11.45 am. Musketry. 11.45 to 12 noon. Ceremonial Drill. Lt-Col. H.M. Smith D.S.O. from Leave, resumes Command of Battn. Major E. Turnor M.C. Second in - Command. Capt. C.S. Smith. Command of 'B' Coy.	

Army Form C. 2118.

WAR DIARY
or
INTELLIGENCE SUMMARY.
(Erase heading not required.)

Instructions regarding War Diaries and Intelligence Summaries are contained in F. S. Regs., Part II. and the Staff Manual respectively. Title pages will be prepared in manuscript.

Place	Date	Hour	Summary of Events and Information	Remarks and references to Appendices
SUZANNE.	5-1-18.		Battn. in Huts at SUZANNE:- Parades. 9.0 am to 10-0 am. P.T. & B.T.	
		10/11 am.	Outpost & Attack Practice. 11/11-45 am. Musketry. 11-45 to 12 noon. Ceremonial Drill. Capt. C.S. Smith admitted to Hospital. 2/Lt. N.W.D. Evans assumes Command of "C" Coy. No. 237698 Pte. Carlin, J.V. absentia relatives.	
SUZANNE.	6-1-18.		Battn. in Huts at SUZANNE:- Battn. Paraded for Divine Service.	
SUZANNE.	7-1-18.	9/10 am.	Battn. in Huts at SUZANNE:- P.T. & B.T. 10/12 noon. Attack Practice. 12 noon to 1-0 pm. Musketry. Ceremonial Drill. Demonstrating Mutual Support. 3 Other Ranks reinforcements. 2/Lt. E.G. Fairbairn rejoins from leave.	
SUZANNE	8-1-18.		Battn. in Huts at SUZANNE:- Snow interfered with training. 2/Lt. J.E.O. Flynn proceeds on leave.	
SUZANNE.	9-1-18.	9/10. am.	Battn. in Huts at SUZANNE:- P.T. & B.T. 10/12 noon. Outpost & Attack Practice. 12 noon to 1-0 pm. Range Practice & Musketry. Capt. C.S. Smith assumes Command of "C" Coy.	
SUZANNE.	10-1-18.		Battn. in Huts at SUZANNE:- Parades. 9/10 am. P.T. 10/12 noon. Attack Practice. 12/1 pm. Musketry.	
SUZANNE.	11-1-18.		Battn. in Huts at SUZANNE:- Parades: 9/10 am. P.T. 11/12 noon. B.T. 12/1 pm. Musketry. 2/Lieut. N.W.D. Evans proceeds on leave.	

Army Form C. 2118.

WAR DIARY
or
INTELLIGENCE SUMMARY.
(Erase heading not required.)

Instructions regarding War Diaries and Intelligence Summaries are contained in F. S. Regs., Part II. and the Staff Manual respectively. Title pages will be prepared in manuscript.

Place	Date	Hour	Summary of Events and Information	Remarks and references to Appendices
SUZANNE.	12-1-18.		Battn. in Huts at SUZANNE:- Parades:- 9/10 a.m. P.T. 10/11 a.m. Platoon & Coy. Drill. 11/12 noon. B.F. 12/1 p.m. Musketry.	
SUZANNE	13-1-18.		Battn. in Huts at SUZANNE:- SUNDAY. CHURCH PARADE.	
SUZANNE	14-1-18.		Battn. in Huts at SUZANNE:- Parades:- 9/10 a.m. P.T. & B.F. 10/12 a.m. Wiring and Trench Revetting. Outpost Scheme. 12 noon to 1-p.m. Musketry. 2/Lieut. W.H. Day. proceeds on Leave.	
SUZANNE	15-1-18.		Battn. in Huts at SUZANNE:- Parades. 9/9.30 a.m. Battn. Drill. 9.30 to 10.30 a.m. Musketry. 10/30 to 11/30 a.m. Section & Platoon Drill. 11.30 am to 1-p.m. Attack Practice.	
SUZANNE	16-1-18		Battn. in Huts at SUZANNE:- Rain interfered with training. The following is an extract from LONDON GAZETTE dated 21-12-17:- MENTIONED IN DESPATCHES:- T/Lt.Col. H.M. Smith. D.S.O. Major. C.E. Aickman. D.S.O. (since K. in A. 24-8-17). A/Capt. E.J.R. Lloyd. D.S.O. T/Lieut. J.J. Jackson. T/Lieut. N.R. Cosgrove (since to England sick. 17-8-17.) No. 11135 A/Sgt. Pemberton. E. _do_ 7-10-17) " 8811 L.Cpl.M.S. Throsgale. J.	

WAR DIARY
or
INTELLIGENCE SUMMARY.
(Erase heading not required.)

Army Form C. 2118.

Place	Date	Hour	Summary of Events and Information	Remarks and references to Appendices
SUZANNE	17-1-18		Battn. in Huts at SUZANNE:- Rain interfered with training	
SUZANNE	18-1-18		Battn. in Huts at SUZANNE:- Parade:- 9/10a.m. Platoon & Coy. Drill. 10/11.o.a.m. Musketry. Judging Distance & Visual Training. 11/12 noon. Wiring. 12. noon to 1-0pm. Guard Mounting. 9/11 a.m. & 11 a.m to 1-0pm. Range Practice. 7/O. Prize from Leave. 5th H.S.L.I. Transport won Brigade (142nd Infy) Transport Competition. Challenge Cup.	
SUZANNE	19-1-18		Battn. in Huts at SUZANNE:- Parade:- 9/10 a.m. & 11/12 noon. P.T. & B.F. 11/1 p.m. Practice in Patrolling, Skirmishing, Machine Support & Fire Control. Range Practice. Lieut Hughes from Leave. 7/O. Mackenzie proceeds on Leave.	
SUZANNE	20-1-18		Battn. in Huts at SUZANNE:- Church Parade. Warning Order received re MOVE.	
SUZANNE	21-1-18		Battn. in Huts at SUZANNE:- Parade 9 a.m to 10 a.m & 11a.m to 12. noon. P.T. + B.F. 10. a.m to 11. a.m. Musketry. 12 noon to 1.0 pm. Range Practice 130 Runners. Report Specialists across their own Section Instruction. 10 mins. Gas Drill.	
SUZANNE	22-1-18		Bn. marched off from SUZANNE at 9-15 a.m. arriving at ROSIERE-EN-SANTERRE at 2-15 p.m. a distance of about 12. miles. One man fell out on march - Faintness.	

Army Form C. 2118.

WAR DIARY
or
INTELLIGENCE SUMMARY.
(Erase heading not required.)

Instructions regarding War Diaries and Intelligence Summaries are contained in F. S. Regs., Part II. and the Staff Manual respectively. Title pages will be prepared in manuscript.

Place	Date	Hour	Summary of Events and Information	Remarks and references to Appendices
ROSIERE-EN-SANTERRE.	23/1/15		Battn. stayed one night at ROSIERE-EN-SANTERRE, marching off at 12.15 p.m. for GUERBIGNY arriving there 2.45 p.m. (8 miles). No men fell out on march.	
Ref. France 1/100,000 Amiens.				
GUERBIGNY.	24-1-15		Battn. in billets at GUERBIGNY. Order received to remain till 25th inst. Transport moved to CANDOR by road 24-1-15. Marching orders issued by B.T.O.	
GUERBIGNY.	25-1-15		Bn. marched off from GUERBIGNY to a distance of about 2 kilos. where they were met by Motor Lorries and conveyed to BERLANCOURT, where they de-bussed and marched to BEINE, billeting there for the night.	
BEINE.	26-1-15		Battn. moved off from BEINE by march route to MONTESCOURT, a distance of 10 miles. at 1.45 p.m. Starting Point: 3 Cross Roads, arriving MONTESCOURT. 5-30 p.m. No men fell out on march. All Ranks warned for Trenches.	
(Ref. Map. ST. QUENTIN. 1/100,000 + 66.C.N.W.)				

Army Form C. 2118.

WAR DIARY
or
INTELLIGENCE SUMMARY.
(Erase heading not required.)

Instructions regarding War Diaries and Intelligence Summaries are contained in F. S. Regs., Part II. and the Staff Manual respectively. Title pages will be prepared in manuscript.

Place	Date	Hour	Summary of Events and Information	Remarks and references to Appendices
MONTESCOURT Rf. St. QUENTIN 1/100.000 & 56. C. N. W.	27-1-18		Battn. in Huts at MONTESCOURT. From 5-20pm to 6-57pm, the Battn marched up to the trenches to relieve the French 413 the Regt., where they took over the LEFT sector from B.30.C.64. to I.L.a.0.0. both inclusive. Dispositions: Bn. Hqrs. at H.5.C.5.3. "D" Coy. about M.6.C. one Platoon at H.6.C.0.7. "C" Coy. — "—" H.5.a.0.0. "A" and "B" Coys in Reserve at H.14. Capt. Groves returns from leave.	
LEFT SECTOR. B.30.C.64 to I.L.a.0.0.	28/1/18		Battn. in position in trenches. Bn. Hqrs. at H.5.C.5.3. "D" Coy. about H.6.C. with one Platoon H.6.C.0.7. "C" Coy. about H.5.a.0.0. "A" & "B" Coys. in reserve at 14. Central. ("A" Coy. First Reserve. "B" Coy. Second Reserve.) All quiet during day, several bursts of artillery fire during night. 6 th R. B's on LEFT FLANK. 9th. K.R.R.C. on RIGHT FLANK.	

Army Form C. 2118.

WAR DIARY
or
INTELLIGENCE SUMMARY.
(Erase heading not required.)

Instructions regarding War Diaries and Intelligence Summaries are contained in F. S. Regs., Part II. and the Staff Manual respectively. Title pages will be prepared in manuscript.

Place	Date	Hour	Summary of Events and Information	Remarks and references to Appendices
Rly. St. QUENTIN 11/10, and P. 66.c. N.W.	29-1-18		Bn. in Trenches, LEFT SECTOR. from B 30.c.64 to I.2.a.0.0. both inclusive.	
			Bn. Hqrs. at H.6.c.5.3.	
			'D' Coy. about H.6.c. with 1 Platoon at H.6.c.0.7.	
			'B' Coy. about H.5.d.0.0.	
			'A' & 'B' Coys in Reserve at 14 Central.	
			'A' Coy. Front Reserve. 'B' Coy. Front Reserve.	
			All quiet during day, some Artillery fire at night. 2 P.O.W. arriving rejoined from leave.	
-do-	30-1-18		Bn. in Trenches. LEFT SECTOR. from B.30.c.64 to I.2.a.0.0. both inclusive.	
			Bn. Hqrs. at H.5.c.5.3.	
			'D' Coy. about H.6.c. with 1 Platoon at H.6.c.5.7.	
			'B' Coy. about H.5.d.0.0.	
			'A' & 'B' Coys in Reserve at 14 Central.	
			('A' Coy. 1st. Reserve. 'B' Coy. 2nd Reserve.)	
			Nothing unusual to report. 'D' Coy. relieved by 'C' Coy. in Front Line at 7-15pm.	

Army Form C. 2118.

WAR DIARY
or
INTELLIGENCE SUMMARY.
(Erase heading not required.)

Instructions regarding War Diaries and Intelligence Summaries are contained in F.S. Regs., Part II. and the Staff Manual respectively. Title pages will be prepared in manuscript.

Place	Date	Hour	Summary of Events and Information	Remarks and references to Appendices
Rgf St Quentin	1/1/18		Bn. in Trenches. LEFT SECTOR. B. 30. c. 64. to I. 2. a. 0.0. both inclusive.	
+ 66.c.N.W.	31.1.18		Battn. Hqrs. at H.5.3.5.c.	
			"D" Coy. about H.5.d.0.0.	
			"C" Coy. about H.6.c. with 1 Platoon at H.C.2.a.7.	
			"A" & "B" Coys. in Reserve at "H" CENTRAL.	
			"A" Coy. 1st Reserve. "B" Coy. 2nd Reserve.	
			Nothing unusual to report.	

Hu Smith
LIEUT. COL.
Commanding, 5th Battn. K.S.L.I.

War Diary.

5th King's Shropshire L.I.

February 1918.

Volumn 27.

WAR DIARY
or
INTELLIGENCE SUMMARY.
(Erase heading not required.)

Army Form C. 2118.

Place	Date	Hour	Summary of Events and Information	Remarks and references to Appendices
Ref St. QUENTIN & 66c.N.W. Left Sector from B.30.c. 64 to I.1.a. o.o. both inclusive.	1/2/18		Battalion in trenches. Battn H.Q. at H.5.c.5.3. D. Coy about H.5.d.0.0. C. " H.6.c. with 1 platoon at H.c.b.o.7. A & B Coys in reserve at 14 Central A Coy 1st reserve B " 2nd reserve Nothing unusual to report. All quiet on front. 8th R.B. on left flank, and 9th K.R.R.C. on right flank.	
Ref ST QUENTIN & 66c.N.W. Left sector from B.30.c. 64 to I.1.a.o.o. both inclusive	2/2/18		Battn in trenches Battn H.Q. at H.5.c.5.3. D Coy about H.5.d.0.0. C " H.6.c. with 1 platoon at H.c.B.0.7. A & B Coys in reserve at 14 Central A Coy 1st Reserve B " 2nd " Instructions received for Battalion to be disbanded at once. 5th Oxs & Bucks L.I. to relieve 5th K.S.L.I. at 8-30 pm. The Battalion marched off idependently by Coys to billets at JUSSY. Arrangements made to distribute	

Army Form C. 2118.

WAR DIARY
or
INTELLIGENCE SUMMARY.
(Erase heading not required.)

Instructions regarding War Diaries and Intelligence Summaries are contained in F. S. Regs., Part II. and the Staff Manual respectively. Title pages will be prepared in manuscript.

Place	Date	Hour	Summary of Events and Information	Remarks and references to Appendices
			Coys to other Battalions of the K.S.L.I., viz; - A Coy to 6th K.S.L.I.: B Coy to 7th K.S.L.I.: C Coy to 1/4th K.S.L.I.: D. Coy to 1st K.S.L.I.: H.Q.(composed of Orderly Room, Signallers & Transport) to remain behind for disposal by G.H.Q.	
JUSSY	3/2/18		Battalion paraded at 7-30 am, outside Battalion H.Q. for purpose of checking and calling roll. The Battalion embussed and entrained at 9 am for their various units. Prior to their departure a Farewell Letter by the Commanding Officer was read to the troops, viz :- FAREWELL ORDER. I regret to inform the Battalion that we are all being disbanded tomorrow. The only bright spot is that we are all going, to different Battalions it is true, but still to the same regiment. In bidding you goodbye I wish to tell you a little of the work you have done. You have fought gallantly and never lost a trench, or failed to do what was required of you. You have often been hungry and thirsty, had to endure intense cold and rain, mud and discomfort, had to work	

WAR DIARY
or
INTELLIGENCE SUMMARY.
(Erase heading not required.)

Army Form C. 2118.

Place	Date	Hour	Summary of Events and Information	Remarks and references to Appendices
			and march in the course of your duty, till you had hardly a strength to stand. You have done all this without a murmur, and with a cheerfulness which has been beyond all praise.	
			I know full well that you will carry on the same splendid work in the other Battalions of the dear old Corps that you are going to. No regiment in the British Service has a finer record, and remember this, it is each one of you who help to keep that record unsullied, and its honour bright.	
			It has been the proudest and happiest time of my life during which I have had the honour of commanding you, and I still hope I may continue to soldier with you.	
			I wish especially to thank the staff of the Battalion for their unfailing devotion and the loyal way in which they have always supported me. The Orderly Room staff, the Quartermaster's staff, Medical staff, and Stretcher Bearers, the Transport (who have recently won fresh laurels) the Orderlies and Battalion Cooks, have each and all helped to make the Battalion what it is today.	
			Words fail me to thank you all adequately for what you have done.	
			I wish you all the best of luck and happiness in the future, and May God Bless you all.	
			(sd) H.M. Smith,	
			Lieut-Col., Commdg	
			5th K.S.L.I.	
	2/2/18.			

Army Form C. 2118.

WAR DIARY
or
INTELLIGENCE SUMMARY.

(Erase heading not required.)

Instructions regarding War Diaries and Intelligence Summaries are contained in F.S. Regs., Part II. and the Staff Manual respectively. Title pages will be prepared in manuscript.

Place	Date	Hour	Summary of Events and Information	Remarks and references to Appendices
JUSSY	4/2/18.		Details of 5th K.S.L.I. awaiting instructions from G.H.Q. Letter of regret received from 42nd Inf Bde :-	
			To/Lieut-Col.H.M. Smith, D.S.O., Officers, W.O's, N.C.O's and men of the 5th K.S.L.I.	
			It is with great regret that I have to write this letter to you. It is a hard blow both to you and the 42nd Inf Bde that a Battalion who was one of the First Hundred Thousand has been ordered to disband. My confidence in the Battalion has always been great, and when I say this, I am certain that I can speak not only for myself but for my predecessor, and the other three Battalions in the Brigade.	
			When I state that I have always considered you, in slang terms a Battalion of "stickers", I wish you to take it as one of the compliments that can be paid you - you have always been so both in Attack and Defence, and have always done what you have been called upon to do.	
			This disbandment is hard on you, but your one consolation must be that it is being done for the best for our beloved Country's sake, and I hope you will take it in a cheerful spirit, in the same spirit which you have always shown when we have had bad times.	
			I wish you all the best of luck wherever you go, and I hope you will always remember with pride when you belonged to the 42nd Inf Bde.	
			I am very sorry to lose you, and I thank you all for the loyal support you have always given me at all times.	
			(sd) G.N.B. FORSTER, Brig-General,	
	2/2/18.		Commdg 42nd Inf Bde.	

Army Form C. 2118

WAR DIARY
or
INTELLIGENCE SUMMARY.
(Erase heading not required.)

Instructions regarding War Diaries and Intelligence Summaries are contained in F. S. Regs., Part II. and the Staff Manual respectively. Title pages will be prepared in manuscript.

Place	Date	Hour	Summary of Events and Information	Remarks and references to Appendices
JUSSY	7/2/18.		Lieut-Col. H.M. Smith DSO., leaves Battalion for 3rd Corps H.Q. for duty.	
			Captain, Commdg 5th K.S.L.I. (details).